Essays on Interest Rates

NATIONAL BUREAU OF ECONOMIC RESEARCH

Number 88, General Series

Essays on Interest Rates

VOLUME I

Edited by

JACK M. GUTTENTAG & PHILLIP CAGAN

New York  *1969*

NATIONAL BUREAU OF ECONOMIC RESEARCH

Distributed by Columbia University Press   New York & London

Relation of the Directors to the Work and Publications
of the National Bureau of Economic Research

1. The object of the National Bureau of Economic Research is to ascertain and to present to the public important economic facts and their interpretation in a scientific and impartial manner. The Board of Directors is charged with the responsibility of ensuring that the work of the National Bureau is carried on in strict conformity with this object.

2. The President of the National Bureau shall submit to the Board of Directors, or to its Executive Committee, for their formal adoption all specific proposals for research to be instituted.

3. No research report shall be published until the President shall have submitted to each member of the Board the manuscript proposed for publication, and such information as will, in his opinion and in the opinion of the author, serve to determine the suitability of the report for publication in accordance with the principles of the National Bureau. Each manuscript shall contain a summary drawing attention to the nature and treatment of the problem studied, the character of the data and their utilization in the report, and the main conclusions reached.

4. For each manuscript so submitted, a special committee of the Board shall be appointed by majority agreement of the President and Vice Presidents (or by the Executive Committee in case of inability to decide on the part of the President and Vice Presidents), consisting of three directors selected as nearly as may be one from each general division of the Board. The names of the special manuscript committee shall be stated to each Director when the manuscript is submitted to him. It shall be the duty of each member of the special manuscript committee to read the manuscript. If each member of the manuscript committee signifies his approval within thirty days of the transmittal of the manuscript, the report may be published. If at the end of that period any member of the manuscript committee withholds his approval, the President shall then notify each member of the Board, requesting approval or disapproval of publication, and thirty days additional shall be granted for this purpose. The manuscript shall then not be published unless at least a majority of the entire Board who shall have voted on the proposal within the time fixed for the receipt of votes shall have approved.

5. No manuscript may be published, though approved by each member of the special manuscript committee, until forty-five days have elapsed from the transmittal of the report in manuscript form. The interval is allowed for the receipt of any memorandum of dissent or reservation, together with a brief statement of his reasons, that any member may wish to express; and such memorandum of dissent or reservation shall be published with the manuscript if he so desires. Publication does not, however, imply that each member of the Board has read the manuscript, or that either members of the Board in general or the special committee have passed on its validity in every detail.

6. Publications of the National Bureau issued for informational purposes concerning the work of the Bureau and its staff, or issued to inform the public of activities of Bureau staff, and volumes issued as a result of various conferences involving the National Bureau shall contain a specific disclaimer noting that such publication has not passed through the normal review procedures required in this resolution. The Executive Committee of the Board is charged with review of all such publications from time to time to ensure that they do not take on the character of formal research reports of the National Bureau, requiring formal Board approval.

7. Unless otherwise determined by the Board or exempted by the terms of paragraph 6, a copy of this resolution shall be printed in each National Bureau publication.

(Resolution adopted October 25, 1926 and revised February 6, 1933,
February 24, 1941, and April 20, 1968)

Advisory Committee on the Interest Rate Study

In the planning and review of its studies of interest rates, the National Bureau has benefited from the advice and guidance of this committee. The committee's concurrence with the views expressed in this report, however, is not to be assumed. The members of the committee are:

Contents

Tables

Charts

Figures

Acknowledgments

The essays in this volume have benefited from the support of the Life Insurance Association of America, as well as computer time contributed by IBM and the University of Pennsylvania.

The editors are most appreciative of the assistance of H. Irving Forman in preparing the charts, and of Gnomi Schrift Gouldin in editing the papers.

They also wish to thank the members of the National Bureau Board Reading Committee: R. A. Gordon, Lester V. Chandler and Robert V. Roosa.

Introduction and Summary

The six essays in this volume, as well as those planned for a second volume, arise out of the Bureau's study of interest rates and reflect the general orientation of the project. A major decision was made at the outset to eschew further theorizing on determinants of "the" interest rate and to concentrate on specific rates on well-defined capital market instruments. This decision implied considerable diversity in approach, method, and proximate objectives of the several studies — diversity which is characteristic of the six essays included here.[1]

Two essays on the mortgage market — Shipp's on the nonresidential market and mine on the residential market — are drawn from larger studies that will be forthcoming at a later date. Both are based on new statistical series covering mortgage rates and terms of loans authorized by large life insurance companies. Shipp's study can be viewed as an introduction to the structure of the nonresidential market, about which few systematic studies have been made. It examines loan, property and borrower characteristics during four quarterly periods (the first in 1954, the last in 1965). Shipp discloses that loan terms such as contract rate, maturity, loan-value ratio, service fee, and amortization provisions vary markedly between large and small loans, and also between loans on different types of properties (apartment houses, motels, stores, etc.). In general, loans that are viewed as less risky obtain more liberal terms. The "capitalization rate" appears to be a good statistical proxy for lenders' over-all judgment regarding risk. These

---

[1] Other studies in the project, published or in preparation, include Joseph W. Conard, *The Behavior of Interest Rates: A Progress Report,* 1965; Reuben A. Kessel, *The Cyclical Behavior of the Term Structure of Interest Rates,* 1965; Phillip Cagan, *Changes in the Cyclical Behavior of Interest Rates,* 1966; Avery Cohan, *Yields on Corporate Debt Directly Placed,* 1967, and "New Series on Residential Mortgage Yields Since 1951" by Jack Guttentag and Morris Beck.

and other insights into institutional practices in this market will lay a foundation for future studies of the interrelationship between this and other markets.

My own paper deals with the operations of the residential mortgage market and its interrelationship with other markets, examining comparative behavior of various yield series over the period 1951–66. Although not the first analysis of this type, it is the first to make use of rate series that are essentially comparable. (A forthcoming volume will provide the technical foundations of the new mortgage series, the data themselves, and a more extensive analysis of their behavior.) These new data confirm the general view that mortgage yields tend to lag behind bond yields over the cycle. Furthermore, for the period up to 1961, cyclical fluctuations in mortgage yields were milder than fluctuations in bond yields — probably because mortgages originate in negotiated rather than in dealer markets. The behavior of mortgage yields since 1961, however, reflects a sharp break with past patterns. The prolonged 1961–65 decline in mortgage yields, and the marked rise in 1966, were as sharp as the corresponding movements in bond yields. The changing position of commerical bank portfolios over that period may have been responsible for this shift in yield patterns. Heavy mortgage acquisitions by banks during 1961–65, associated with marked increases in time deposits, intensified the downward pressure on mortgage yields, while in 1966 the banks attracted an unprecedented volume of funds from savings institutions which were forced, as a result, to sharply curtail their own mortgage acquisitions.

The Conard-Frankena paper undertakes to examine the *prima facie* puzzling fact that new corporate bond issues often carry a yield above that of similar outstanding issues. The authors show that higher coupon rates on new issues accounted on the average for roughly half of the yield differential during the period since 1952. Bonds with high coupon rates carry high yields because of the greater danger that they will be called for refunding should prices rise in the future, and because of the smaller likelihood of capital gains. The balance of the yield spread not explained by coupon rates evidently is due to imperfections in the market for outstanding issues, and to the sometimes cautious policies of underwriters in pricing new issues in weak markets.

Before his untimely death in 1965, Conard had completed and circulated a preliminary draft of this study, as well as a summary which appeared later as a chapter in his progress report on the project as a whole. He was never able to revise the manuscript. Fortunately, Frankena, who was Conard's research assistant during the summer of 1964 and knew the problems as well as the data, undertook to revise the draft with some help from me. Although the revisions were extensive and often based on additional statistical tests performed by Frankena, we did not attempt to break new ground beyond what Conard had marked out. Ordinarily we would have hesitated to take such liberties in the absence of the senior author, but we were confident that he would have wanted us to do so. Respect for evidence and doggedness in digging further when others would have stopped were characteristic of the man. Moreover, the basic results of Conard's initial work have stood the test of further analysis, although Frankena points out that some of the findings must be interpreted cautiously because of shortcomings in the statistical procedures.

The three essays by Cagan are products of his study of the cyclical behavior of interest rates. In the first, he develops a statistical procedure for separating the effects of interest rates on business activity from the reverse effect of activity on rates. The test relates the timing of cycles in bond yields to the duration of business cycles. Bond yields over a long history have typically, though not always, reached cyclical peaks and troughs some months after the corresponding peaks and troughs in business activity. If, as we expect, interest rates influence investment expenditures and thus aggregate activity, a rise in interest rates early in a business expansion should restrain aggregate expenditures and shorten the duration of the expansion. Cagan's test compares the length of the lag in the turning points of rates to the duration of the accompanying cyclical phase in business activity. One advantage of this procedure is that the data allow coverage of an unusually long period, beginning in 1856. The results indicate that the timing of cyclical changes in bond yields does affect the duration of business cycles.

Cagan's second essay was suggested by the results of Kessel's earlier study of liquidity premiums (NBER Occasional Paper 91). Kessel found that liquidity premiums on Treasury bills fluctuate with the level of interest rates, thus exhibiting positive conformity to the business cycle. To explain this result, Kessel presented a theory of liquidity premiums based on treating Treasury bills as partial substitutes for money balances. Cagan elaborates this theory and compares it with an alternative that has been presented in the literature. He then tests both theories, using data on Federal securities at the short end of the yield curve — as Kessel did — and, more relevant to the practical application of the theories, at the long end as well. Measuring liquidity premiums at the long end encounters certain statistical difficulties, which the essay discusses. Although tentative, the findings support Kessel's explanation. Besides developing new evidence on the behavior of liquidity premiums, the essay describes certain implications of the theory for changes in the relative supply of securities of different maturity.

Cagan's third essay deals with the well-known inverse association between short-term rates and bank reserve ratios. Until the mid-1930's the association was cited as evidence of the effect of monetary policy on market rates, but since then it has been attributed to the opposite effect, that of market rates on reserve ratios. The latter effect is usually explained by short-run profit incentives to banks: When market rates are high, banks lend excess reserves and borrow from Federal Reserve Banks at the (usually) lower discount rate, and conversely when market rates are low in relation to the discount rate. Cagan reexamines the association in the light of the two theories and finds that most of it reflects common cyclical fluctuations in the variables rather than a direct causal relationship. He attributes cycles in bank reserve ratios mainly to cyclical variation in the demand for bank loans. Since the pattern of bank loan demand over the cycle is similar to that of interest rates, this creates the appearance of an inverse association of reserve ratios with interest rates.

While the various parts of the interest rate study diverge greatly in approach, method, and proximate goals, they tend to converge on ultimate objectives. One objective, of course, is to illuminate the effect of financial variables on economic activity. Our contribution to this comes at several levels. For one thing, our studies of the structure of rates and other transaction characteristics of specific instruments have illuminated the problems involved in properly measuring financial influences on specific types of real output. We have examined the problem of recording lags in rate series, of changes in composition of the instruments underlying rate series that affect their homogeneity, of nonrate dimensions of loan transactions that may be used to "ration" credit, and of the needed degree of disaggregation in series on financial variables. In the process, we have invested in the collection of new data on rates and other transaction characteristics in cases where the available data were badly deficient. New time series have been developed that can be used in studies of the influence of financial variables on activity.

As an illustration, consider the contribution of Shipp's work to the study of financial influences on multifamily residential construction. His tabulations strongly suggest that rates and other terms on mortgage loans secured by multifamily properties differ considerably from those on other income-producing properties, and that some characteristics have changed over time quite differently among the various property types. This implies that studies of multifamily construction should use financial series covering multifamily properties and not proxy series that cover corporate bonds, or FHA mortgages, or mortgages on all types of income-producing properties. In a forthcoming study Shipp will provide, for the first time, series on multifamily properties. The series will cover not only rates but other important transaction characteristics and will pertain to the time when funds are committed rather than when disbursed, which was the basis on which all prior series on nonresidential loans had been constructed. It will be possible, through cross-section analyses of yields and transaction characteristics, to determine the homogeneity of the series and improve them in this respect. The technical aspects of such adjustments were pioneered by Avery Cohan in his study of *Yields on Corporate Debt Directly Placed,* (NBER, 1967).

In addition, we have examined a number of approaches toward assessing the effect of financial variables on the real sector which help avoid some of the shortcomings that have plagued earlier investigations. Cagan's imaginative essay on the relationship of the longevity of business cycles to prior rate behavior is in this spirit.

A second objective on which our studies converge, closely related to the first, is to help illuminate the channels through which monetary policy influences the economy, and the extent and effectiveness of this influence. Almost all the essays in this volume have something to say about this. Thus Cagan's paper on interest rates and the business cycle suggests that the monetary authorities can affect the duration of business cycle expansions by the speed at which they shift gears from monetary ease to restraint after the preceding cyclical trough. The long upswing beginning in 1961, while not examined thoroughly but noted in his paper, fits in neatly with this hypothesis. The Conard-Frankena paper indicates that, owing to imperfections in the market for seasoned corporate bonds, monetary policy has its most immediate and direct effect on the new issue market. My own paper suggests a lag in the transmission of market changes from bonds, which receive the first impact of open market operations, to residential mortgages. Except for this lag, the residential sector would be much more sensitive to monetary policy. Cagan's paper on interest rates and bank reserve ratios suggests that the Federal Reserve's control over the money supply is not significantly weakened by bank action to alter free reserves in response to changes in market interest rates. On the other hand, variations in customer loan demands do affect free reserves and therefore the money stock, and this may require substantial offsetting by the Federal Reserve. These selective remarks are meant only to be suggestive of the types of monetary policy questions on which the papers in this volume may help shed some light.

A third problem to which we hope to contribute some understanding is the economic efficiency of major financial markets. Work is just beginning on this very difficult area and only scattered and highly tentative inferences come out of the essays in this volume. Yet progress depends on the gradual accumulation of knowledge of how the major financial markets work, one study building on the enlarging the scope of others. The studies reported here move us a notch forward on this front.

JACK M. GUTTENTAG

Essays on Interest Rates

1

The Influence of Interest Rates on the

Duration of Business Cycles   *Phillip Cagan*

Introduction

FINANCIAL EFFECTS ON INVESTMENT. In economic theory the cost of capital has an important influence on decisions to invest and, therefore, on business cycles. Increases in capital costs may curtail investment undertakings thus contributing to a downturn in aggregate activity, and conversely for decreases. Since the rate of interest is a major item in capital costs, empirical studies have looked for rate effects on investment decisions and expenditures. Short-term rates are supposed to influence inventory investment and trade credit, while long-term rates influence plans for plant and equipment installations and for residential housing. Such an effect would show up first in orders and contracts, later in appropriations and expenditures.

The typical cyclical pattern of interest rates does not at first sight support the foregoing theory. Interest rates and investment series generally conform to business activity on a positive basis, and so their correlation with each other is positive rather than negative as the theory implies. A negative effect could still occur, and be consistent with this behavior, if offsetting factors intervened for some time to delay the effect. For example, during business upswings, at first investors look favorably upon capital projects despite the accompanying rise in interest rates; but, if the rising cost of capital eventually exceeds expected returns, the resulting reduction in investment expenditures could bring on a downturn in general activity. Then, as the downturn

NOTE: I benefited greatly from the comments and suggestions of F. Thomas Juster, Jacob Mincer, and Geoffrey H. Moore. Josephine Trubek and Jae Won Lee provided invaluable research assistance.

gathers momentum, business prospects dim even further and the remnants of optimism fade. Investment undertakings previously held back by high interest rates no longer appear attractive even when rates are much lower. If cutbacks in the demand for capital funds are large, interest rates will decline. Interest rates and investment expenditures can therefore display a positive association over cycles, even though the rates have a delayed, inverse effect which contributes to fluctuations in investment.

This view of the cyclical role of interest rates can be expressed in terms of traditional supply and demand analysis. Price in that framework would represent interest rates, and quantity would be capital borrowing per period of time. A positive association between price and quantity reflects cyclical shifts in a downward sloping demand curve combined with an upward sloping supply curve. A restriction on business expansions due to rising capital costs implies that the supply curve shifts leftward; if at a later stage of the expansion those shifts came to outweigh the rightward shifts in demand, capital borrowing and expenditures would then decline, contributing to a downturn in aggregate activity. A recession in activity, no matter how initiated, usually leads to substantial leftward shifts in the investment demand curve, overcoming all other effects on supply and demand to make interest rates and investment fall. Notwithstanding the over-all positive association between price and quantity, countercyclical shifts in the supply curve, by further raising rates and eventually reducing the quantity demanded, could be a factor in the downturn of business activity.

Deriving evidence of such supply effects, however, presents severe difficulties. To disentangle the shifts in demand and supply, econometric studies specify and attempt to measure the separate curves. Even for the more successful studies, the data requirements usually restrict the coverage to recent periods, which limits the significance of the results. It is desirable to draw on the evidence of long periods. This study reports experiments with a new test for supply effects utilizing the cyclical behavior of series just of interest rates and investment or business activity, and so allows coverage of a long period. The results are promising, though tentative because of some remaining difficulties in measurement and interpretation.

A TEST FOR SUPPLY EFFECTS. One might, in principle, draw conclusions about supply and demand effects simply from the cyclical behavior of these series at turning points. If investment and the interest rate turn down, for example, the decline reflects a predominant, leftward shift in

demand—if the rate continues to rise, a predominant, leftward shift in
supply. In practice, however, such inferences are subject to doubt. The
interest rate may not correctly reflect the cost of financing the particular items covered by the investment series, and a comparison confined
to concurrent movements does not allow for lags. A downturn in capital
borrowing while the rate is, at the moment, still rising might indicate a
leftward shift in the supply curve, for example, or it might indicate a
decline in investment demand which reduces orders immediately but
has a delayed effect on the interest rate. With lags, such comparisons
have ambiguous interpretations.

The test for supply effects presented here is designed to allow for
long lags, in both demand effects on interest rates and rate effects on
quantities, as well as to simplify the data requirements. The test treats
each cyclical phase in the rate or in investment or business activity as
one observation, and is based on the assumption that cyclical fluctuations in interest rates reflect largely reinforcing shifts in both the demand and the supply curves of capital funds (that is, the demand shifts
procyclically and the supply countercyclically). While such shifts in
demand tend to prolong the accompanying cyclical movement in investments, those in supply tend to limit it. Cyclical fluctuations in demand and supply do not, however, have identical timing, and disparate
turning points in interest rates and related investment series are often
observed. Much of the independent behavior of the supply curve can
be attributed to monetary and other financial factors. At business re-
vivals, for example, the supply of capital funds often continues to expand following an upturn in investment demand, as indicated by a fall
in interest rates while borrowing increases; but such a procyclical shift
in supply soon ends and then is reversed, and interest rates rise. The
tightening of credit restricts and eventually may help to end the expansion in investment. Therefore, for each month that the leftward shift in
supply is delayed the expansion in investment would tend, other things
the same, to last longer. A test of this supply effect is to determine
whether investment and business expansions are longer when interest
rates start to rise later. A similar test may be used for contractions.

Shifts in demand also affect rates and the duration of phases, of
course, but presumably not in the same way. Demand factors may well
account for the tendency of interest rates to lag at business cycle turns,
contrary to the assumption here that supply shifts are responsible. But
there is no reason to expect the timing of, say, an upturn in investment
demand to determine the date of the subsequent downturn in business
activity unless, as the test here assumes, expansion in the supply of

capital funds was limited and thus restricted the duration of the up-swing.

Although the logic of such a test applies in general to the price-quantity fluctuations of any sector of the economy, it uses a small part of the potentially available information and therefore appears useful primarily where the complexity of relationships and lack of data preclude a more complete analysis. Aggregate investment is such a sector. Even after making the simplifications, there are difficulties in representing the cost of financing particular investment activities by any of the available interest-rate series. Generally the investment series which cover a fairly long period pertain to certain industries. Since this study is mainly concerned with the financial effects on general business activity, most of it compares interest-rate movements with the National Bureau's chronology of business cycles, on the assumption that total investment demand in the economy is closely related to general business activity and has largely the same turning points. Later the analysis is extended to some series on residential and business construction. Since business cycles depend upon a variety of economic relationships, such a test cannot establish whether monetary and financial effects on capital costs play a dominant role in cyclical turns. But it can suggest whether they make an important independent contribution.

Cyclical Fluctuations in Interest Rates and the Duration of Reference-Cycle Phases

THE LAGGED TIMING OF INTEREST RATES. Reasonably accurate estimates of the duration of business cycles extend back to the mid-1800's, providing a large number of observations. The estimates are used here with series on commercial paper rates and high-grade bond yields. Those rates are assumed to reflect the relative movements of demand and supply in the financial market as a whole. Paper rates are relevant to short-term business loans for inventory investment; bond yields, to long-term capital financing. The bond series is Macaulay's high-grade railroad average, through 1937, and Moody's Aaa public utility average, thereafter. Before the 1930's, railroad bonds were much in favor with investors seeking safety; but after the experiences of that decade, preferences shifted, in particular to public utility bonds. During the 1930's no group of corporate bonds was widely viewed as high grade. For that and other reasons, to be noted later, none of the cyclical movements between 1933 and 1945 are retained for bonds in the subsequent analysis. The turning points selected for bond series are shown in Chart 1-1. Those for commercial paper (not shown) are similar.

Turning points present certain problems of identification. First of all, cyclical turns are not always clearly defined, and the selection of a particular date may involve considerable error. Second, interest rates sometimes have extra cyclical movements corresponding to the same reference phase, and it is not always clear which movement corresponds to the reference phase. The choice of one turn rather than another can make considerable difference in the length of leads or lags. To avoid arbitrary matchings when the rate has multiple turns, the highest peak has been matched with reference peaks, the lowest trough with reference troughs; the extra turns are ignored. This procedure cannot be defended as always being appropriate, but multiple turns in rates are not numerous. A few of the special cases could unduly influence the statistical results, and they have been excluded. Reference phases skipped by the interest rates are also excluded; they will be discussed later.

The rate series conform to most reference cycles, but usually with a lag of variable length. For the conforming movements, the median lag for bonds is six months at troughs and fourteen at peaks; for commercial paper, five and four months, respectively. A long, fairly regular lag is characteristic of few other economic variables. The lags may be attributed in part to monetary and other financial developments on the supply side.[1] Demand factors are less likely to run counter to general business activity for long and therefore to produce lags in rates.

A REGRESSION TEST. For conforming movements in the interest rate, the relevant variables may be denoted by L_t, A_t and D_t as defined in Figure 1-1. L has usually been positive, indicating that the interest rate lags behind the reference-cycle turn. (Sometimes the lag is so long that L even exceeds D.) Occasionally, when rates have led, L is negative. The amplitude of movement in the interest rate during the lag segment is represented by A. According to the test for supply effects outlined above, both the length and the amplitude of the segment should affect the duration of the corresponding reference phase. We may separate the joint effect by treating the lag L and the amplitude per month A/L

---

[1] See my "Changes in the Cyclical Behavior of Interest Rates," *Review of Economics and Statistics,* Aug. 1966, reprinted as Occasional Paper 100, New York, NBER.

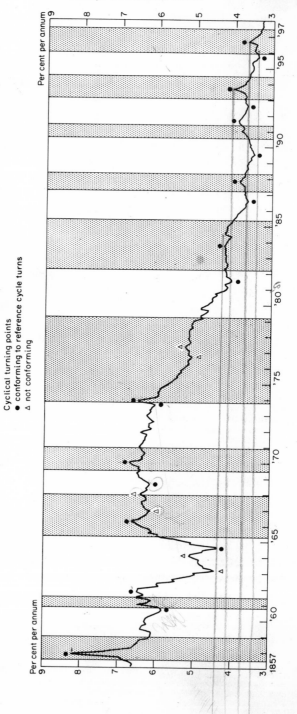

CHART 1-1. Cyclical Turning Points in High-Grade Corporate Bond Yields, 1857–1965

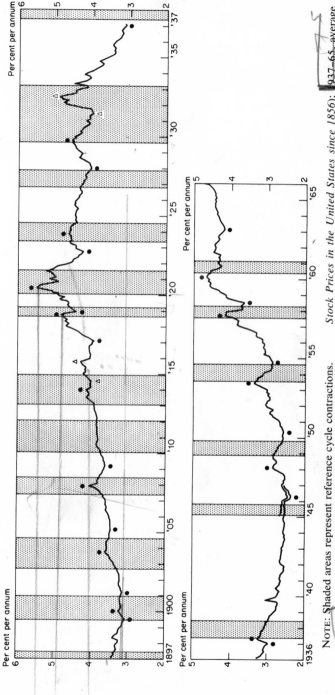

NOTE: Shaded areas represent reference cycle contractions. SOURCE: 1857–1937, average high-grade railroad bonds (F. R. Macaulay, *The Movements of Interest Rates, Bond Yields and Stock Prices in the United States since 1856*); 1937–65, average of Aaa public-utility bonds (1937–45 from S. Homer, *A History of Interest Rates*, 1945–65 from *Moody's Public Utility Manual*).

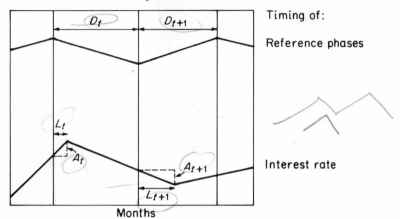

FIGURE 1-1. Movement of Interest Rates at Reference-Cycle Turns

as independent variables. An effect of interest rates on duration may then be expressed by the regression equation (assumed linear):

$$D = \alpha L + \beta \frac{A}{L} + C + \epsilon \qquad (1)$$

where α and β are constant parameters, C is a constant term, and ϵ is a random variable representing all the other factors which produce variations in the duration of phases. The sign of A/L is defined to be positive when rates are rising between peaks in the rate and business or when rates are declining between troughs; and negative for the opposite movements. By this designation of the sign, positive movements in A/L tend to shorten the accompanying reference phase, so the sign of β should be negative.

Charts 1-2 and 1-3 present scatter diagrams of D and L for the two interest rates. Skipped phases, as mentioned earlier, have been excluded.[2] A few extreme observations pertain to unusually long durations: 1873–79, 1933–37, and 1938–45, except that bond yields skipped the last one. The latter two had long lags in the interest rates which exaggerate the apparent correlation with duration, while the 1873–79 contraction had a leading turn in the interest rates which re-

[2] One could mechanically include them by relating the skipped phase to the nearest appropriate turn in the interest rate, but that would relate the same turn to two phases which has the implausible implication that the timing of the same interest-rate movement affects the duration of two separate phases. For this reason it seems preferable simply to exclude the few skipped phases.

duces the apparent correlation. The 1873–79 contraction was a special case: There is reason to believe that the business trough actually came earlier than 1879. Also, the interest rates had multiple cyclical turns and began a secular downtrend during that phase, casting doubt on whether our selection of the first of those turns is appropriate. In any event, the extreme observations are best excluded when examining the association for most cycles. The 1937–38 contraction is also excluded for bonds, as noted earlier, because of doubt about the data used for that period.

For the remaining forty-two phases for bonds and forty-six for com-

CHART 1-2. Lead or Lag in Bond Yields at Reference Cycle Turns, and Duration of References Phases, 1857–1960

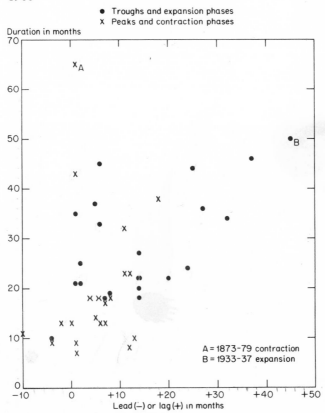

SOURCE: Same as Chart 1-1.

CHART 1-3. Lead or Lag in Commercial Paper Rate at Reference Cycle Turns, and Duration of Reference Phases, 1857–1960

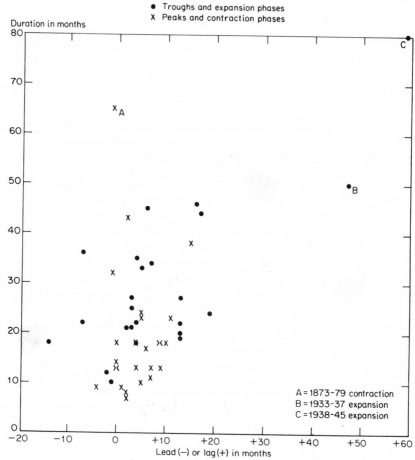

SOURCE: Commercial paper rate from Macaulay to February 1936, thereafter from weekly data in *Commercial and Financial Chronicle*.

mercial paper, Table 1-1 presents regressions of the duration on the lead or lag and average amplitude as in equation (1). Lack of independence in the residuals, often a serious problem in time series regressions, should be largely absent here because the observations represent separate cyclical phases spaced fairly far apart in time. However, the residuals may not be normally distributed, particularly if some effects on duration are relatively large and do not follow a normal distribution. Consequently, use of the t test of significance may involve bias.

Table 1-1 indicates a relationship in the expected direction, though, as might be expected from our disregard of demand effects, the correlation is low. Yet by the t test it is significant ($t > 2$) for all phases together and for bonds in expansions. The coefficient of the amplitude variable has the correct sign but is not significant. Apparently the amplitude, as distinct from the direction of movements early in the

TABLE 1-1. Interest Rates and Duration of Reference Phases 1857–1960, Regression Equations

Interest Rate and Reference Phases [a]	Regression Coefficient [b] (and t value)		Con- stant Term (months) (C)	Total Cor- rela- tion Co- effi- cient	No. of Obser- vations
	Lead or Lag (L)	Amplitude Per Month [c] (A/L)			
Bonds	.58(3.8)	−.25(0.8)	18	.52	42
Commercial paper	.52(2.2)	−.04(1.0)	20	.34	46
Bonds					
All phases	.62(3.8)		17	.52	42
Expansions	.45(2.4)		22	.49	21
Contractions	.64(1.8)		14	.38	21
Commercial paper					
All phases	.49(2.1)		19	.31	46
Expansions	.41(1.6)		24	.35	22
Contractions	.58(1.4)		15	.29	24
Bonds, Expansions Added to:					
Subsequent contractions	.48(2.0)		37	.43	19
Previous contractions	.36(1.9)		37	.43	18
Commercial paper, Expansions Added to:					
Subsequent contractions	.25(0.8)		42	.17	21
Previous contractions	.27(1.1)		40	.24	21

SOURCE: Same as Charts 1-1 and 1-3.

[a] Excluding 1873–79, 1933–37, and 1938–45 reference phases for commercial paper rate and first two of those phases and 1937–38 for bond yields, as well as adjacent phases for the bottom four regressions.

[b] Regression equation is eq. (1) in text. See accompanying figure for definition of variables. Signs of t values have been dropped. For 19 or 20 degrees of freedom, the value of t significant at the .05 level is 2.09; for 40 degrees of freedom it is 2.02.

[c] Sign is positive if change in rate during period of lead or lag relative to reference turn works to shorten corresponding reference phase, negative if to lengthen it (that is, increases relative to peaks and declines relative to troughs are positive, declines at peaks and increases at troughs are negative). If L is zero, A/L is also made zero.

phase, is an unimportant part of the total effect of supply shifts during the entire phase. We cannot disentangle that total effect from demand effects in a test of this kind.[3] The amplitude variable has been omitted from the other regressions in the table, which show roughly similar results for expansions and contractions separately.

The bottom group of four regressions is designed to test for possible bias due to secular variations in trend. Reference cycle turns are derived from series with growth trends whereas interest rates, being pure numbers, have no natural growth. Although bond yields exhibit long swings of 15–30 years duration, they have no clear trend over the period covered as a whole. An upward trend in a series shifts peaks forward and troughs backward, thus lengthening expansions and shortening contractions. Hence, when the intercyclical trend in business activity is relatively strong (assuming the trend in the rates is negligible), business cycles have longer expansions and shorter contractions than interest rates do. This by itself would tend to increase lags in interest rates at troughs and to reduce lags at peaks. If the magnitude of the trend varied secularly, there would appear to be a positive association between the duration of phases and the corresponding lag in interest rates, as found here. And this effect of trend could pertain separately to expansions and contractions. If we add together the L's for adjacent expansions and contractions, the shifts in timing due to such trend will cancel out. The bottom four regressions in Table 1-1 give the results two ways, pairing expansions (1) with subsequent contractions and (2) with previous contractions. For each pair, the regression related the sum of the two D's to the sum of the two L's. Either method of pairing produces a reduction in correlation, suggesting that trend may have affected the previous results, though less for bonds than for commercial paper. The trend-adjusted relation for bonds remains on the borderline of signifi-

---

[3] Various regressions (not presented) were run to measure the effect on duration of the amplitude of change per month in the interest rate from its turning point to the end of the reference phase and of the amplitude for the initial sections of that segment. The partial correlation of such variables were usually negative (showing, as expected, that a larger amplitude produces a shorter phase), but on the whole they were not significant. This may not indicate unimportance, however, because the concurrent positive effect of business activity on interest rates tends to hide the inverse effect of their changes on duration. A vigorous business expansion, for example, generates momentum to prolong the upswing while it also raises interest rates. The separate effects of demand and supply on rates cannot readily be distinguished. Indeed, the tests of Table 1-1 are specifically designed to avoid that problem by examining the early stages of the phase, before rates have turned, during which L and A/L measure the extent to which shifts in supply exceed those in demand. During the lag segment, supply conditions contribute to a continuation of the phase and have not yet begun to restrict it.

cance (at the .05 level). That for commercial paper rates remains positive but falls below the significance level; turns in that series appear to reflect cyclical shifts in the supply curve of total credit less strongly.

The remainder of this section discusses the problem of skipped phases and of the shift in timing of bond yields after 1914.

SKIPPED PHASES. In a few cases, the interest rates have no identifiable cyclical movement corresponding to a reference phase. Such an uninterrupted rise or decline in the rate, if supply shifts are mainly responsible, tends to shorten or prolong the phase. Table 1-2 gives the expected and actual effects for the skipped phases. In five of the six

TABLE 1-2. Reference-Cycle Phases Skipped by Interest Rates, 1857–1960

	Reference Phase			Direction of Cyclical Movement and Effect on Reference Phase Skipped	
Date	Direction	Duration (months)	Relation to Average Duration[a]	Commercial Paper Rates	Corporate Bond Yield
Jan. 1910–Jan. 1912	Cont.	24	Long		Up, Prolong
Jan. 1912–Jan. 1913	Exp.	12	Short		Up, Shorten
July 1924–Oct. 1926	Exp.	27	Equal		Down, Prolong
Oct. 1926–Nov. 1927	Cont.	13	Short		Down, Shorten
June 1938–Feb. 1945	Exp.	80	Long		Down, Prolong
Feb. 1945–Oct. 1945	Cont.	8	Short	Up, Prolong	Down, Shorten
Oct. 1945–Nov. 1948	Exp.	37	Long	Up, Shorten	

SOURCE: Same as Chart 1-1 for bond yields; Chart 1-3 for commercial paper rates.
[a] Average of all reference phases, 1857–1960: 26.9 months for expansions, 17.2 for contractions.

phases skipped by the bond series, the relative duration of the phase was consistent with the expected effect of the movement in bond yields: rising bond yields appeared to shorten, and falling yields to prolong, business expansions; and conversely for business contractions. (The evidence for the sixth phase, which is equal to the average, is neutral.) Commercial paper rates skipped but two reference phases, both in the early post-World War II years when the Federal Reserve pegged government bond prices. Those two phases had lengths inconsistent with the upward movements in commercial paper rates, but those movements were extremely small and understandably exerted little restraint on business activity. On the whole, the skipped phases are consistent with supply effects on the duration of reference phases.

THE SHIFT IN TIMING OF BOND YIELDS. Although the statistical evidence clearly indicates a financial effect by bond yields on business activity, the yields nevertheless raise questions of interpretation that require further consideration. As shown in Table 1-3, the lagged timing of bond yields, typically quite long before World War I, has shortened noticeably since then.[4] The regression results suggest that such a shortening of lags would reduce the duration of later reference phases,

TABLE 1-3. Timing of Bond Yields at Reference Turns and Average Duration of Reference Phases, Before and After 1914 (*months*)

	Median Lag (+) at		Average Duration of Reference Phases
	Peaks	Troughs	
1857–1914	+9.5	+14	23
1915–60	+1	+3.5	23

NOTE: Coverage same as for Table 1-1, that is, excluding 1873–79, 1933–37, and 1937–38, as well as skipped phases.

yet the average duration has not changed. Evidently the regression lines shifted between the two periods, as is confirmed by the separate fits reported in the top part of Table 1-4. The slope of the line and the constant term increased from the earlier to the later period. For expansions and contractions fitted separately (not shown), there is the same increase in the constant term; the slope also increases for expansions though not for contractions. Such a major shift in the relationship seems to indicate that interest-rate movements do not affect duration. But that conclusion then leaves no apparent explanation for the correlations within each period.

Another interpretation is that the correlations do indicate an effect of supply shifts on investment and business activity but that the reflection of those shifts in bond movements has speeded up, altering our measuring rod. Why the timing of bond cycles changed is not clear, though, presumably, growth in the size and activity of the bond market contributed to greater sensitivity of yields to financial developments.

[4] See also "Changes in the Cyclical Behavior of Interest Rates."

TABLE 1-4. Regression of Reference-Phase Duration on Lead or Lag in Bond Yields and in Monetary Growth Rate, Before and After 1914

	Regression Coefficient (and *t* value) of Lead or Lag (*L*)	Constant Term (months)	Total Correlation Coefficient	No. of Observations
Bonds				
1857–1914	.70(4.4)	14	.67	26
1915–60	.98(2.5)	20	.56	16
Monetary Growth Rate (inverted)				
1870–1960	.73(5.6)	17	.69	37
1870–1914	.61(3.2)	17	.60	21
1915–61	.85(4.3)	17	.75	16

SOURCE: Bond yields, same as for Table 1-1; money, currency outside banks plus demand and time deposits from M. Friedman and A. Schwartz, *A Monetary History of the United States, 1867–1960,* Princeton for NBER, 1963, Table A1 series revised and extended. The monetary series is annual before 1907, making the turning points less reliable in the earlier period. The dates of some of the monetary turns are different than those shown in "Changes in the Cyclical Behavior of Interest Rates," Chart 3, because of revisions.

This interpretation is further suggested by the related behavior of the growth rate of the money stock. Cycles in monetary growth contribute to cyclical shifts in the supply of loanable funds and help to account for the lagged cyclical behavior of interest rates. My earlier study [5] found that troughs in interest rates tend to coincide with peaks in monetary growth, and peaks in rates with monetary troughs — that is, monetary growth has an inverted relation to interest rates. We may therefore expect to find a relation between turns in monetary growth (inverted) and the duration of reference phases. (Chart 1-4 presents the scatter diagram.) Monetary growth (inverted) tends over the period covered there to lag behind matched reference turns, in the same way that interest rates do, and to exhibit a similar correspondence to phase durations. Correlations of this relation, shown in the lower panel of Table 1-4 which excludes the three extreme observations marked on the chart, are significant. The relation for bond yields therefore parallels a similar relation for monetary growth.

[5] *Ibid.,* Chart 1-3 and Table 1-7. That study also presented evidence that the cycles in monetary growth are not themselves produced by interest-rate movements.

CHART 1-4. Lead or Lag in the Rate of Change in the Money Stock at Non-war Reference Cycle Turns, and Duration of Reference Phases, 1870–1960

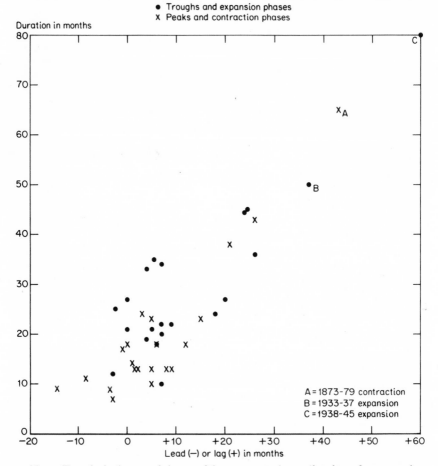

NOTE: Troughs in the rate of change of the money stock are related to reference peaks, and peaks to reference troughs.

SOURCE: Same as Table 1-4.

This similarity suggests the following interpretation: A cyclical downturn in monetary growth during business expansion contributes to an upturn in interest rates and exerts a growing restraint on investment which eventually helps to bring on a recession in activity; and, conversely, a cyclical upturn in monetary growth during a recession contributes to a decline in interest rates, stimulates investment, and subsequently leads to a business revival. The money correlations are pertinent to the shift in timing for bonds, mentioned above, because the constant term of the money regressions is not larger after 1914 than it was before. That the timing of the monetary cycles and their relation to duration have remained the same suggests that the change in timing for bonds did not reflect a change in the cyclical effect of the supply of loanable funds on business activity.[6]

To be sure, the evidence is far from conclusive and must be viewed as tentative. Other interpretations cannot be ruled out, though two alternatives examined in the next section, at first sight appealing, are found not to be supported by the evidence.

Alternative Interpretations of the Evidence

The fact that D can be viewed as the sum of two correlated segments, L and $D - L$, suggests two alternative interpretations of the data. One is that D is spuriously correlated with L because both are influenced by the same cyclical factors. Another is that the association is purely mechanical and without economic significance, because turns in interest rates occur at random somewhere within each reference phase. Thus, although D is independent of L, if for any reason D should be larger L would also tend to be larger. We may consider these two alternative interpretations in turn.

COMMON INFLUENCES ON D AND L. Some business phases, one might argue, proceed slowly and some rapidly, and interconnections across the economy maintain a similar rate of movement in each sector. In slowly developing phases which have long durations, interest rates tend to move sluggishly and to have delayed turning points; and rapidly developing phases behave conversely. There could be an association between L and D, therefore, even though neither was directly related to the other. Since interest rates obviously depend on developments in the economy at large, this rationalization of the preceding results is plausible on the surface and deserves consideration.

To judge its importance in the correlations of Tables 1-2 and 1-4, a variable representing the pace of general business activity in each phase can be added to those regressions. Such a variable may be

---

[6] This conclusion disregards the increased slope of the later regressions for both bonds and money, which seems to suggest that in the later period the lag in the turning point is more nearly additive to the phase duration. It is not clear what might produce such a change.

represented by the average change per month in an index of general business activity and is denoted by *B*. If it accounted for the previous results, it would be the only variable having a significant partial correlation with duration. The results are presented in Table 1-5.

TABLE 1-5. Bond Yield and Duration of Reference Cycle Phase: Regression of Duration on Lead or Lag and Severity of Reference Phase

	Partial Correlation Coefficient (and *t* value)		
	Lead or Lag (*L*)	Severity of Reference Phase (*B*)	Multiple Correlation Coefficient
Expansions	.48(2.3)	−.66(3.6)	.74
Contractions	.27(1.2)	−.36(1.6)	.50
All phases	.41(2.8)	−.54(3.9)	.69

SOURCE: Bond yield, same as Chart 1-1; severity of reference phase, G. H. Moore (ed.), *Business Cycle Indicators,* Vol. I, Princeton for NBER, 1961, p. 104, and unpublished extensions and revisions.

NOTE: Regression equation is

$$D = \alpha L + \beta B + C,$$

where *L* is lead (−) or lag (+) of interest rate from reference-cycle turn, *D* is duration of reference phase, *B* is an index of severity of the reference phase per month, and α, β, and *C* are regression coefficients. Signs of *t* values have been dropped.

Coverage is the same as for Table 1-2.

As expected, the index of business activity has a significant (negative) association with duration. The index does not, however, account for the effects found above for interest rates. The partial correlation coefficient of *D* on *L* is still significant in all phases, taken together, and for expansions, taken separately. Although the measure used for the average amplitude of business activity may not perfectly represent the common cyclical influences on the variables, it should be a reasonable proxy, and its failure to make a significant difference suggests that such influences are not important here.

EFFECTS OF *D* ON *L*. It is conceivable that the financial system operates in such a manner that interest rates tend to have cyclical upturns when business activity expands and downturns when it contracts. If, in addition, the turns in rates occur at random during the concurrent

reference phase, *L* would tend to vary with *D*. There are some difficulties in specifying the economic conditions under which such a
dependence could happen,[7] but the possibility has disarming simplicity
and should be examined.

Evidence is afforded by the behavior of other economic series. If
the correlation between *D* and *L* for interest rates reflects a mechanical relationship rather than financial influences on business cycles,
nonfinancial series should be correlated with *D* in the same way. A
group of representative economic time series was examined for such
correlation.[8] The selection favored series with a long coverage and
included a broad sample of economic activity. Only one gave evidence
of a systematic correlation between the lead or lag from reference
turns and the duration of the concurrent reference phase.[9] Since bond
yields and monetary growth exhibit a rare relationship to reference
phases, it cannot be dismissed as simply a mechanical characteristic
of cycles observable in a variety of series.

Some Statistical Properties of the Relationship

If, as the evidence suggests, increases in interest rates restrain business
expansions and decreases stimulate recovery from business contractions, such effects seem to imply a cyclical pattern of rates having an
inverted conformity to reference cycles and a lead in timing. How-

---

[7] As a purely statistical proposition, L_t can be defined as a stochastic variable drawn
at random from a population whose mean value is some fraction of D_t. The two would
then be correlated over time, consistent with the results here. But if this were taken to
imply an effect of *D* upon *L*, the inference would face difficulties in economic interpretation. Since the mean of the distribution of *L* is proportional to the length of the concurrent business phase not yet ended, an event early in the cycle is made to depend upon
future developments. For developments early in a phase to be determined by its ultimate
duration seems far fetched. In addition, contrary to this determination of *L*, the turn in
rates does not always occur during the phase; it sometimes occurs earlier or later.

[8] Those examined were new incorporations 1861–1960; wholesale prices 1857–1960;
common stock prices 1873–1960; bank clearings outside New York City 1879–1960;
new orders of durable goods 1921–60; contracts for total commercial and industrial
building 1919–60; labor costs per unit of output 1919–60; capital expenditures for new
plant and equipment 1918–60; production worker employment 1914–60.

[9] New incorporations, 1861–1960 (with extreme observations for 1873–79, 1933–37,
and 1938–45 excluded), was the only series to show a significant correlation between
D and *L* at the .05 level, though unlike bonds and money (inverted), generally this series
leads reference turns (*L* is usually negative).

ever, movements in business activity also exert a strong pull (from the demand side) on interest rates, which tends to produce positive conformity and coincident or lagging timing. Which pattern predominates may be judged from the stability of the timing relation on each basis. σ_L^2 is the variance of the timing relation on a positive basis; σ_{D-L}^2 is the variance of the timing on an inverted basis. Table 1-6 shows that σ_L is smaller than σ_{D-L} (though about the same in expansions, taken alone). Interest rates conform more closely to reference cycles on a positive than on an inverted basis.[10] By implication, the effect of business activity on interest rates is slightly more powerful than the effect of the rates on activity in determining the relation between the two.

TABLE 1-6. Stability of Timing in Bond Yields at Reference Cycle Turns on Positive and Inverted Basis (*standard error of lead or lag, months*)

	Positive Basis σ_L	Inverted Basis σ_{D-L}	Ratio of Standard Errors σ_L/σ_{D-L}
Expansions	11.2	10.8	1.03
Contractions	5.7	9.2	.62
All phases	9.3	10.1	.92
1852–1914	8.5	6.3	1.36
1915–61	7.6	11.0	.69

SOURCE: Same as for Tables 1-1 and 1-4.

It is just this—the strong effect of activity on the rates—that makes the reverse effect elusive and difficult to identify. Nevertheless, activity effects on rates do not result in a perfect positive conformity, partly because of deviations produced by monetary and other financial influences. Because of the frequent occurrence of deviations from perfect positive conformity, the preceding test of a rate effect on duration becomes possible.

The fact that $D - L$ varies more than L is one reason for the low correlation with D, since the ratio of segment variances and the slope of the regression line jointly determine the correlation coefficient.

---

[10] It is easily shown that this implies $R_{D,L} < R_{D,D-L}$, which expresses the general rule that the sum of two nonidentical series has a greater correlation with the component having the larger variance.

This may be demonstrated. By definition we have

$$R_{D,L}^2 = \hat{\alpha}^2 \frac{\sigma_L^2}{\sigma_D^2}$$

where $\hat{\alpha}$ is the estimate of the regression slope, $\sigma_{D,L}/\sigma_L^2$. The variance of D can be decomposed into

$$\sigma_D^2 = \sigma_{D-L}^2 + \sigma_L^2 + 2\sigma_{D-L,L}.$$

Since $\sigma_{D-L,L} = \sigma_{D,L} - \sigma_L^2 = \hat{\alpha}\sigma_L^2 - \sigma_L^2 = -(1 - \hat{\alpha})\sigma_L^2$, we have

$$\sigma_D^2 = \sigma_{D-L}^2 + \sigma_L^2(2\hat{\alpha} - 1). \tag{1}$$

Hence

$$R_{D,L}^2 = \frac{\hat{\alpha}^2}{(\sigma_{D-L}^2/\sigma_L^2) + 2\hat{\alpha} - 1} \tag{2}$$

The ratio of segment variances, $\sigma_{D-L}^2/\sigma_L^2$, and the slope α are usually greater than unity. Consequently, $R_{D,L}$ is less than α.[11]

A regression slope below unity means that an increase in L is associated on the average with a smaller numerical increase in D, suggesting that financial effects on duration are not additive to other effects but interact with them. Interest rates appear to influence business activity by speeding up or slowing down the effects of other factors, which in turn constrain the financial effects. Without taking those other factors into account, we cannot take full advantage of the information provided by movements in interest rates. The statistical result of specifying such a nonlinear relationship as linear is to introduce a negative correlation between L and ϵ. Since they are assumed to be uncorrelated by the least squares regression procedure, the negative correlation shows up between L and $D - L$, the remainder of the reference phase after the turn in the interest rate.[12]

Because of this negative correlation and the relatively high variability in $D - L$, L provides a weak prediction of D. The regression is nevertheless significant, and therefore a better predictor than the mean length of past phases. If the probability distribution of phase durations does not change over time, the error of such a prediction can be esti-

[11] It is not clear which of these quantities are independent and which are determined by the others. We might plausibly expect economic factors to determine the segment variances and the slope of the relationship between D and L, which would make the correlation coefficient the dependent quantity. In view of the increase in $\hat{\alpha}$ after 1914, however, it is not clear whether that reasoning is correct.

[12] Since, $\sigma_{D-L,L} = -(1 - \hat{\alpha})\sigma_L^2$ as shown above, $R_{L,D-L} < 0$ if $\alpha < 1$.

mated by the standard deviation of past durations, σ_D. Under the assumption of no change in the probability distribution, however, the regression equations of Tables 1-1 and 1-4 give a better prediction, namely $\hat{\alpha}L_t + \hat{c}$, where $\hat{\alpha}$ and $\hat{c}$ are the estimated regression coefficients. The standard error of their predictions is less than σ_D by the fraction $\sqrt{1 - R^2}$, where R is the correlation coefficient of the regression fit. For bonds in all phases it is 85 per cent ($\sqrt{1 - .52^2}$); and in the earlier and the later period separately, 74 and 83 per cent, respectively. That provides a slight improvement over simply projecting the mean value of past durations, though the comparison disregards the few phases listed in Table 1-2 in which the interest rate failed to give any prediction at all because of no cyclical turn. It is also true that the regression prediction can be made only after the interest rate turns — and L_t becomes known. While this usually occurs during the phase, not at its beginning, the evidence still suggests that a phase is most unlikely to end before the interest rate turns.

Interest-Rate Effects on Construction Contracts

Changes in bond yields mainly affect the capital or durable goods sector of the economy where interest costs are relevant to purchasers. Therefore, the previous evidence will be extended to examine the relation between cycles in interest rates and investment. Unfortunately, there are few monthly or quarterly series on investment having a broad and fairly long coverage. Construction is one sector that partially meets those criteria. We have series on the value of construction contracts, subdivided into business and residential construction. Since cycles in these series often deviate considerably from general business activity, their use does not involve a repetition of the previous test. Indeed, contracts are signed well before any expenditures are made and represent an early stage of investment undertakings.

The three sections of Chart 1-5 show scatter diagrams of the lead or lag in bond yields at cyclical turns in the contract series and the duration of the corresponding phase in contract cycles. Skipped or nonmatching cyclical movements in the series have been excluded. In some cases there is no turn in bond yields during a contract phase, and it is not always clear whether an earlier or later turn in bonds should be matched with the phase in contracts. All matchings which appear at all reasonable are included in Chart 1-5. It would be desirable, in

CHART 1-5. Lead or Lag in Bond Yields at Turning Points in Value of Total, Residential and Nonresidential Construction Contracts, and Duration of Phases in Construction.

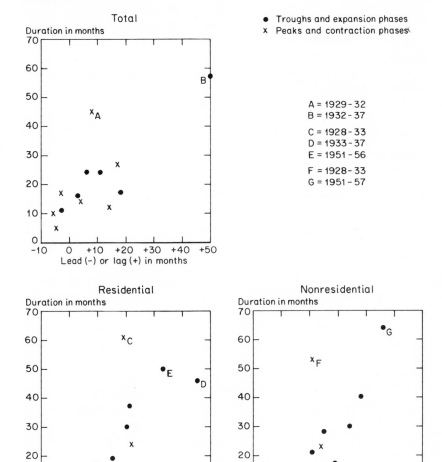

SOURCE: F. W. Dodge Corporation. Periods covered are total construction 1912–60, residential 1916–60, nonresidential 1919–60.

addition, to examine many other series covering a variety of capital-goods industries, and different interest rates. The chart nevertheless provides one sample of the timing relationship between interest rates and investment.

For the cyclical phases covered, the scatter diagrams reveal a positive association between the lead or lag in interest rates and the duration of the phases in contracts similar to the previous findings for reference phases. There are a few extreme observations dated on the chart. Most of these pertain to the 1930's as before, but one is for the 1950's: Residential and total construction contracts skipped the 1953–54 recession (except for a mild decline in 1951, not matched in bond yields), which produces an unusually long expansion from 1951 to 1956 or 1957. These dated observations would strongly influence regression estimates and have been excluded from the correlations presented in Table 1-7.

TABLE 1-7. Relation Between Interest Rates and Duration of Cyclical Phases in Value of Construction Contracts: Regression of Duration on Lead or Lag in Rates, and Stability of Timing

			Standard Error of Lead or Lag			
	Regression Coefficient (and t value) (1)	Correlation Coefficient (2)	Positive Basis σ_L (3)	Inverted Basis σ_{D-L} (4)	Ratio σ_L/σ_{D-L} (5)	No. of Observations (6)
Total, 1912–60	.84(5.3)	.83	8.7	5.2	1.7	15
Nonresidential, 1919–60	.49(2.5)	.64	8.4	6.5	1.3	11
Residential, 1916–60	.55(3.5)	.73	10.7	8.6	1.3	13

SOURCE: Same as Chart 1-3 excluding dated points.

The table gives results broadly similar to those of Tables 1-4 and 1-6 for reference phases. There are some differences: The regression coefficients are smaller and the correlation coefficients higher here than in Table 1-4 for the later period.

One indication that bond yields are related more closely to investment than to general business activity is the smaller variation in timing on an inverted basis (Table 1-7, Col. 4). Troughs in interest rates lead corresponding peaks in construction contracts, and peaks in rates lead troughs in contracts, with less variation in the length of leads $(D - L)$ than is true for reference phases (Table 1-6). As was shown by identity (2) on page 23, however, these statistical measures are not independent of each other. When the ratio of timing variances (Table

1-7, Col. 5) favors the positive basis, the correlation coefficient tends to be higher, while it tends to be lower for a smaller slope of the regression. Because of the limited coverage, these differences may be in the nature of random variations. The over-all results here for construction activity nevertheless support implications of the previous tables and suggest, if tentatively, an interest-rate effect on investment undertakings.

Summary

Business commentators have long pointed to the importance of financial effects in business cycles. Yet it has proved difficult to measure these effects statistically because of their complex interaction with other cyclical developments. This paper examines one aspect of the financial role, and partly avoids some of the difficulties, by comparing turning points in interest rates with the duration of cyclical phases in business activity. Most interest rates have, as a rule, lagged business-cycle turns. On the assumption that shifts in the demand for loanable funds conform closely to movements in business activity, the lagged turns reflect nonconforming movements in the supply function for funds. If autonomous shifts in supply play an important role in cycles, they will affect the timing of interest-rate cycles and contribute with a lag to the turning points in business activity. The test of such effects presented here is whether delayed upturns in rates prolong business expansions and delayed downturns prolong contractions, and whether the converse is true for early turns in rates. To be sure, the test ignores much relevant information about business cycles, but it has the important advantage of not requiring a large variety or high quality of data and therefore allows the coverage of a long period. The analysis relates bond yields and commercial paper rates to business cycles for the period 1857 to 1960, and to cycles in construction contracts for the period since World War I.

The statistical results point to a weak but significant association between the duration of business cycle expansions and contractions and the corresponding lag in rates at the initial turn of the phase. The association appears to reflect a financial influence on business activity rather than some mechanical characteristic of cyclical movements. The finding that turns in bond yields account for variations in the duration of cyclical phases in the value of construction contracts supports the results for business cycle phases.

The expansion of business activity since 1961 (not included in the analysis) dramatically illustrates the relationship, though of course no single instance is conclusive by itself. The cyclical upturn in bond yields came in early 1963 (Chart 1-1), two years after the business cycle trough and uncommonly late, while by the end of 1968 the business expansion had lasted nearly six years, the longest on record. On the previous interpretation, the supply of loanable funds in the early 1960's kept pace with the demand for funds and prevented financial restraint from impeding investment undertakings until 1963, and even then the restraint did not become strong, judging by the rate of rise in interest rates, until the second half of 1965.

The results suggest that interest-rate effects on business are not simply added to other factors but interact with them. If the upturn in interest rates is delayed so many months, the business expansion is not prolonged, on the average, by an equal number of months, but only by a fraction of the time. This makes interest-rate turns a less than ideal predictor of cycle duration; indeed, the predictive power of the relationship was found to be very small, except that business phases are unlikely to end while interest rates continue a cyclical movement in the opposite direction. Turning points in interest rates contain only a minimal amount of information about financial developments, and are often difficult to pinpoint even well after they have occurred. Consequently, interest rates cannot be seriously proposed as more than of marginal value for short-term forecasting.

The findings also require qualification for other reasons. Turning points in interest rates are sometimes ambiguous even by hindsight and may involve considerable error. Attempts to extend the analysis to the amplitude of movements in interest rates were not entirely successful, though in theory the amplitude as well as the direction of movements should be important. Finally, the regression for bond yields shifted after 1914, the explanation and relevance of which is not entirely clear. Despite these qualifications, the findings have value in lending concrete statistical support to other studies which point to financial influences in the business cycle. A similar relationship between turning points and the duration of reference phases also holds true for the monetary growth rate (inverted), which represents an autonomous source of fluctuations in the supply of loanable funds. Although indirect, the evidence suggests that monetary and other financial factors produce cyclical variations in bond yields which have important effects on business activity.

2

The Behavior of Residential Mortgage

Yields Since 1951 *Jack M. Guttentag*

This chapter reports some selected findings drawn from a study of the behavior of residential mortgage interest rates in the period since 1951. The findings reported here are based in part on new monthly and quarterly time series on residential mortgage rates and terms drawn from the internal records of some large life insurance companies.[1] These new data have a combination of important attributes heretofore not available in any single series.

First, the date of record is the date when loans were committed or authorized by lenders, rather than the date on which funds were disbursed. Hence the long and erratic lag characteristic of a series recorded on a disbursement basis is largely eliminated.

Second, the data cover all three types of residential mortgages (FHA, VA, and conventional); separate series are also available on mortgages acquired through correspondents as opposed to those originated directly by life insurance companies.

Third, the data include loan-value ratios and maturities, as well as fees and charges collected and paid by the lender over and above the contract rate. The contract rate, adjusted to take account of net fees

NOTE: This is a revised draft of a paper presented at a joint meeting of the American Real Estate and Urban Economics Association and the American Finance Association in San Francisco, California, on December 27, 1966. I am indebted to Phillip Cagan, Avery Cohan, and Richard Selden for helpful comments.

[1] The larger study upon which this paper is based, prepared in collaboration with Morris Beck, "New Series on Residential Mortgage Yields Since 1951," will provide a more detailed discussion of the technical features and analytical characteristics of these data, along with the series themselves.

and charges received by the lender, is referred to as "effective yield" or simply "yield." [2]

Fourth, the data have a broad geographic base, since the lenders covered by the series operate nationwide.

These new series are supplemented by data on FHA mortgages provided by that agency, and on FHA and VA mortgages provided by the Federal National Mortgage Association. These are sometimes referred to as "secondary market" series, since they are based on transactions covering more or less completed mortgages for "immediate delivery"; [3] in contrast, the National Bureau series is based on a commitment, which implies delivery of the mortgage sometime in the future. I have also used new series on conventional mortgages compiled by the Federal Home Loan Bank Board beginning in December 1962. [4]

The paper is divided into six sections. Following the summary, there are three sections on the relationship between mortgage yields and bond yields, and two sections on relationships between FHA, VA, and conventional mortgage yields.

Summary and Conclusions

The new commitment data show that for the period prior to 1961 conventional mortgage yields had a narrower cyclical amplitude than high grade bond yields. The new data thus confirm the findings of earlier investigators, but they do not support the various hypotheses advanced

---

[2] The effective yield is determined by the following factors: contract rate, fees and charges expressed as a per cent of the loan amount, face maturity, method of repayment (most home mortgages are on uniform monthly payment basis), and actual life (most mortgages are prepaid in full prior to maturity). The *Mortgage Yield Table* published by the Boston Financial Publishing Company shows the yield on uniform monthly payment mortgages for various combinations of these variables. Except where indicated otherwise, all effective yields referred to in this paper are based on the assumption of uniform monthly payments and prepayment in full after ten years.

[3] The FHA series are based on opinions of FHA insuring office directors regarding the prices prevailing in their areas. The FNMA quotations are based on sales reported by mortgage companies, mainly to life insurance companies and mutual savings banks, and may include commitments as well as over-the-counter purchases. FNMA quotations are said to be adjusted to a common service fee.

[4] These series are based on the date of the approval of a borrower's loan application, which is the same as the date of authorization, except in cases where commitments are given to builders. The Federal Home Loan Bank Board series used in this paper cover direct loans by life insurance companies secured by newly built homes.

by them to explain this phenomenon. The relatively narrow cyclical amplitude of mortgage yields, at least on loans by life insurance companies, is not due to failure to allow for cyclical changes in fees and charges. Nor does the evidence suggest that cyclical yield variability is dampened by variability in loan-value ratios and maturities, in borrower characteristics affecting risk, or in the composition of loan aggregates by region or by individual lender. The hypothesis that relatively high origination costs dampen mortgage yield variability is another one which does not withstand close scrutiny. Cyclical changes in risk premiums could play a role in dampening mortgage yield amplitude relative to that of bonds, but most of the available evidence suggests otherwise.

The hypothesis suggested here is that the narrow cyclical amplitude of mortgage yields relative to bond yields reflects differences in market organization. Yields tend to be less volatile in negotiated markets where the borrower and the lender are in direct contact, than in dealer-type markets. Some of the reasons for this also underlie the tendency for mortgage yields to *lag* bond yields at cyclical turning points.

The new authorizations data confirm that mortgage yields tend to lag behind bond yields at cyclical turning points. This is not explained by the hypothesis that small changes in mortgage market conditions register first in such nonrate dimensions of mortgage loans as loan-value ratios, maturities or fees and charges. The evidence indicates that these characteristics may be even less sensitive than the contract rate. The hypothesis suggested to explain the lag in mortgage yields is that the basic demand for mortgage credit is relatively stable and that short-run developments affecting general yield levels ordinarily originate in the bond markets. The transmission of bond yield changes to the mortgage market is entirely dependent on the activities of the primary lenders (there is no dealer arbitrage). Since these lenders respond only to what they consider pervasive movements in bond yields, which must prove out over time, the transmission process takes time and mortgage yields lag. The transmission lag may account in part for the smaller cyclical amplitude of mortgage yields than of bond yields, since the lag prevents the full range of bond yield changes from being transmitted to the mortgage market.

The 1961–66 behavior of mortgage yields, however, represents a sharp break with past patterns. During the long stretch of easy money extending from 1961 to 1965, mortgage yields continued to decline far beyond the lower turning point of bond yields. Then as tight money emerged in 1966, mortgage yields rose with unprecedented rapidity.

In contrast to the prior three cycles, the amplitude of conventional mortgage yields (measured in basis points) was comparable to that of bonds in both phases of the 1961–66 cycle.

Structural changes affecting the commercial banking system may have been largely responsible for this. During 1961–66, commercial banks underwent a marked shift in policy toward time deposits. With their secondary reserves of government securities largely depleted, time deposits became a valuable source of funds over which commercial banks could exercise some degree of control. The importance of time deposits in the bank liability structure, which had been growing steadily for some time, accelerated markedly. The higher deposit costs and reduced liquidity requirements associated with time deposits encouraged a portfolio shift into relatively high-yielding mortgages. This shift put added downward pressure on mortgage yields during the easy money period of 1961–65.

When tight money emerged in 1966 banks did not withdraw wholesale from the mortgage market as they had in earlier periods of restraint; probably, because by then many banks considered mortgages a permanent part of their portfolios. Under the same pressures to meet business loan demands as in earlier periods of restraint, the banks had no buffer of government securities to liquidate. As a result they competed for time deposits with unprecedented aggressiveness and considerable success, in good part, at the expense of savings institutions which invest most of their funds in mortgages. Whereas government securities liquidation in earlier periods had dispersed market pressures rather widely, the withdrawal of funds from savings institutions impinged directly on the mortgage market and resulted in an unprecedented rise in mortgage yields.

There is some indication that the yield advantage of conventional over FHA mortgages declined secularly over the period 1949–66. Presumably the decline reflected favorable repayment experience over the period, which would have reduced *ex ante* risk premiums on conventional loans.

The conventional-FHA yield differential does not show any systematic cyclical pattern. During two periods of extreme credit stringency, in late 1959–60 and 1966, FHA mortgages came to yield appreciably more than conventional ones, however. This appears to be a real market phenomenon rather than a statistical accident; it shows up in data covering individual lenders, and in data for individual states — both states with low usury ceilings and states with high or no ceilings. One explanation is that those mortgage lenders who prefer

FHAs to conventionals are sensitive to yield differentials between mortgages and bonds and shift out of mortgages when capital markets become very tight. Mortgage lenders who prefer conventionals are willing to absorb the overhang of FHAs only at premium rates.

At various times, FHA mortgages have carried a higher contract rate than VAs, and this has affected their relative yield. Prior to mid-1952, FHAs and VAs carried premiums. Under these conditions FHAs, having a higher contract rate, carried higher yields. This probably resulted from the risk aversion of conservative lenders to the uncertainty associated with realized yield when mortgages sell above par. (The yield realized on a mortgage that is not priced at par depends not only on the contract rate and the size of the premium or discount, but also on the life of the mortgage which is not known in advance. Most mortgages are prepaid in full well before maturity.) When mortgages carry premiums yield is an increasing function of mortgage life and may be very low, even zero or negative, if the mortgage is paid off soon after origination. An over-estimate of mortgage life can thus have a seriously adverse effect on realized yield. If the market is dominated by conservative lenders, concerned with the "worst that can happen," the premium paid on a high contract rate mortgage will not be large enough to provide a yield equal to that on a low contract rate mortgage when yields are calculated on the basis of any reasonable estimate of expected life.

During 1957–61 FHA contract rates were again higher than VAs, but in this period both carried discounts. When mortgages carry discounts, yield is a decreasing function of life and the lowest possible yield, realized if the mortgage runs to maturity, is not much lower than the yield based on its expected life. Hence, yield uncertainty associated with uncertainty regarding mortgage life probably does not have much influence on the relative yields of mortgages carrying different contract rates.

Discounts raise public relations problems, however, particularly with regard to larger lenders in the public eye such as the life insurance companies covered by our interest rate study. These lenders, sensitive to public censure, took discounts on VAs that were smaller than those necessary to equalize the yield with the higher contract rate FHAs, but they sharply reduced their VA volume. Hence, for these lenders FHAs yielded more than VAs. Data provided by FNMA reveal, however, that in the "free" market where discounts on VAs rose to the level needed to clear the market, VAs yielded more than FHAs. It is ironical that the public pressures on large institutions to limit discounts on VA mortgages, by causing them to sharply reduce their VA volume, had the effect of increasing pressure on VA discounts in the free market.

There are indications, however, that during 1958–59 life insurance company attitudes toward discounting began to change in that they began to accept the discounts required to bring VA yields into an appropriate relationship to FHA yields. By 1961 the mortgage market had evidently learned to live with discounts.

Cyclical Amplitude of Mortgage Yields and Bond Yields

In an earlier study, Klaman noted that conventional mortgage interest rates have a smaller cyclical amplitude than bond yields.[5] The same observation was made earlier by Grebler, Blank and Winnick.[6] Although Klaman's data were recorded on the disbursement date, which tends to dampen amplitude,[7] the observation also applies to mortgage yields recorded on an authorization basis. As shown in Table 2-1, the change in conventional mortgage yields (measured in basis points) in each of six cyclical phases between 1949 and 1960 was smaller than the change in yields on U.S. government bonds, outstanding corporate bonds (both Aaa and Baa), and outstanding state and local bonds (both Aaa and Baa). (In the most recent cycle, conventional mortgage yield amplitude was comparable to that of bonds, but special factors were at work that will be discussed later in this paper.) Cyclical changes expressed in terms of percentage changes in yields would show even more marked differences in amplitude because of the higher absolute level of mortgage yields.

There are several possible explanations for the relatively narrow cyclical amplitude of mortgage interest rates. First, the data used by earlier investigators did not take account of fees and charges received or paid by lenders over and above the contract rate. Grebler, Blank and Winnick noted that "since the data show contract interest rates rather than yields on mortgages, they fail to reflect changes in premiums and discounts on mortgage loans, at times important in the

---

[5] Saul B. Klaman, *The Postwar Residential Mortgage Market,* Princeton for NBER, 1961, pp. 75–78.

[6] Leo Grebler, David M. Blank and Louis Winnick, *Capital Formation in Residential Real Estate: Trends and Prospects,* Princeton for NBER, 1956, p. 223.

[7] When mortgage rates are recorded on the disbursement date the recorded peak and trough values are actually averages of rates authorized during a number of months preceding the turning point month.

TABLE 2-1. Changes in Yields During Specific Cycles, Selected Series (*basis points*)

Period of Rise (R) or Decline (D)	Life Insurance Co. Mortgages— Authorization Basis		FHA Secondary Market	U.S. Govt. Long-Term	Corporate		State & Local	
	Conventional (1)	FHA (2)	(3)	(4)	Aaa (5)	Baa (6)	Aaa (7)	Baa (8)
1949–51 D	−10	−20	−28	−26	−27	−37	−63	−97
1951–53 R	56	62	85	94	83	72	134	168
1954 D	−15	−11	−33	−66	−53	−43	−74	−73
1954–58 R	97	104	110	126	125	164	153	155
1958 D	−31	−16	−31	−61	−55	−56	−74	−78
1958–60 R	72	81	94	125	104	81	80	72
Average, 3 cycles	47	49	64	83	75	76	96	107
1960–65 D	−60	na	−85	−64	−42	−56	−60	−101
1965–66 R	105	na	156	106	130	140	104	106
Average, 1 cycle	83	na	121	85	86	98	82	104

SOURCE: Col. 1 and 2, data supplied to NBER in a survey of life insurance companies and to appear in a forthcoming publication, plus Federal Home Loan Bank Board; col. 3, FHA; col. 4, Federal Reserve System; cols. 5, 6, 7, 8, Moody's.

NOTE: Dates refer to years containing turning points in conventional mortgage series. Cyclical changes are measured between peaks and troughs of each series. Averages are calculated without regard to sign.

na = not available.

mortgage market." [8] Furthermore, an a priori argument for cyclical sensitivity in fees and charges is that local institutions would feel less comfortable about raising rates than about raising fees and charges. The going rates on mortgages in any given area are widely known, while fees and charges are not. [9]

The new authorization series, which take account of fees and charges, do not bear out this supposition. On conventional loans, the inclusion of fees and charges has virtually no effect on cyclical amplitude. This is illustrated in Chart 2-1 which shows effective yield, contract rate, and the difference between them. (Note that the difference

[8] Grebler, Blank and Winnick, p. 223.
[9] I owe this point to Avery Cohan.

CHART 2-1. Gross Yields and Contract Rate on Conventional Loans, 1951–63

is on an enlarged scale.) It is clear that virtually all cyclical variability in conventional yields stems from variability in the contract rate.

Whether fees and charges are cyclically insensitive for lender groups other than life insurance companies is not clear. Federal Home Loan Bank Board data covering the period of marked rate increase, September–October 1965 to December 1966–January 1967, suggest that cyclical changes in fees and charges may be significant for savings and loan associations and, perhaps, commercial banks. During that period, the average effective yield on new-home loans approved by savings and loan associations rose by about 68 basis points, the increase in fees and charges accounting for about 10 basis points and the increase in contract rate for the balance. For commercial banks, the rise in fees accounted for 5 basis points of a 76 point rise in yield. For the three other lender groups—life insurance companies, mortgage companies and mutual savings banks—fees and charges did not rise significantly. This evidence is hardly conclusive, however, since the data cover only one cyclical phase; and the Board's definition of fees and charges is not comprehensive.[10]

The popular notion that small changes in market conditions are better revealed in fees and charges on conventional loans than in contract rates, seems to derive from the fact that fees and charges are infinitely divisible while lenders very seldom write loans at contract rates that are not multiples of $\frac{1}{4}$ per cent. Indivisibility does not, however, imply inflexibility in an aggregate, i.e., an average contract rate can rise .01 per cent when a small proportion of the mortgages in the aggregate, which previously had barely qualified for a $5\frac{1}{2}$ per cent rate, are jumped to $5\frac{3}{4}$ per cent, the others remaining unchanged.

A second possible explanation of the relatively narrow cyclical amplitude of conventional mortgage yields was suggested by Klaman.

the element of administrative costs . . . has its own place in the relative stickiness of mortgage rates. In general, the larger such costs are relative to the interest rate the more stable the interest rate is likely to be. The reason is simple: a minimum margin must be maintained between the interest rate and a lender's fixed administrative costs to assure him a reasonable return . . . On residential loans, administrative costs of acquisition, servicing, and record-keeping, perhaps 75 basis points compared to 10 on corporate securities, create a relatively stable state in residential mortgage interest rates.[11]

This reasoning is not convincing. Since mortgage rates at their lowest levels are several times higher than mortgage costs, it is not clear just how these costs dampen rate variability. Even if there is such a rate-dampening mechanism, which is not yet understood, one would think that the extent of the rate dampening effect would depend not on the absolute cost but on its size relative to the average rate level on that instrument. Viewed in this way it is not at all clear that costs would have more of a dampening effect on mortgages than on bonds. The rate differential between mortgages and bonds (Baa and higher) is almost always greater than the 65 basis point cost differential mentioned by Klaman.

---

[10] In the Board's series, fees and charges cover only payments received by lenders, excluding payments made by lenders to third parties as "finder's fees." In the Bureau series, fees paid are netted from fees received. It is possible that fees paid by some lenders are cyclically sensitive.

[11] Klaman, p. 78.

A third explanation, also suggested by Klaman, is that adjustments in nonrate dimensions of the mortgage loan contract retard or offset rate adjustments.

As we move away from standardized to more differentiated markets and commodities the number of variables, in addition to price, to be negotiated multiplies. The market for residential mortgages is an example of the most differentiated because few markets are characterized by more one-of-a-kind deals. The credit of each borrower must be established, and 'credit worthiness' becomes a function of the relative tightness of capital markets. Numerous contract terms other than price are subject to individual negotiation — down-payment requirements, amortization provisions, contract maturities, prepayment penalties and non-interest costs. The nature and location of the particular residential unit securing the mortgage, moreover, are important factors in a mortgage transaction.

All these elements are more sensitive than the mortgage interest rate is to changes in financial market conditions. Down-payment and maturity provisions are particularly responsive . . .[12]

This argument is illustrated in the upper panel of Figure 2-1. If the aggregate yield series constitutes a weighted average of components *A*(high yield) and *B*(low yield), and the mix shifts toward *B* when yields rise and toward *A* when they fall, cyclical variability in the aggregate will be dampened.

Examination of cyclical variability in the mix of available loan characteristics helps to test this hypothesis. Table 2-2 shows that cyclical variability was negligible for loan-value ratios and maturities on conventional mortgages by life insurance companies during the 1951–63 period. For example, during the 1954 period of declining yields, the average maturity on conventional loans rose by sixteen months and the loan-value ratio by only two-tenths of a percentage point. Cross-section regression analysis (not shown here) suggests that such increases would affect yields by less than .01 per cent.

Cyclical changes in borrower characteristics associated with risk could affect cyclical yield variability. This appears to be the case in at least one other negotiated loan market. It has been found that a larger proportion of commercial bank business loans are to prime borrowers at interest rate peaks than at troughs; and that this tends to dampen variability in average business loan rates.[13] There is no evidence of a

---

[12] *Ibid.*, pp. 77 and 78.

[13] Albert M. Wojnilower and Richard E. Speagle, "The Prime Rate," in *Essays in Money and Credit*, Federal Reserve Bank of New York, 1964, pp. 50–51.

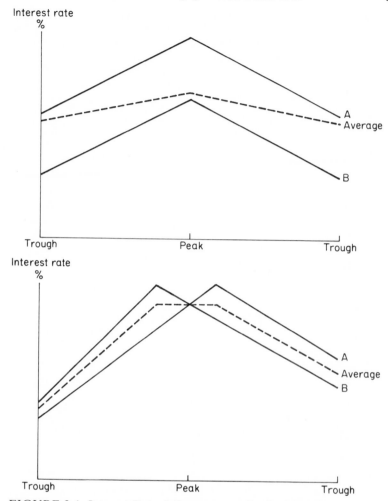

FIGURE 2-1. Interest Rate Adjustments to Cyclical Change

similar tendency in the case of conventional mortgage loans by life insurance companies, however. The only measure of borrower risk available from the time series is the average property value underlying the series.[14] Trend-adjusted cyclical fluctuations in average property

[14] On a cross-section basis property value appears to be a better measure of borrower risk than current income, probably because property value is a better proxy for permanent income. When effective yield on conventional loans is regressed separately on property value and income, coefficients are negative for both and always larger for value;

TABLE 2-2. Changes in Maturities and Loan-Value Ratios During Periods of Cyclical Rise and Decline in Mortgage Yields, 1953–63

	Part A: Periods of Rise in Yields						
	1951–54		1954–58		1958–60		Average
	Change	Per Month	Change	Per Month	Change	Per Month	Per Month
Changes in Maturity (months)							
Conventional	9.10	.26	18.80	.48	11.60	.55	.42
FHA	42.20	1.32	.40	.01	14.00	.78	.65
VA	−6.70	−.21	−10.00	−.27	4.80	.27	−.14
Changes in Loan-Value Ratio (percentage points)							
Conventional	1.00	.03	2.00	.05	3.40	.16	.07
FHA	2.60	.08	4.30	1.20	.60	.03	.09
VA	−3.00	−.09	−4.30	−.12	−.70	−.04	−.09

	Part B: Periods of Decline in Yields						
	1954	Per Month	1958	Per Month	1960– 63	Per Month	Average Per Month
Changes in Maturity (months)							
Conventional	16.10	1.61	11.90	1.49	30.10	.75	1.20
FHA	9.90	.66	22.50	3.75	8.50	.19	.63
VA	48.60	3.20	29.50	4.91	−2.50	−.06	1.15
Changes in Loan-Value Ratio (percentage points)							
Conventional	.20	.02	.30	.04	.00	.00	.01
FHA	.60	.04	1.50	.24	1.60	.04	.06
VA	1.90	.13	7.20	1.20	−1.40	−.03	.12

SOURCE: Data supplied to NBER in a survey of life insurance companies and to appear in a forthcoming publication.

NOTE: Changes are calculated from three-month averages centered on turning points in conventional yields (for changes in conventional terms), and in FHA yields (for changes in FHA and VA terms). Terminal date for the 1960–63 decline is November 1963.

value are in the wrong direction. Values rose considerably faster during the three periods of declining yields, 1951–66, than during the four periods of rising yields, thus tending to *increase* cyclical amplitude rather than dampen it.[15]

Applying the shift-in-mix hypothesis to shifts in lender and geographical mix is potentially more promising, since these are the most important sources of yield variability on a cross-section basis. To test whether shifts in the geographical and lender mix affected cyclical yield variability, conventional yields for each turning-point quarter were recalculated on the assumption that loan distribution among thirty-six separate strata—four lenders and nine regions—was the same as in the previous turning-point quarter. The results, shown in Table 2-3, indicate that cyclical changes in lender and geographical mix also have a negligible effect on over-all cyclical yield variability.

TABLE 2-3. Cyclical Changes in Conventional Mortgage Yields at Current and Fixed Lender and Regional Weights, 1951–63

Cyclical Rise (R) or Decline (D)	Current Weights	Fixed Weights
I 51 to I 54 (R)	.49 [a]	.48 [a]
I 54 to IV 54 (D)	−.15	−.14
IV 54 to I 58 (R)	.97	.94
I 58 to IV 58 (D)	−.23	−.19
IV 58 to III 60 (R)	.65	.65
III 60 to IV 63 (D)	−.59	−.60

SOURCE: Same as Table 2-2.
[a] Contract rate.

The change-in-mix hypothesis implies that FHA mortgage series should have greater amplitude than conventional series when they are measured on a comparable basis. Since cross-section yield variability

when value and income are included in the same regression, the latter is much smaller and frequently not significant. On a time series basis, of course, property value is affected by changes in price levels as well as by changes in the composition of home buyers.

[15] It is unlikely in any case that the effect is of any quantitative importance. The relationship between property value and yield for life insurance companies is smaller than for other lender groups, reflecting the companies' tendency to maintain relatively conservative standards.

is lower on FHAs than on conventionals and the mix of FHA yield determinants has less cyclical sensitivity (see Table 2-2), changes in mix might be thought to dampen yield variability less in FHAs. In fact, the amplitude of the FHA authorization series is not significantly different from that of the conventional authorization series (see Table 2-1).

The fourth explanation of the problem is that the relatively narrow cyclical amplitude of mortgage yields arises from greater differentiation within the mortgage category which causes differences in cyclical phasing among the various components of the aggregate. (This is illustrated in the lower panel of Figure 2-1.) Without any change in mix, the two components of the total may reach a turning point at different times, in which case the amplitude of the average will be smaller than the amplitude of either component. The greater the number of component series and the greater the timing differences between them, the stronger will be this dampening tendency. It is likely that conventional mortgage loan series are more heterogeneous than bond series, and thus, in effect, contain more component series with independent cyclical phasing.

This explanation, however, implies that high-grade bond yield series will have a wider cyclical amplitude than lower-grade series, since the former tend to be more homogeneous; similarly, FHA series would be expected to have a wider amplitude than conventional series. Table 2-1 shows that this is not the case for either bonds or mortgages.

A fifth possible explanation of the relatively narrow amplitude of conventional mortgage yields is based on cyclical changes in risk premiums. It could be argued that risk premiums between mortgages and bonds will be smaller at cyclical peaks, which are associated with high levels of business activity, than they are at troughs. Conventional mortgages are generally riskier than high-grade bonds and, when economic conditions become increasingly favorable, risk premiums narrow more on riskier instruments. To put it somewhat differently, the quality of conventional mortgages improves more than does that of high-grade bonds during periods of economic expansion.

This hypothesis may be tested indirectly. If a decline in risk premiums accounted for the reduction in yield differentials between conventional mortgages and high-grade bonds during business expansions, similar reductions should also have occurred as between high-grade and low-grade bonds, and between FHA and conventional mortgages. A comparison of yield differentials at business cycle peaks and troughs does not support this hypothesis, as Table 2-4 shows. The difference in

TABLE 2-4. Yield Differentials at Business Cycle Peaks and Troughs

Yield Differential	Average of 3 Reference Cycle Peaks	Average of 3 Reference Cycle Troughs	Difference: Troughs Less Peaks
Conventional mortgage			
less Aaa corporate	1.53	1.86	.33
less Aaa state and local	2.42	2.86	.44
Aaa corporate less Baa corporate	.71	.83	.12
Aaa state and local less Baa state and local	1.04	1.01	−.03
Conventional mortgage less FHA mortgage	.05	−.01	−.06

SOURCE: Appendix Table.

the conventional mortgage-high-grade bond yield differential at reference cycle peaks and troughs was significant at the 1 per cent level, while the other differences are not significant (in two cases they have the wrong sign).[16]

This test, however, depends heavily upon the assumption that lender reevaluations of security risk can be tied to reference cycle turning points. Another test — cruder but perhaps more meaningful in

[16] Avery Cohan's paper on the quality of directly placed bonds points out that changes in the yield differential are not a perfect proxy for changes in "quality" if quality is defined in terms of the probability that a loan will be repaid. Assume, for example, that the yield differential between a riskless one-year security and a risky security of the same maturity reflects only the probability of loss attached to the latter. At the end of the year the value of the riskless security will be $1 + G$ where G is the contract rate on that security, while the value of the risk security will be $(1 + r)p$, where r is the contract rate on the risk security and p is the probability that the principal and interest will be paid. Since the risk premium included in r is by hypothesis just large enough to equate the future value of both securities, $1 + G = (1 + r)p$ and $p = \dfrac{1 + G}{1 + r}$. $\Big($ It can be shown, similarly, that if both securities have a maturity of n years, $p = \left[\dfrac{1 + G}{1 + r}\right]^{n}\Big)$. This means that if the level of G rises, r must rise by even more to maintain a constant p. The risk premium expressed in terms of basis points of yield must get larger even though the probability of loss is constant. The required change in the yield differential, however, is very small. For example, a cyclical rise in G of the general order of magnitude shown in the Appendix Table would require a rise of 2–3 basis points in the conventional mortgage-Aaa bond yield differential in order to maintain a constant risk premium.

light of our ignorance on this point—compares average yield differentials during recession periods with averages during expansions. This test is more favorable to the risk premium hypothesis. As shown in Table 2-5, the yield differential between Aaa and Baa issues of

TABLE 2-5. Yield Differential Between Baa and Aaa Bonds and Between Conventional and FHA Mortgages During Business Expansions and Recessions (*basis points*)

Recession (R) or Expansion (E)	Baa Less Aaa		Conventional Less FHA
	Corporate	State and Local	
(R) Nov. 48–Oct. 49	75	102	8
(E) Nov. 49–June 53	57	85	24
(R) July 53–Aug. 54	62	109	9
(E) Sept. 54–June 56	50	97	10
(R) July 57–April 58	98	108	4
(E) May 58–April 60	75	94	−8
(R) May 60–Feb. 61	79	96	−11
(E) March 61–July 67	57	53	−4

SOURCE: Same as Appendix Table.

corporate and of state and local bonds was higher in each of four recession periods than in the subsequent expansion. This suggests that some cyclical reevaluation of risk may well have occurred on bonds. No such pattern was evident, however, for the yield differential between conventional and FHA mortgages.

Cyclical changes in mortgage delinquencies are perhaps even more relevant. One would not expect a recession to raise the *ex ante* risk premium on conventional mortgages if the repayment experience on mortgages held in portfolio was not appreciably affected by the recession. The evidence on delinquencies, by and large, does not support the risk premium hypothesis. For major lender groups, including life insurance companies, there has been a modest tendency for delinquencies to rise during recent recessions, but this appears to be accounted for entirely by FHA and VA mortgages.[17] A study of monthly

[17] Some of the evidence on this is shown in James S. Earley, "The Quantity of Postwar Credit in the United States," NBER, September 1965 (mimeograph). A complete compendium of delinquency and foreclosure series is listed in Edgar R. Fiedler with the assistance of Maude R. Pech, "Measures of Credit Quality," NBER, July 1967 (mimeograph).

time series covering conventional mortgages does not reveal any cyclical sensitivity during the period since 1953, for which monthly data are available.

The final hypothesis considered here is that the narrow cyclical amplitude of mortgage yields relative to bond yields reflects differences in market organization. It can be argued that, for a number of reasons, rates tend to be relatively sluggish in negotiated markets where borrowers and lenders are in direct contact, as opposed to impersonal dealer-type markets. First, negotiated markets involve some bilateral bargaining which will moderate changes in rates if there is any continuity in the relationship between borrower and lender, as in the case of commercial banks and their business loan customers, or of life insurance companies that acquire mortgages through correspondents. Concern for maintaining relationships over the long run blunts the tendency to maximize market position in the short run.

Second, lenders in negotiated markets are likely to have heavy, nontransferable overhead costs geared to the specific market, as in the case of life insurance companies that acquire mortgages through their own network of branch offices. Such lenders find it profitable to maintain stable rates in those markets.

Third, lenders in negotiated markets tend to lag in adjusting their offer functions to yield changes in dealer markets (see below). If basic credit demands are less stable in the dealer markets, the full range of rate changes in these markets will not be transmitted to the negotiated market. Because of the transmission lag, peaks and troughs in the dealer market are in effect "lopped off." Here, the explanation of why mortgage yields have smaller cyclical amplitude merges with the explanation given below of why mortgage yields *lag* bond yields.

Clearly this hypothesis goes beyond our immediate focus into largely unexplored terrain. It would explain, however, not only the small amplitude of mortgage yields relative to bond yields, but also the narrower amplitude of commercial bank business loan rates than of rates on open market paper of comparable maturity.[18] It is also of interest that the FHA secondary market yields series is more volatile than FHA authorization series though less volatile than bond yields (Table 2-1). The market organization underlying the FHA secondary market lies somewhere between the organization of the markets underlying

---

[18] For evidence on this, see Phillip Cagan, *Changes in the Cyclical Behavior of Interest Rates,* NBER Occasional Paper 100, New York, 1966, p. 9. An alternative explanation is given by Donald Hodgman, *Commercial Bank Loan and Investment Policy,* Urbana, Ill., 1963, pp. 126–131.

the life insurance company authorization series and that underlying the bond yield series.[19]

Lag of Mortgage Yields Relative to Bond Yields at Turning Points

Klaman noted that "Changes in mortgage interest rates lagged continually behind changes in bond yields throughout the postwar decade." [20] This lag is reduced by one to six months when transactions are recorded as of the date of loan authorization rather than the date of disbursement. The lag is not eliminated, however, as Table 2-6 indi-

TABLE 2-6. Lag at Turning Points, Conventional Mortgage Yields Relative to Bond Yields (*months*)

Turning Point in Conventional Yields	U.S. Govt. Long Term	Corporate		
		Aaa	Aa (New)	Baa
(P) Dec. 1949 [a]	14	13		12
(T) Feb. 1951	14	13		0
(P) Jan. 1954	7	7	8	4
(T) Nov. 1954	4	1	8	−2
(P) Feb. 1958	4	5	3	3
(T) Oct. 1958	6	4	4	3
(P) July 1960	6	6	10	5
(T) Sept. 1965 [b]	53	30	32	6
1954–60 Average	5	5	7	3

(The rows (P) Jan. 1954 through (P) July 1960 are bracketed and labeled "Normal")

SOURCE: Same as Table 2-2, plus Federal Reserve System, Moody's.
[a] Based on data for one company.
[b] Based on FHLBB series on new house purchases.

cates. At five turning points during the 1954–60 period, conventional yields lagged government bond yields by from four to seven months. These might be considered "normal" lags. Lags at the 1949, 1951 and 1965 turning points were considerably longer, but they were affected by special developments that changed the underlying relationship be-

[19] Thus, there are no dealers in the FHA secondary market but brokers are often used, and buyers and seller tend to canvass the market for the best available deal on any given day.

[20] Klaman, p. 78.

tween mortgage and bond yields. The 1965 case will be discussed below.[21]

Since the dating of turning points is sometimes unavoidably arbitrary, another measure of cyclical sensitivity is employed in Table 2-7.

TABLE 2-7. Changes in Yields on Direct Mortgage Loans and on Bonds Following Turning Points in U.S. Government Bond Yields

		Changes in Yield (basis points)				
	No. of Months After Turning	Long-Term	Cor-	Cor-	Mortgages (Direct Authorization)	
Turning Points in Long-Term Government Bond Yields	Point in Bond Yields	Govern-ments (1)	porate Aaa (2)	porate Aa New (3)	Conven-tional (4)	FHA (5)
Troughs						
July 1954	+5	+12	+1	+4	−4	+1
	+10	+34	+15	+26	−3	+6
	+15	+40	+21	+27	+8	+18
April 1958	+5	+63	+49	+83	−24	−19
	+10	+80	+54	+50	+1	+3
	+15	+99	+87	+108	0	+8
Peaks						
June 1953	+4	−26	−24	−58	+21	+16
	+8	−51	−45	−75	+21	+13
	+12	−58	−50	−78	+13	+7
Oct. 1957	+3	−49	−50	−119	+8	+8
	+6	−61	−50	−106	+4	+6
	+9	−37	−43	−93	−5	−7
Jan. 1960	+4	−21	−16	−4	+7	+5
	+8	−55	−36	−30	+5	−3
	+12	−48	−29	−40	−1	−8

SOURCE: Same as Table 2-6.

This table uses only one turning point — that on long-term government bond yields — and measures yield changes in all the series during periods of specified length (e.g., five, ten and fifteen months) beginning with that date. Relative sensitivity is measured by the rise (or decline)

[21] The changing relationship between mortgage and bond yields during 1949–51 was discussed in Jack Guttentag's, "Some Studies of the Post-World War II Residential Construction and Mortgage Markets," unpublished Ph.D. dissertation, Columbia University, 1958, pp. 82–86.

during the periods following troughs (or peaks) in government bond yields.[22] These comparisons show mortgage yields relatively insensitive at every one of the five turning points in the table. As an example, ten months after the April 1958 trough in government bond yields, these bond yields were up 80 basis points, high-grade corporates were up 50–54 basis points, while direct conventional mortgage yields were up only 1 basis point.

One hypothesis used to explain the lag in conventional mortgage yields suggests that small changes in market demand and supply register first in changes in loan-value ratios and maturities, and this retards the adjustment of yields. If this is true, terms will reach a cyclical turning point before yields. Table 2-8 shows cyclical turning points in loan-value ratios and maturities corresponding to turning points in yields (taken from the new NBER series, separately for each type of loan and for weighted totals covering all loans). Some of these observations are obscured by the effects of changes in legal limits while, in other cases, there was no clearly defined turning point in terms. With these exclusions, there are twenty-two usable observations. Terms led yields at eight turning points; terms lagged behind in five cases; in nine cases, the turning points in terms were within one month of the turning point in yields. If these were independent observations, an 8–9–5 distribution could easily occur by chance and would provide little support for the hypothesis that sensitivity of terms retards yield adjustments.

Since the twenty-two observations are not in fact independent, it is useful to view this evidence in another way, by taking each of the five turning points in yield as one observation. From this standpoint, the evidence provides no support for the hypothesis at all. At only one of the turning points, the interest rate peak in early 1958, was there a clear tendency for terms to precede yields; seven of the eight "lead" observations come from this turning point.[23] Terms lagged behind yields at the other four turning points, although the 1953 turning point has only one valid observation.

---

[22] These comparisons use series on direct conventional mortgage loans only, since the correspondent loan component may have some residual recording lag. The periods following yield peaks are shorter than those following troughs to avoid extending past the subsequent turning point. The most recent trough is not included in this table because the trough dates are dispersed over an extraordinary long period in the different series.

[23] Furthermore, as shown in Table 2-6, the lag of mortgage yields behind bond yields at this turning point was shorter than usual, whereas the sensitivity-of-terms hypothesis used to explain this lag implies that it should have been longer.

TABLE 2-8. Cyclical Turning Points in Loan-Value Ratios and Maturities Corresponding to Turning Points in Yields

	Cyclical Peaks and Troughs in Yield					Number of Cases		
						Terms Lead Yields	Terms Lag Yields	Same Turning Points [c]
	P	T	P	T	P			
Gross Yield								
FHA and VA	Nov. 53	Feb. 55	March 58	Sept. 58	March 60			
Conventional	Jan. 54	Nov. 54	Feb. 58	Oct. 58	July 60			
All, weighted	Dec. 53	Oct. 54	Feb. 58	Oct. 58	May 60			

Cyclical Troughs and Peaks in Terms [b]

	T	P	T	P	T	Terms Lead Yields	Terms Lag Yields	Same Turning Points [c]
Conventional								
Maturity	Nov. 53	Dec. 54	Aug. 56	Jan. 59	March 61	2	2	
Loan value	ntp	ntp	Aug. 57	Sept. 59	ntp	1	1	1
FHA								
Maturity	June 53 [a]	May 55	Feb. 57 [a]	Sept. 58	ntp		1	1
Loan value	July 54 [a]	June 55	Jan. 57 [a]	Sept. 58	ntp		1	1
VA								
Maturity	May 53 [a]	Dec. 54	Jan. 57	ntp	ntp	2		
Loan value	Aug. 53 [a]	Oct. 54	ntp	ntp	ntp	1		
All, weighted								
Maturity	Aug. 52 [a]	Oct. 54	Sept. 57	Dec. 59	Dec. 60	1	2	1
Loan value	Aug. 52 [a]	Oct. 54	Aug. 57	Dec. 59	Dec. 60	1	2	1

SOURCE: Same as Table 2-2.

ntp = No well-defined turning point.

[a] Affected by changes in legal limits.

[b] Peaks (troughs) in terms corresponding to troughs (peaks) in yields.

[c] Within one month of corresponding yield series.

The new FHLBB series on conventional loans provide additional evidence to test the theory that sensitivity in terms retards adjustments in rates. Although, as yet, these data cover only one turning point, series are available for five lender groups, separately for new and existing properties, or ten cases for each loan characteristic. For maturities there were eight identifiable turning points which lagged the turning point in their respective contract rate in every case (Table 2-9). Similarly, six identifiable turning points in loan-value ratio all lagged their respective contract rate. Thus, the data do not support the hypothesis that sensitivity in terms retards adjustments in yields at cyclical turning points.

TABLE 2-9. Leads and Lags of Loan-Value Ratios, Maturities, and Fees and Charges Relative to Contract Rate at the 1965 Contract Rate Trough in Ten Conventional Home Loan Series

| | Number of Identifiable Turning Points in Characteristic | Number of Cases | | |
| | | Char. Leads Rate | Char. Lags Rate | Same Turning Point [a] |
Characteristic				
Maturity	8	0	8	0
Loan-value	6	0	6	0
Fees and charges	6	1	4	1

SOURCE: Federal Home Loan Bank Board.
[a] Within one month of corresponding rate series.

Neither is the lag in conventional yields explained by a special sensitivity of fees and charges. The NBER conventional contract rate series has exactly the same turning points as the gross yield series except at the 1958 peak when the contract rate series leads by one month. The FHLBB series show fees lagging rates at the 1965 trough in most cases (Table 2-9).

Short-term developments affecting general yield levels normally originate in the bond markets, and this may be an important factor underlying the tendency of mortgage yields to lag behind bond yields. The basic demand for mortgage credit is affected mainly by demographic factors and by "normal" income, changing little in the short run.[24] Demands on the capital markets by the federal government and

[24] See Sherman Maisel, "A Theory of Fluctuations in Residential Construction Starts," *American Economic Review,* June 1963, pp. 374–376.

nonfinancial corporations, in contrast, are subject to sharp cyclical fluctuations.[25]

Bond yield changes could, of course, be transmitted immediately to the mortgage market; but, in fact, there is a lag. For a number of reasons there is virtually no arbitrage between the bond market and the mortgage market.[26] Rate adjustments in the mortgage market depend almost entirely upon the activities of primary lenders. These lenders appear to be responsive to pervasive changes in bond yields, though not to short-lived ones. As one lender expressed it, "To attempt to follow every wiggle in bond yields would unduly disrupt our market relationships." However, a pervasive movement in bond yields cannot usually be distinguished from a reversible one until the passage of time proves it out; the result is that mortgage yields lag. As noted earlier, this lag, in conjunction with the relatively stable mortgage credit demand, may be partly responsible for the narrow cyclical amplitude of mortgage yields.

Longer-Run Changes in the Relationship of Conventional Mortgage Yields to Bond Yields and the 1961–66 Experience

The relationship between conventional mortgage yields and high-grade bond yields is examined in two ways. Chart 2-2 shows the yield differential (mortgages less long-term government bonds), monthly during the period 1948–66. This series is affected by the tendency of mortgage yields to lag bond yields by periods of varying length. Table 2-10 shows differentials at cyclical peaks and troughs only, with the yield on each instrument measured at its respective peak or trough. Thus at peak 4, the yield on conventional mortgages in July 1960 is compared to the yield on long-term government bonds in January 1960. These are referred to as "matching differentials."

During the period 1949–60, the monthly series shows marked

---

[25] See Jack M. Guttentag, "The Short Cycle In Residential Construction," *American Economic Review,* June 1961, pp. 292–294.

[26] First, because of differentiation within the mortgage market, yield relationships are not reliable enough to permit effective arbitrage. (Arbitrage transactions must be carried out in individual securities, and depend on reasonably reliable yield relationships between the instruments being arbitraged.) Second, the cost of arbitrage transactions involving mortgages is high because the market for outstanding mortgages is rudimentary. Brokers exist who will attempt to sell mortgages on a commission basis but I do not know of dealers who will take seasoned mortgages into portfolio. Third, the secondary mortgage market, such as it is, has no direct organizational links to the bond market.

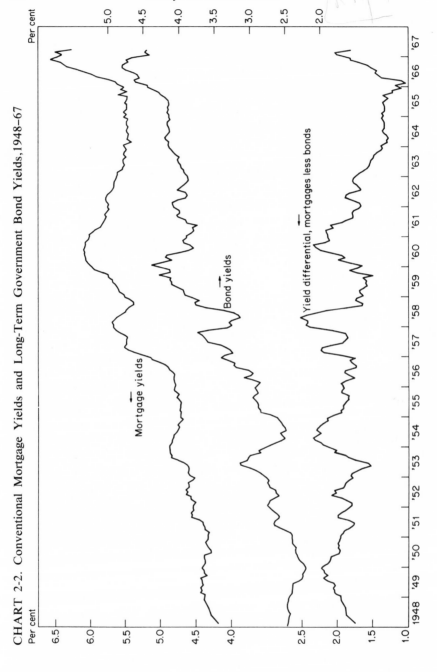

CHART 2-2. Conventional Mortgage Yields and Long-Term Government Bond Yields, 1948–67

TABLE 2-10. Yield Differentials Between Conventional Mortgages and Bonds, at Cyclical Peaks and Troughs

	Dates					Yield Differentials				
	(1)	(2)	(3)	(4)	(5)	(1)	(2)	(3)	(4)	(5)
Part A: Cyclical Peaks										
Conventional Mortgages	Dec. 49 [a]	Jan. 54	Feb. 58	July 60	Nov. 66					
U.S. Govt. Long Term	Oct. 48	June 53	Oct. 57	Jan. 60	Sept. 66	1.96	1.74	1.96	1.73	1.77
Corporate Aaa	Nov. 48	June 53	Sept. 57	Jan. 60	Sept. 66	1.59	1.47	1.57	1.49	1.07
Corporate Aa (New)		May 53	Oct. 57	Sept. 59	Dec. 66		.99	.78	.62	.63
Corporate Baa	Dec. 48	Sept. 53	Nov. 57	Feb. 60	Dec. 66	.90	.99	.60	.76	.38
Part B: Cyclical Troughs										
Conventional Mortgages	Feb. 51	Nov. 54	Oct. 58	Oct. 65						
U.S. Govt. Long Term	Dec. 49	July 54	April 58	May 61		2.09	2.21	2.26	1.77	
Corporate Aaa	Jan. 50	Oct. 54	June 58	March 63		1.74	1.81	1.81	1.31	
Corporate Aa (New)		March 54	June 58	Jan. 63		–	1.77	1.57	1.30	
Corporate Baa	Feb. 51	Jan. 55	July 58	March 65		1.15	1.23	.85	.72	

SOURCES: Conventional mortgages are the NBER series except at Trough (4) and Peak (5) which are the FHLBB series for life insurance companies covering purchase of new homes (contract rate); Long-term government bonds are the Federal Reserve Board series; Corporate bond series are from Moody's.

NOTE: Yield differentials are measured at peaks and troughs of each series.

[a] Based on data for one company.

cyclical fluctuations with some indication of widening amplitude, but there is no indication of trend. Similarly, the matching differentials at the first three troughs and four peaks show no indication of trend.

During the cyclical decline in yields that began in 1960, however, mortgage yields continued to fall long past the point at which bond yields began to drift upward.[27] As a result, the 1960–65 decline in the monthly differential was larger than any earlier cyclical decline (as measured in basis points from peak to trough), and brought the differential some 45–48 basis points below the previous lows reached in 1959 and 1953. Similarly, the matching differential at trough 4 was markedly lower than at any of the previous troughs. An observer at the end of 1965 might have speculated, as was done in an early draft of this paper, that perhaps the yield differential had been "permanently" reduced.

The dramatic events of 1966 — mortgage yields rose more in one year than they had declined in the previous five — added an additional dimension to this experience. The rise in the yield differential during 1966 was larger than during any earlier cyclical rise, and it brought the differential back to high levels, although still below earlier peaks. Thus it appears less certain now than it did at the end of 1965 that a permanent decline in the differential has occurred. What needs explaining is the amplitude of the yield differential, greater throughout the period 1961–66 than in earlier periods, which reflects the increased amplitude of the mortgage yield series during this period.

The hypothesis offered here to explain the wide amplitude of mortgage yields during 1961–66 takes the following crude "facts" as a point of departure. In the 1961–65 period of decline in mortgage yields, net mortgage acquisitions on one- to four-family properties rose to $72.3 billion from $65.7 billion in the preceding six years, or rose by $6.6 billion. Commercial banks accounted for most of the increase, their acquisitions rising by $5.1 billion. During 1966, when mortgage yields rose precipitously, total net acquisitions dropped $4.6 billion, all of it accounted for by savings institutions. Commercial bank acquisitions held up in 1966, in contrast to earlier periods of monetary restraint when banks tended to desert the mortgage market.

The hypothesis advanced here is that structural changes involving commercial bank policy toward time deposits, and a marked increase

---

[27] The dispersion of turning points in various yield series at trough 4 is extremely wide, with several of the series showing multiple bottoms. While timing comparisons at this turning point are hazardous, the value of matching yield differentials is not significantly affected by the choice of turning point.

in the relative importance of time deposits in the bank liability mix, were responsible for the marked variability in mortgage yields during the 1961–66 period. The shift in the bank liability mix encouraged a portfolio shift into mortgages which put downward pressure on mortgage yields during 1961–65. When tight money emerged in 1966, commercial banks were able to bid savings accounts away from savings institutions, which channel most of their funds into mortgages, thus placing upward pressure on mortgage yields — stronger pressure than in earlier periods of monetary restraint when banks had raised funds by liquidating government securities.[28]

The marginal value of time deposits to commercial banks has grown steadily over the last decade or so, while their government securities portfolios have trended downward. Beginning in the late 1950's and early 1960's, one bank after another found it could no longer rely on the liquidation of government securities to meet loan demand in excess of deposit growth. Demand deposit growth, furthermore, had lagged throughout the entire post-World War II period. As a result, time deposits emerged as a valuable source of funds over which banks could exercise some degree of control.

The shift to time deposits was most pronounced after 1961. In that year New York City banks began to issue large-denomination negotiable certificates of deposit, and they were followed by large banks in other cities. Both large and small banks began to compete vigorously with savings institutions for smaller accounts. Rate differentials between savings accounts at commercial banks and those at savings institutions narrowed; rate advertising increased in intensity; and, probably, elasticity of substitution rose.

Table 2-11 shows three measures of change in bank liability structure during each of three complete cycles in mortgage yields. Each of the three measures shows a marked shift toward time deposits in the 1961–66 cycle, relative to the two earlier cycles. Thus the ratio of time deposits to total deposits rose by .63 percentage points per quarter during the 1961–66 cycle, compared with increases of .27 points and .26 points in the two preceding cycles.

As their liability mix shifted toward time deposits, the asset pref-

---

[28] An underlying condition was, of course, the willingness of the Federal Reserve to allow the commercial banks to compete vigorously for time deposits by keeping Regulation Q ceiling rates above constraint levels. Late in 1966 the System decided that competition for savings had gone so far as to threaten disaster to the residential sector, and the ceilings on some types of accounts were reduced.

TABLE 2-11. Measures of Change in Bank Liability Structure During Cycles in Mortgage Interest Rates, 1953–66

Mortgage Interest Rate Cycle	$\dfrac{TD_1}{D_1} - \dfrac{TD_0}{D_0}$	$\dfrac{TD_1 - TD_0}{TD_0} - \dfrac{DD_1 - DD_0}{DD_0}$	$\dfrac{TD_1 - TD_0}{D_1 - D_0}$
	(1)	(2)	(3)
Decline IV 1953 – I 1955	.25	1.27	.52
Rise II 1955 – IV 1957	.28	1.41	.80
Total Cycle	.27	1.36	.70
Decline I 1958 – III 1958	.67	3.20	.73
Rise IV 1958 – I 1960	.06	.26	.46
Total Cycle	.26	1.24	.55
Decline II 1960 – III 1965	.68	4.39	.81
Rise IV 1965 – IV 1966	.41	1.76	.77
Total Cycle	.63	3.90	.80

SOURCE: Federal Reserve System, Flow of Funds Accounts.
TD = Time deposits
DD = Demand deposits
D = Total deposits
Subscripts 0 and 1 refer to beginning and end of period, respectively. Measures (1) and (2) show differences per quarter.

erences of commercial banks also changed. It is a traditional tenet of bank management that mortgages can be prudently acquired with funds obtained from time deposits.[29] Cross-section analysis using balance sheet data invariably shows a positive correlation between the relative importance of time deposits on the liability side and mortgages on the asset side.[30] This appears to reflect a combination of cost and liquidity considerations. If deposit costs are high, bankers feel they must invest in higher yielding assets.[31] In addition, time deposits are generally viewed as requiring smaller liquidity provision than demand deposits, so that asset structure can safely be made less liquid.

[29] See Fred G. Delong, "Liquidity Requirements and Employment of Funds," in Kalman J. Cohen and Frederick S. Hammer (eds.), *Analytical Methods in Banking,* Homewood, Ill., 1966, pp. 38–53.
[30] For 416 individual member banks in the Philadelphia Federal Reserve District on December 31, 1960, the coefficient of correlation between the ratio of time to total deposits and the ratio of mortgages to total assets was .55.
[31] This implies profit target behavior by banks rather than profit maximization, which many economists find difficult to accept.

More direct evidence on this relationship, focusing on *changes* in mortgage holdings and *changes* in time deposits during the period under study, is provided by the following experiment. The percentage change in mortgage loans during the period from December 1960 to June 1964 was regressed on various combinations of deposit change for 416 member banks in the Philadelphia Federal Reserve District.[32] To avoid the effects of relationships between changes and levels in these magnitudes, the initial ratios of mortgages to assets and time deposits to total deposits (both in December 1960) were also included as variables in the regressions. As a sort of control, the same procedure was used to explain the percentage change in state and local securities, which the banks also acquired in substantial volume during this period, except that the equations included the initial ratio of state and local securities to assets rather than the ratio of mortgages to assets. Some results are shown in Table 2-12.

In equation (1), the percentage change in mortgages and in state and local securities is regressed on the percentage change in time deposits and the percentage change in total deposits. The regression coefficient for the change in time deposits is positive and statistically significant in the mortgage equation, but not in the state and local equation, suggesting that only mortgage acquisitions were sensitive to the composition of deposit increase.

Equation (2) used the percentage change in time deposits and those in demand deposits as separate variables in the regression. In the mortgage equation, the coefficient for time deposits was three times as large as the coefficient for demand deposits, while in the state and local equation the coefficient for time deposits was not statistically significant.[33]

Since mortgage acquisitions by individual banks were influenced by changes in their time deposits,[34] it can be inferred that mortgage

---

[32] I am indebted to the Federal Reserve Bank of Philadelphia for these data. Note that real estate loans in these data cover loans on nonresidential as well as residential properties.

[33] Equations were also run in which the dependent variable was the change in real estate loans as a percentage of the initial level of total assets rather than the initial level of real estate loans. The results were very much the same.

[34] There is some reason to believe that the relationship is dominated by small banks. A study of fifty-three large banks by Morrison and Selden did not reveal any positive relationship between changes in real estate holdings and changes in time deposits during 1960–63. See George R. Morrison and Richard T. Selden, *Time Deposit Growth and the Employment of Bank Funds,* Association of Reserve City Bankers, Feb. 1965, Tables A-1 and A-4.

TABLE 2-12. Regression Results Showing Relationship Between Changes in Real Estate Loans and in State and Local Securities, Held by 416 Member Banks, to Changes in Deposits, December 1960 to June 1964

Independent Variables	Real Estate Loan Equations			State and Local Securities Equations		
	b-Coef.	T	R^2	b-Coef.	T	R^2
Equation (1)						
Change in total deposits	.39	7.1		2.13	1.7	
Change in time deposits	.50	22.3	.39	−.57	.2	.07
Equation (2)						
Change in time deposits	.67	120.8		.19	.1	
Change in demand deposits	.22	8.1	.39	1.56	3.3	.07
Equation (3)						
Change in total deposits	1.22	98.8		.07	.0	
Change in demand deposits	−.27	5.4	.36	1.63	1.7	.07

NOTE: Dependent variables are: per cent change in real estate loans in real estate loan equations, and per cent change in state and local securities in state and local securities equations. All equations include, in addition to the independent variables listed, the December 1960 ratio of time deposits to total deposits, size class of bank, and the December 1960 ratio of real estate loans (or state and local securities) to total assets.

acquisitions by the banking system as a whole were boosted by the pronounced shift that occurred in the bank deposit mix. This supports the view that the sharp decline in mortgage yields during the 1961–65 period was due, at least in part, to the marked increase in time deposits relative to demand deposits during the period, and to a related shift in bank portfolio preferences for mortgages.

It might appear at first glance that these structural changes affecting commercial banks would *retard* the rise in mortgage yields during a period of monetary restraint, such as emerged in 1966. Presumably banks would not reduce mortgage acquisitions as sharply as they did in earlier periods of restraint when mortgages were viewed more as "residual" assets. Indeed, commercial banks maintained a high level of mortgage acquisitions in 1966, as Table 2-13 shows.

This view, however, neglects the effect that more intensive bank competition for time deposits would have on inflows to savings institutions and on mortgage lending by those institutions. Although the

TABLE 2-13. Changes in Holdings of One- to Four-Family Residential Mortgages and in Time and Savings Deposits by Commercial Banks and Savings Institutions During Cycles in Mortgage Interest Rates, 1953–66 (*amounts in billions of dollars, annual rate*)

Mortgage Interest Rate Cycle	Commercial Banks		Savings Institutions		Time Deposits as Per Cent of Total Time and Savings Deposits
	Time and Savings Deposits	Mort-gages	Time and Savings Deposits	Mort-gages	
Decline IV 53 – I 55	3.6	1.6	6.7	6.4	35
Rise II 55 – IV 57	3.1	0.8	7.1	5.7	30
Decline I 58 – III 58	9.2	1.5	8.8	6.9	51
Rise IV 58 – I 60	1.4	1.1	8.5	7.7	14
Decline II 60 – III 65	13.7	2.0	13.2	10.0	51
Rise IV 65 – IV 66	14.3	2.1	8.4	4.4	63

SOURCE: Federal Reserve System, Flow of Funds Accounts.
NOTE: Savings institutions are mutual savings banks, savings and loan associations, and credit unions. Mortgages lead one quarter.

status of mortgages in bank portfolios has risen, they remain less attractive than business loans, the demand for which increased very sharply in 1966. The banks' determination to meet these demands, in the face of depleted liquidity positions caused them to bid a substantial volume of funds away from the savings institutions, which led to a corresponding reduction in mortgage lending by these institutions.[35] As shown in Table 2-13, the maintenance of bank mortgage lending did not begin to counterbalance the decline in lending by savings institutions losing funds to banks.[36]

[35] The shift in funds became so large in the summer and fall that the Federal Reserve "took a variety of steps to redress the balance in the flow of funds between business borrowers and the housing industry . . ." (*Federal Reserve Bulletin,* February 1967, p. 189). For a discussion of these measures, see the cited article.

[36] Table 2-13 shows a marked reversal in the pattern of change in savings flows and mortgage lending in the most recent cycle in mortgage yields, as compared to the two earlier cycles. In the earlier cycles, the net flow of savings and mortgages at savings institutions was about as large during the period of rising yields as it was during the preceding period of falling yields; but in the most recent cycle both flows were markedly lower during the period of rising yields. The pattern for commercial banks changed in the opposite way. In earlier cycles, their time deposits and mortgage lending fell during tight money periods, while in the recent cycle both flows were maintained.

The liquidation of government securities by commercial banks in earlier periods of restraint had, of course, indirectly affected the flow of funds into mortgages by changing the yields on alternative investments. This pressure must have been more diffused and less intense than the withdrawal of funds from savings institutions, which invest most of their funds in mortgages. Government securities liquidation in earlier periods probably was absorbed by reductions in "idle balances," whereas the response of lenders such as life insurance companies to changes in the alternative investment yields probably was much more gradual than the response of savings institutions to a reduction in their inflows. A good case can be made that the change in the bank response to tight money, from an emphasis on reducing investments to an emphasis on increasing time deposits, has had the result of transmitting the effects of tight money to the mortgage market more promptly and fully than ever before.

Relationship Between FHA and Conventional Yields

Our new data permit an analysis of changes in the relationship between FHA and conventional yields over the cycle, and over the eighteen year period, 1949–66. The dotted line on Chart 2-3 covering 1951–63 shows the differential based on the new National Bureau series. The solid line covering the period 1949–66 is based on the FHA secondary market series, and three linked conventional series.[37] Table 2-14 shows yield differentials calculated at the specific cycle peaks and troughs in both series. Since the cyclical amplitude of FHA yields is sensitive to the prepayment assumption, the conventional-FHA yield differential in this table is computed on four different prepayment assumptions.

It would generally be expected that conventionals would carry higher yields than FHAs because the latter are virtually free of default risk. The risk on conventional loans made by life insurance companies, however, is quite small since these loans typically carry down payments of 25 per cent or more. (Largely for this reason conventional loans by life insurance companies typically are in the lower range of yields on conventional loans in general.) For some lenders the modest risk advantage of FHAs is more than counterbalanced by its disadvantages.

---

[37] The Bureau series is used for 1951–63, the FHLBB series covering loans by life insurance companies on new properties for 1964–66, and data on one company for 1949–50. Yields in this chart are calculated on a uniform prepayment assumption of ten years.

CHART 2-3. Yield Differential Between Conventional and FHA Loans, 1949–67

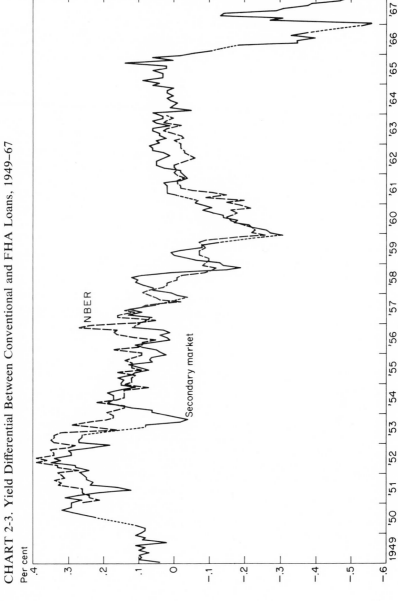

TABLE 2-14. Gross Yields on FHA and Conventional Mortgages at Specific Cycle Peaks and Troughs

			Part A: Peaks		
FHA	*Jan. 50* [a]	*Nov. 53*	*March 58*	*March 60*	*Dec. 66*
Contract rate	4.50	4.49	5.25	5.75	6.00
Discount (points)	−1.57	1.32	2.47	3.45	6.80
Effective yield−8 years	4.25	4.72	5.69	6.37	7.17
10 years	4.28	4.69	5.63	6.28	7.01
Half of maturity	4.28	4.68	5.58	6.20	6.80
Maturity	4.34	4.64	5.52	6.12	6.67
Conventional	*Dec. 49* [a]	*Jan. 54*	*Feb. 58*	*July 60*	*Nov. 66*
Contract rate	4.59	5.02	5.75	6.12	6.55
Discount (points)	−1.27	−.96	−.37	−.13	b
Effective yield−8 years	4.39	4.85	5.68	6.09	6.55
10 years	4.41	4.87	5.69	6.10	6.55
Half of maturity	4.41	4.87	5.69	6.10	6.55
Maturity	4.44	4.90	5.70	6.11	6.55
Conventional less FHA					
Effective yield−8 years	.14	.13	−.01	−.28	−.62
10 years	.13	.18	.06	−.18	−.46
Half of maturity	.13	.19	.11	−.10	−.25
Maturity	.10	.26	.18	−.01	−.12

			Part B: Troughs		
FHA	*Jan. 51*	*Feb. 55*	*Sept. 58*	*Aug. 65*	
Contract rate	4.27	4.50	5.25	5.25	
Discount (points)	−1.21	.61	1.45	1.40	
Effective yield−8 years	4.06	4.60	5.51	5.48	
10 years	4.08	4.59	5.47	5.45	
Half maturity	4.09	4.58	5.44	5.42	
Maturity	4.10	4.57	5.41	5.38	
Conventional	*Feb. 51*	*Nov. 54*	*Oct. 58*	*Nov. 65*	
Contract rate	4.48	4.82	5.44	5.50	
Discount (points)	−1.20	−.83	−.33	b	
Effective yield−8 years	4.29	4.66	5.37	5.50	
10 years	4.31	4.68	5.38	5.50	
Half maturity	4.32	4.68	5.38	5.50	
Maturity	4.34	4.70	5.39	5.50	
Conventional less FHA					
Effective yield−8 years	.23	.06	−.14	.02	
10 years	.23	.09	−.09	.05	
Half maturity	.23	.10	−.06	.08	
Maturity	.24	.13	−.02	.12	

NOTE: Data are based on NBER authorization series except for the 1966 peak and 1965 trough, which are based on the FHA secondary market series and the Federal Home Loan Bank Board conventional loan series.

[a] Data cover one company.

[b] Assumed equal to zero to maintain comparability.

FHA loans have somewhat higher origination costs because of the need to comply with the insuring agency's reporting and other requirements. Higher delinquency ratios on FHAs raise servicing costs while higher foreclosure ratios are also viewed unfavorably. While financial loss on foreclosed FHAs is quite small, most life companies prefer to avoid foreclosure for public relations and other reasons. In addition, conventional loans may carry prepayment penalties that are attractive to lenders, while borrowers can often be offered faster processing, and the $\frac{1}{2}$ per cent insurance premium is avoided. The evidence indicates that conventionals have usually yielded more, but with some notable exceptions.

There is some suggestion in Chart 2-3 of a secular decline in the yield differential over the period 1952–59. Yields declined erratically, but persistently over this period. A secular decline might be expected from the favorable repayment experience on conventional mortgages, which would have reduced their risk premiums relative to federally underwritten mortgages.[38]

The yield differential rose during 1950–52, but for very special reasons. With FHA $4\frac{1}{2}$ per cent mortgages carrying premiums, the maximum contract rate on these mortgages was reduced to $4\frac{1}{4}$ per cent in April 1950. Since premiums on high contract-rate mortgages are never large enough to reduce yields to the level of lower contract-rate mortgages (for reasons discussed in the next section), the reduction in contract rate also reduced FHA yields and raised the yield differential. The rise in yield differential during this period can be disregarded, therefore, as essentially reflecting an administrative action by the FHA. This strengthens the case for a secular decline.

The data do not reveal any tendency for the yield differential between FHA and conventional mortgages to change systematically over the cycle. Thus the average differential at the four peaks and three troughs covered by the authorization data is about the same, as shown at the top of page 64. However, Chart 2-3 shows that during two periods of extreme credit stringency—during late 1959–60 and during 1966—the yield differential fell sharply to the point where FHAs were yielding appreciably more than conventionals. What could account for this apparent aberration?

The most obvious possibility is that it is a statistical accident, arising from the lack of statistical comparability between FHA and

---

[38] An alternative hypothesis is that the liberalization of terms on conventional mortgages during this period kept pace with the increasingly sanguine views of lenders, so that no reduction in risk premiums occurred.

Conventional Less FHA Yields [a]

Prepayment	4 Peaks 1950–60	3 Troughs 1951–58
8 years [b]	−.01%	.05%
10 years [b]	.05	.08
One-half of maturity	.08	.09
At maturity	.14	.12

[a] Calculated from Table 2-14.   [b] After the loan is closed.

conventional series. The most convincing evidence that this is not the case is that the phenomenon appears in data covering individual lenders, both in 1959 and in 1966. It also appears in data covering individual regions and states.

In some degree, the conventional loans acquired during a period of market tightness are of higher over-all quality than those acquired in more normal periods, as lenders limit themselves to the best risks. This might cause a *decline* in the yield differential but would not explain why FHAs come to yield more.[39]

A third possibility, suggested to me by market practitioners, is that usury laws in some states constrained the rise in yields on conventional loans more than on FHA loans. Discounting had become an accepted practice on FHAs by 1959, but on conventionals charges exceeding customary levels encounter borrower resistance and various kinds of institutional frictions.[40]

If this explanation was correct, we would expect to find rates on conventional mortgages rising more slowly, and the margin between FHA and conventional rates increasing most sharply in states with relatively low usury ceilings. In states with high or no ceilings, in contrast, conventional rates should rise enough so as to maintain a margin over FHAs. Data available on a state basis for the 1959–60 period of market stringency do not support this explanation. Table 2-15 shows that in the two year period ending in the first quarter of 1960 rates on conventional loans did not increase any more in three states with a 10 per cent usury ceiling than in three states with a 6 per cent ceiling.

[39] The decline would be small in any case, since life insurance companies do not change their risk standards on conventional mortgages very much in the short run.

[40] Many lenders are reluctant to charge discounts on conventional mortgages because of adverse public relations arising from complaints by borrowers that they had been forced to pay a usurious charge in disguise. Under the FHA program, only sellers are allowed by law to pay discounts. Even though this requirement is frequently violated by adjusting transactions prices, FHA approval provides the lender with a *prima facie* valid defense against the charge that the borrower paid the discount.

TABLE 2-15. Yields on FHA and Conventional Home Mortgages in Selected States, 1958 and 1960

	First Quarter, 1958						First Quarter, 1960					
	FHA		Conventional			Conv. Less FHA (yield)	FHA		Conventional			Conv. Less FHA (yield)
State	Yield	No. of Loans	Yield	Contract Rate	No. of Loans		Yield	No. of Loans	Yield	Contract Rate	No. of Loans	
	6% Usury Law											
New York	5.39	10	5.58	5.64	48	.19	a	a	a	5.88	44	a
New Jersey	5.44	61	5.59	5.61	29	.15	6.04	10	5.94	5.94	43	−.10
Pennsylvania	5.44	69	5.48	5.57	43	.04	6.06	24	5.96	5.95	50	−.10
	10% Usury Law											
California	5.65	55	5.70	5.83	245	.05	6.27	132	6.05	6.15	178	−.22
Florida	5.65	45	5.76	5.78	26	.11	6.29	27	6.07	6.07	37	−.22
Texas	5.69	71	5.82	5.83	71	.13	6.34	72	6.15	6.15	119	−.19

SOURCE: Same as Table 2-2.

a Only one FHA loan was authorized in this period.

FHA yields came to exceed conventional yields in both groups of states, and in fact the margin was wider in states with high usury ceilings.

Any explanation must begin with the proposition that many individual lenders have an institutional preference for conventionals over FHAs at the same rate. Otherwise, barring differences in the timing of transactions or other statistical quirks, conventionals could *never* yield less. Discussions with lenders indicate that some do indeed prefer conventionals, for reasons discussed earlier. Under "normal" market conditions, the impact of lenders with an institutional preference for conventionals is more than offset by that of lenders with a preference for FHAs, so that conventionals yield more. Lenders who prefer FHAs, however, tend to maintain more diversified portfolios, and are sensitive to rate differentials between mortgages and bonds. Under conditions of extreme market stringency, such lenders tend to shift out of FHA mortgages; these mortgages must then, in large degree, be absorbed by lenders with a preference for conventionals who will accept them only at premium rates. Unfortunately there is no way at present to test this hypothesis.

Relationship Between FHA and VA Yields

The relationship between FHA and VA yields is affected by factors bearing on their relative loan quality, and by their contract rates. Klaman noted that VA yields tended to be higher, and prices to be lower during 1953–56 when their maximum contract rates were the same.[41] He noted that "in general, contract terms — maturities, down payments, and loan-to-value ratios — have been more liberal for VA loans than for FHA loans. Lenders generally have regarded VA property appraisals also as tending to be more liberal than those made by FHA. The fact that the VA guarantee is for 60 per cent of a loan (not to exceed $7500) and FHA insurance for 100 per cent of a loan may also have influenced investors' judgments about the quality of these mortgages."[42]

Our new data confirm that VA prices were lower, and discounts larger, during the 1953–56 period of contract rate equality (Table

[41] Klaman's comparisons were based on secondary market price quotations reported by the Federal National Mortgage Association, described above.

[42] Klaman, pp. 90–91.

2-16).[43] Such comparisons are not possible during the next five years because FHA and VA contract rates differed most of the time, but during 1962–66 contract rates were again the same. In this later period, the price differential was negligible. This may reflect the fact that FHA terms became more liberal during the intervening period relative to VA terms. By 1964, average down payments were only a few percentage points lower on FHA than on VA mortgages, and FHA maturities were several years longer. It is also possible that lenders became less concerned with terms during this period.

At various times, FHA mortgages have carried a higher contract rate than VAs, and this has affected their relative yield. In part, this is because the yield realized on a mortgage that is not priced at par is uncertain; it depends not only on the contract rate and the size of the premium or discount, but also on the life of the mortgage, which is not known in advance. Most mortgages are prepaid in full well before maturity. The larger the deviation from par the more important is variability in life as a determinant of realized yield.[44] Lender reaction to this uncertainty will affect relative yields.

It is quite possible that lender reactions to yield uncertainty will be different when mortgages sell at premiums than when they sell at discounts from par. When mortgages sell at discounts, yield is a decreasing function of life, and the lowest possible yield, which is realized if the mortgage runs to maturity, is not much lower than the yield at some intermediate "expected" life based on past experience or on reasonable expectations. The maximum yield in this case approaches infinity as life approaches zero. This is illustrated by the top line in Figure 2-2. When mortgages carry premiums, on the other hand, yield is an increasing function of life, as illustrated by the lower line on Figure 2-2; the lowest possible yield approaches minus infinity as life approaches zero. The maximum yield, which is realized if the mortgage goes to maturity, is not much higher than the expected yield.

The consequence of miscalculating mortgage life is thus quite different when mortgages sell at premiums than when they sell at discounts. When mortgages carry premiums, an error in the wrong direc-

---

[43] Prices are used in these comparisons because differences in maturities and expected life as between FHA and VA mortgages over the period covered were too small to have any significant effect on yield differences.

[44] See Jack M. Guttentag, "Mortgage Interest Rates: Trends and Structure," *1964 Conference on Savings and Residential Financing,* United States Savings and Loan League, p. 128.

TABLE 2-16. Discounts on FHA as Compared to VA Mortgages During Periods of Equal Maximum Contract Rate

Period	National Bureau Series					FNMA Series		
	Average Contract Rate		Average Discount			Average Discount		
	FHA	VA	FHA	VA	VA Less FHA	FHA	VA	VA Less FHA
June–December 1953	4.49	4.49	.93	1.83	.90	2.2	2.6	.4
1954	4.49	4.49	.86	1.31	.45	1.1	1.5	.4
1955	4.48	4.48	.98	1.67	.69	1.2	1.8	.6
January–November 1956	4.48	4.49	1.72	2.17	.45	2.2	2.8	.6
1962	5.26	5.25	3.13	3.40	.27	3.2	3.3	.1
1963	5.25	5.25	1.80	1.77	-.03	2.1	2.1	.0
1964						1.8	1.9	.1
1965						1.9	1.9	.0
1966						6.1	6.1	.0

NOTE: FNMA quotations apply to $4\frac{1}{2}$ per cent mortgages during 1953–56, $5\frac{1}{4}$ per cent mortgages during 1962–65, and $5\frac{1}{4}$–6 per cent mortgages during 1966 (current rate used in all cases).

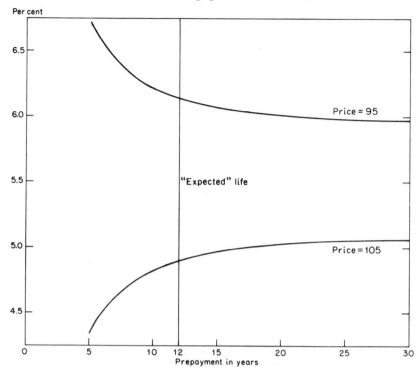

FIGURE 2-2. Yield on a 5½ Per Cent Thirty-Year Mortgage Priced at 95 and 105

tion can be very serious, since yield can be zero or negative. If the market is heavily influenced by conservative lenders, concerned with the "worst that can happen," the premium paid on high contract rate mortgages may not be large enough to equalize yield with low contract rate mortgages.

When mortgages carry discounts, in contrast, the consequence of a mistake in estimating mortgage life in the wrong direction is not serious. Other factors, however, including public relations aspects of accepting discounts from borrowers, may influence the yield.

The evidence examined here can be divided broadly into two phases, in both of which, for periods of varying length, the FHA contract rate was higher than the VA rate. These periods are prior to mid-1952, when FHAs and VAs carried premiums; and 1957–61 when they carried discounts.

THE CASE OF PREMIUMS. The data [45] confirm the supposition advanced above that lenders will be reluctant to pay a premium on a high contract rate mortgage large enough to equalize yield with a lower contract rate mortgage. Prior to April 1950, FHA Section 203 mortgages carried a maximum rate of $4\frac{1}{2}$ per cent, while the VA rate was 4 per cent. One large life insurance company paid an average premium of 0.8 per cent for VAs during this period and 1.6 per cent for FHAs, producing a yield spread of .37 per cent in favor of the high-rate FHAs (Table 2-17). Put differently, the premium on FHAs would have had to have been about 4.0 points to equalize the yield with that on VAs. The FHA rate was only .14 below the conventional rate in this period.

TABLE 2-17. Premiums and Yields on FHA, VA and Conventional Mortgages Authorized by Life Insurance Companies, January 1949–April 1950 and January 1951–April 1952

	January 1949–April 1950 [a]			January 1951–April 1952		
	Contract Rate	Premium	Effective Yield	Contract Rate	Premium	Effective Yield
FHA	4.49	1.6	4.26	4.26	.5	4.19
VA	4.00	.8	3.89	4.00	−.3	4.04
Conventional	4.58	1.3	4.40	4.63	1.2	4.45

SOURCE: Same as Table 2-2.
[a] Data limited to one company.

In April 1950 the FHA rate was reduced to $4\frac{1}{4}$ per cent, and the yield on FHAs immediately fell relative to VAs and conventionals. Chart 2-3 shows a sharp rise in the yield differential of conventionals over FHAs following the rate reduction on FHAs. In the sixteen months ending April 1952, the FHA yield for life insurance companies was .07 per cent lower than in the prior period, while the yields on 4 per cent VAs and on conventionals were higher by .15 per cent and .05 per cent, respectively (see Table 2-17). This shift in the spread can be attributed largely to the decline in the FHA rate. Nevertheless, $4\frac{1}{4}$ per cent FHAs continued to yield more than 4 per cent VAs.[46]

It may be asked why, under conditions where mortgages carry

[45] Publishable data prior to 1951 are limited to one large company. Fragmentary data from other sources, however, confirm the relationship shown in the table.

[46] After an adjustment for "quality," the spread would have been wider. It will be recalled that in 1953–56, when contract rates were the same, VAs yielded more.

premiums, the contract rate was not bid down by competition. The rate set by law or regulation on FHAs and VAs is, after all, a maximum rate and not a minimum. Any extended discussion of this would go well beyond the scope of this paper, but clearly, the explanation is rooted in the imperfect character of the residential mortgage market at the primary (origination) level. Among the relevant factors would be the following:

(a) The ignorance and unwillingness or inability of most mortgage borrowers to shop.[47]

(b) The apparent sanction provided the maximum rate by the federal agencies; borrowers are encouraged to believe that the government has set *the* rate, rather than merely the maximum rate.

(c) A tendency for mortgage lenders to view rate cutting as an "unethical practice." One large lender who did cut rates below the maximum in the period when FHAs carried large premiums was taken severely to task by other lenders.[48] The tendency of mortgage lenders was to view the maximum allowable rate much as personal finance companies view the legal rate ceiling on small loans, namely, as a customary rate that is in the best interest of all lenders to observe.

(d) The unwillingness of builders to bargain for a lower contract rate; the builder could usually command part of the premium from the high-rate mortgage. This might or might not be reflected in lower house prices.

It would seem an inevitable implication of the above analysis that, from the standpoint of borrower interest, contract rates on FHA and VA mortgages should never be high enough that these mortgages command premiums. As a matter of fact, they never have commanded premiums since 1953.

THE CASE OF DISCOUNTS. Following the 1953–56 period of contract rate equality between FHA and VA mortgages, rate differences arose again beginning in 1957. For this and later periods, price data on FHAs and VAs are available from FNMA as well as from the new NBER survey. The latter cover loans authorized by the large life insurance companies, while the former are largely based on over-the-counter sales by mortgage companies, mainly to life insurance com-

---

[47] For some evidence on this, see Housing and Home Finance Agency, "Residential Mortgage Financing, Jacksonville, Florida, First Six Months of 1950," *Housing Research Paper No. 23,* Washington, D.C., December 1952, pp. 30–33.

[48] See H. A. Schaaf, "Federal Interest Rate Policy on Insured and Guaranteed Mortgages," unpublished Ph.D. dissertation, University of California, Berkeley, 1955, p. 135.

TABLE 2-18. Discounts on FHA and VA Mortgages as Reported in NBER and FNMA Series, Selected Periods (*percentage points*)

Period	NBER		FNMA		FNMA Less NBER	
	FHA	VA	FHA	VA	FHA	VA
Feb. 57–July 57	2.4	3.0	2.9	7.0	0.5	4.0
Oct. 57–March 58	2.3	3.2	2.6	9.2	0.3	6.0
Sept. 58–June 59	2.4	4.9	3.1	7.2	0.7	2.3
Dec. 59–Jan. 60	3.4	5.3	3.8	7.9	0.4	2.6
Dec. 60–Jan. 61	2.9	4.6	2.4	6.6	−0.5	2.0
April 61–Aug. 61	2.6	4.5	2.2	4.3	−0.4	−0.2

SOURCE: Same as Table 2-2, plus the Federal National Mortgage Association.

TABLE 2-19. Gross Yield on FHA and VA Mortgages as Reported in NBER and FNMA Series, Selected Periods (*per cent*)

Period	Maximum Contract Rate			Gross Yield					
				NBER			FNMA		
	FHA	VA	FHA Less VA	FHA	VA	FHA Less VA	FHA	VA	FHA Less VA
Feb. 57–July 57	5.00	4.50	.50	5.33	4.93	.40	5.43	5.52	−.09
Oct. 57–March 58	5.25	4.50	.75	5.58	4.96	.62	5.63	5.86	−.23
Sept. 58–June 59	5.25	4.75	.50	5.60	5.44	.16	5.69	5.79	−.10
Dec. 59–Jan. 60	5.75	5.25	.50	6.19	6.01	.18	6.31	6.40	−.09
Dec. 60–Jan. 61	5.75	5.25	.50	6.15	5.91	.24	6.09	6.21	−.12
April 61–Aug. 61	5.50	5.25	.25	5.88	5.89	−.01	5.82	5.86	−.04

SOURCE: Same as Table 2-18.

panies and mutual savings banks. The two sources show only modest price differences on FHA mortgages, but very substantial differences on VAs. Thus, during February 1957–July 1957, NBER series show VAs carrying a discount of 3 points, while the FNMA series show VAs carrying a discount of 7 points (Table 2-18). As a result, for the large life insurance companies, the higher contract-rate FHAs yielded more, while for the lenders covered by the FNMA data the lower contract-rate VAs yielded more (Table 2-19). The yield difference was largest during the period October 1957–March 1958, when the contract rate difference between FHAs and VAs was largest (.75 per cent). During this period, FHAs authorized by the life companies yielded .62 per cent *more* than VAs, while on loans sold by mortgage companies FHAs yielded .23 per cent *less* than VAs.

When VA mortgages carried lower contract rates than FHAs, the large life insurance companies reduced their VA volume but took a limited number at relatively small discounts. This action reflected a widespread view, in Congress and elsewhere, that large discounts on VA mortgages were unethical. Klaman noted that "large financial intermediaries, in their widely acknowledged role as public trustees, have been less willing to risk public censure than to ignore the facts of market forces." [49] The result of this policy was, in effect, to create two markets for VA mortgages: a rationed low-discount market by large life insurance companies (and perhaps other lenders with similar compunctions); and a "free" market where discounts rose to the level necessary to clear the market. It is ironical that the public pressures on large institutions to limit discounts on VA mortgages, by causing them to sharply reduce their VA volume, had the effect of increasing pressure on VA discounts in the "free" market.

There are indications that life insurance company attitudes toward discounting underwent a considerable change during 1958–59, in the sense that they began to accept the discounts required to bring VA yields into an appropriate relationship to FHA yields. Comparing the October 1957–March 1958 and the September 1958–June 1959 periods, VA discounts rose by 1.7 points in the NBER series and declined by 2.0 points in the FNMA series (Table 2-18). Perhaps even more dramatic was the shift in the FHA-VA yield relationship in the NBER series (Table 2-19). Yields on VA mortgages rose by .48 per cent as VA discounts rose appreciably despite a rise in contract rate (4.50 to 4.75 per cent). Yields on FHA mortgages rose by only .02 per

[49] Klaman, p. 89.

TABLE 2-20. Prices and Yields on Current and "Old" FHA and VA Home Mortgages, Selected Periods

Period	Mortgage (per cent)	Average Price over Period	Average Yield over Period [c]	Yield Differential [d]
May 1953–Jan. 1955	FHA 4¼	96.2	4.78	
(18 observations) [a]	FHA 4½ [b]	98.6	4.70	.08
	VA 4	94.4	4.80	
	VA 4½ [b]	98.3	4.74	.06
Dec. 1956–June 1957	FHA 4½	93.4	5.47	
(7 observations)	FHA 5 [b]	97.3	5.39	.08
Aug. 1957–Dec. 1958	FHA 5	95.5	5.66	
(17 observations)	FHA 5¼ [b]	97.7	5.58	.08
April–Dec. 1958	VA 4½	92.1	5.67	
(9 observations)	VA 4¾ [b]	94.3	5.59	.08
July–Sept. 1959	VA 4¾	91.5	6.02	
(3 observations)	VA 5¼ [b]	94.8	6.02	.00
Oct. 1959–March 1960	FHA 5¼	93.0	6.30	
(6 observations)	FHA 5¾ [b]	96.2	6.31	−.01
Feb.–May 1961	FHA 5½ [b]	97.2	5.91	
(4 observations)	FHA 5¾	98.6	5.96	−.05
June 1961–Feb. 1962	FHA 5¼ [b]	96.3	5.79	
(10 observations)	FHA 5½	97.8	5.82	−.03
	FHA 5¾	99.4	5.84	−.05
March–April 1966	FHA 5¼	92.6	6.37	
(2 observations)	FHA 5½ [b]	94.5	6.33	−.04
May–June 1966	FHA 5½	92.6	6.63	
(2 observations)	FHA 5¾ [b]	94.6	6.57	−.06

SOURCE: Federal National Mortgage Association.

[a] No observations for July, September or October 1953.

[b] Current maximum rate.

[c] Assumes twenty-five-year maturity, ten-year prepayment.

[d] Low-rate mortgage less high-rate mortgage.

cent, as discounts on FHA mortgages of constant contract rate increased only slightly.

Evidently by 1961 the market had learned to live with discounts. During the period April 1961–August 1961, price quotations on VA loans were about the same in the FNMA series and the NBER series, and differences between FHA and VA yields were small. However, the contract rate difference between FHAs and VAs was only .25 per cent during this period; it is not clear how the market would have reacted to a .75 per cent difference. Since 1961 contract rates have been the same.

There is, however, some additional evidence that lenders' attitudes toward discounting underwent a change during 1959. The evidence consists of FNMA price quotations following a change in the FHA or VA maximum contract rate, on old mortgages carrying the old rate. When the contract rate is changed, new commitments will be at the new rate, but there will also be some overhang of uncommitted mortgages carrying the old rate for which mortgage companies or other originators must find buyers. FNMA continues to report prices on mortgages carrying the old rate for as long as there is any significant activity in the older mortgages. During such periods of dual coverage yield comparisons are possible between old and new mortgages carrying different contract rates (Table 2-20).

These observations reveal that through 1958 yields tended to be about .08 per cent higher on mortgages carrying the lower contract rate. In later periods, however, yields were higher on the high contract rate mortgages. These yield differentials are sensitive to the assumed maturity and prepayment, but there is no ambiguity regarding the change in the differentials. No matter what assumptions are made, a significant decline occurred in the yield on high contract rate mortgages *relative* to low contract rate mortgages, indicating a greater willingness to accept discounts as an offset to a lower contract rate.

APPENDIX TABLE. Yields on Bonds and Mortgages at Reference Cycle Peaks and Troughs

	July 1953	July 1957	May 1960	Average
Part A: Peaks				
Conventional mortgages	4.76	5.48	6.09	
FHA mortgages	4.53	5.38	6.27	
Conventional less FHA	.23	.10	−.18	.05
Corporate Baa bonds	3.86	4.73	5.28	
Corporate Aaa bonds	3.28	3.99	4.46	
Baa less Aaa	.58	.74	.82	.71
State and local Baa bonds	3.60	4.29	4.31	
State and local Aaa bonds	2.56	3.17	3.34	
Baa less Aaa	1.04	1.12	.97	1.04
Conventional mortgages less Aaa corporate bonds	1.48	1.49	1.63	1.53
Conventional mortgages less Aaa state and local	2.20	2.31	2.75	2.42

	Aug. 1954	April 1958	Feb. 1961	Average
Part B: Troughs				
Conventional mortgages	4.74	5.63	5.96	
FHA mortgages	4.60	5.61	6.16	
Conventional less FHA	.14	.02	−.20	−.01
Corporate Baa bonds	3.49	4.67	5.07	
Corporate Aaa bonds	2.87	3.60	4.27	
Baa less Aaa	.62	1.07	.80	.83
State and local Baa bonds	2.94	3.78	4.06	
State and local Aaa bonds	1.90	2.70	3.14	
Baa less Aaa	1.04	1.08	.92	1.01
Conventional mortgages less Aaa corporate bonds	1.87	2.03	1.69	1.86
Conventional mortgages less Aaa state and local	2.84	2.93	2.82	2.86

NOTE: Mortgage yields are from NBER authorization series, with assumed prepayment of ten years. Bond series are from Moody's.

3

The Structure of the Mortgage Market
for Income Property Mortgage
Loans   *Royal Shipp*

Introduction and Summary

At the end of the second quarter of 1967, mortgage debt outstanding on nonfarm multifamily and nonresidential properties (hereafter referred to as income properties) had reached over $100 billion and constituted nearly three-tenths of all mortgage debt outstanding. Over the past decade, mortgage debt on income properties grew at a faster rate than any other major type of indebtedness.

Despite the size and growth of this sector of the capital markets, few comprehensive studies have been made of the market for mortgage loans on income properties, mainly due to a lack of statistical data.

NOTE: This paper was prepared while the author was employed by the Board of Governors of the Federal Reserve System. It expresses his views and not necessarily those of the Board of Governors. The author is indebted to several colleagues at the Federal Reserve and to others associated with the National Bureau of Economic Research for assistance in preparing the paper. From the Board's staff, Erling T. Thoresen gave sound advice regarding the choice and use of a computer program to tabulate the data, Kathryn Morisse wrote a number of computer programs, and Peter M. Keir and Bernard N. Freedman made helpful suggestions. Robert P. Shay of the National Bureau of Economic Research and Richard T. Selden of Cornell University also read and commented on the paper. A particularly large debt is owed to Robert Moore Fisher of the Federal Reserve's Capital Markets Section, and to Jack M. Guttentag, each of whom read several drafts and made extensive comments. Only the author, of course, is responsible for any shortcomings or errors which remain.

Mr. Shipp is senior analyst, Office of Program Evaluation, Bureau of the Budget.

The National Bureau of Economic Research, with a grant from the Life Insurance Association of America, attempted to remedy this situation by including income property loans in its survey of mortgage rates. Monthly data on the rates and terms, as well as property and borrower characteristics, were obtained on income property mortgage loans authorized since 1951 by fifteen large life insurance companies.[1] The Federal Reserve Board expressed an early interest in the project, providing resources to help with the final stage of the data-collecting process and to tabulate and analyze the data.

This paper presents preliminary findings from the first stage of the study which is based on the four cross-section quarters of the historical data for which the most information was obtained.[2] These findings document relationships among certain basic characteristics of income property loans that heretofore have generally been estimated by conventional rules of thumb and from the findings of isolated case studies.[3] The paper presents statistical information about the characteristics of loans, borrowers, and property that not only helps to illustrate how the market for these mortgages has been operating but also provides tentative guidelines for persons concerned with real estate appraisal, market analysis, and lender supervision.

The central conclusions of the paper concern relationships among loan characteristics. First, loan size is an important factor in explaining levels of other loan transaction characteristics. For example,

---

[1] See Appendix A to this chapter for a list of the companies participating in the survey and their share of the total resources of all life insurance companies. These fifteen companies probably account for about 15 per cent of the total mortgage debt outstanding on income properties. While the historical data were being collected, arrangements were made for the same companies to report current data monthly to the Life Insurance Association of America, beginning in July 1965 when the historical series terminated. Robert Killebrew had responsibility for much of the field work necessary to compile the historical data. Barbara Negri Opper, formerly of the LIAA, supervised the initial collection and tabulation of the current data supplied by the reporting companies.

[2] These quarters and the number of loans authorized in each are 3rd 1954 (514), 4th 1959 (720), 3rd 1963 (828), and 1st 1965 (895). Analysis of the data is being broken into three stages. The second stage will be a cross section regression study of the relationship between interest rates and other loan characteristics. (Stages one and two utilize only information from the four quarters mentioned above.) The third stage will consist of the development of an historical interest rate series to link up with the current series being compiled by the LIAA.

[3] These relationships are examined by cross classifying the characteristics. While cross classification is a useful technique for preliminary analysis and description of the data, it usually is limited to a consideration of three or four variables at one time. Obviously, it cannot explain all the relationships, particularly since most of the characteristics are intercorrelated.

loan maturities and loan-value ratios vary directly with loan size. In addition, loan size is related to loan amortization arrangements,[4] the presence or absence of borrower liability, and the period of time between the date of loan authorization and the date of loan closing. Perhaps the most surprising finding is that the relationship between loan size and interest rates, as shown by simple cross classification, is a weak one.

Second, the terms of loan transactions also vary by property type and by property leasing arrangements. These factors are related to loan terms, presumably because they reflect the lender's assessments of size and degree of certainty of estimated property income streams.

Third, capitalization rates can be used as proxy measures of the lender's assessment of mortgage risks. The data show that relatively liberal loan terms are consistently associated with low capitalization rates, and vice versa.

Fourth, the relationship between interest rates and other loan terms is not pronounced. The main reason for this is that loan terms, as well as interest rates, are related to risk, and a good part of the variability in risk is absorbed by changes in terms.

Terms of Loan Transactions

Terms of loan transactions to be discussed in this section are: interest rate, service fee, maturity, loan-value ratio, loan amount, loan repayment provisions, and extent of borrower liability.

INTEREST RATE. Interest rate in this paper refers to the contract, or nominal, interest rate. Although contract rate adjusted for fees and charges, termed "effective yield," is generally viewed as the preferable measure, much of the information from the life insurance companies which would have been necessary to calculate effective yield (i.e., data regarding one-time fees which lenders paid or received in connection with the origination of the loans) was incomplete. In addition, the data available on origination fees suggest that such fees were small in comparison with the contract rate. As a result, the fees, if included, would have caused contract rates to differ little from effective yields.

---

[4] The term "amortization arrangement," discussed in more detail below, refers to the conditions under which repayment of loan principal takes place. For example, the loan principal may be repaid gradually over the life of the loan, it may be repaid in one lump sum at the end of the loan life, or some other arrangements may be made.

Average interest rates varied among the four quarters, with the low being 4.72 per cent in 1954 and the high 6.14 per cent in 1959. The rates for 1963 and 1965 were 5.88 and 5.91 per cent, respectively.[5] As Table 3-1 shows, the average interest rate also varied considerably

TABLE 3-1. Average Interest Rates by Type of Property and Quarter

Type of Property	3rd Quarter 1954	4th Quarter 1959	3rd Quarter 1963	1st Quarter 1965
Elevator apartments	4.47	6.13	5.88	5.96
Nonelevator apartments	4.94	6.19	5.99	6.01
Hotels and motels	5.00	6.44	6.05	6.32
Retail stores	4.61	6.03	5.70	5.72
Shopping centers	4.70	6.17	5.81	5.77
Office buildings	4.53	6.08	5.78	5.80
Medical office buildings	4.82	6.14	5.81	5.90
Warehouses	4.65	6.05	5.79	5.81
Industrial properties	4.61	6.17	5.78	5.81
Misc. commercial properties	4.67	6.11	5.74	5.74
Institutional properties	4.62	6.18	5.86	6.10
All loans	4.72	6.14	5.88	5.91

NOTE: See Appendix B for an explanation of the kinds of properties included in the different categories in this table.

among property types. The highest interest rates (hotels and motels in every quarter) ranged 35–60 basis points above the lowest (retail stores in three of the quarters and elevator apartments in the other).[6]

Interest rates seemed to cluster at different levels. In the later three

[5] Averages used in this paper were weighted by number of loans. In the remainder of the text of this paper only the year will be used to designate the different periods.

[6] Interest rates on most income property mortgage loans were in denominations of one-fourth of 1 per cent (for example, 4.00, 4.25, 4.50). In some instances, they were in eighths of a per cent (for example, 4.125, 4.375), and in a few cases the contract rate was not constant for the entire life of the loan. For example, one loan had a contract rate of 6 per cent for the first four years and 5.75 per cent for the remaining life of the loan. An average contract rate was computed for loans with varying rates by taking the outstanding loan balances at the middle of each year and adding them up for all the years outstanding, assuming that the loan would be repaid in full after one-half its contract maturity. This total was then divided into the sum of dollars of interest payable in each year to give an average interest rate.

quarters, about one-half of the loans were made at 6 per cent. In 1954, nearly one-third were at 4.50 per cent. In every quarter, around nine-tenths of the loans were within a range of 1 percentage point. For example, in 1965, 93 per cent of the loans had interest rates between 5.50 per cent and 6.49 per cent.

SERVICE FEES. Loan servicing [7] is handled by life insurance companies in two different ways. Some loans are serviced by the home office or a branch office of the lending company. These are called direct loans and the cost of servicing them is absorbed as a general overhead expense. In other cases, lenders contract with correspondents (usually mortgage companies) to service the loans. These are known as correspondent loans and the correspondents are paid a fee for servicing the loan which is calculated as a per cent per year of the outstanding amount. (See Table 3-2 for the proportion of correspondent and direct loans in each quarter.)

Two of the life insurance companies in the survey have branch offices throughout most of the United States, thus enabling them to originate and service nearly all of their loans. These two companies accounted for between 70 and 90 per cent of the direct loans during the four quarters. Eight companies used correspondents for nearly all of their servicing needs, and five companies for two-thirds and five-sixths of their needs, servicing the remainder directly.

Fees charged on about half the correspondent loans recorded in the survey were for a constant per cent per year of the outstanding balance. The other half of the service fees varied in percentage terms as the outstanding loan balance declined (called the variable balance type), or as time passed (called variable time type). Five companies in the survey used the variable balance method for at least some of their loans; one of the largest companies used it almost exclusively.

One company used the following variable balance formula to calculate service fee on some of its loans: one-fourth of 1 per cent on the first $100,000 of the loan; one-eighth of 1 per cent on the next $300,000

---

[7] Loan servicing has been defined by Sherman J. Maisel as "The collection of payments on a mortgage. [It] . . . also consists of operational procedures covering accounting, bookkeeping, insurance, tax records, loan-payment follow-up, delinquent-loan follow-up, and loan analysis." See *Financing Real Estate,* New York, 1965, p. 424. For a more extensive discussion of loan servicing, see Henry E. Hoagland and Leo D. Stone, *Real Estate Finance,* 3rd ed., Homewood, Illinois, 1965, pp. 294–295, and also Kurt F. Flexner and Roger B. Hawkins (eds.), *Mortgage Officer Handbook,* The American Bankers Association, 1963, pp. 139–159, 189–211.

TABLE 3-2. Number and Per Cent of Loans by Type of Servicing
Arrangement

Type of Servicing Arrangement	3rd Quarter 1954		4th Quarter 1959		3rd Quarter 1963		1st Quarter 1965	
	Num- ber	Per Cent	Num- ber	Per Cent	Num- ber	Per Cent	Num- ber	Per Cent
Correspondent loans	261	51.1	438	60.9	527	63.7	516	58.0
Direct loans	250	48.9	281	39.1	300	36.3	374	42.0
All loans	511	100.0	719	100.0	827	100.0	890	100.0

NOTE: The number of loans shown in some tables will differ from the numbers given in footnote 2. This is because some information was not available for certain loans. For example, in the case of five loans in the first quarter 1965, the information necessary to determine whether they were correspondent or direct was missing.

of the loan; and one-sixteenth of 1 per cent on the remainder of the loan. If a $1 million twenty-year loan were made, the first year's service fee would be calculated as follows:

$$.0025 \times \$100,000 = \quad \$250.00$$
$$.00125 \times \$300,000 = \quad \$375.00$$
$$.000625 \times \$600,000 = \quad \underline{\$375.00}$$
$$\$1,000.00$$

After the outstanding loan amount declined to $400,000 or less, the .0625 per cent rate would no longer be used. When the outstanding amount was $100,000 or less, the amount of service fee would be .25 per cent of the outstanding balance.

The variable-time method was used by one company (accounting for about one-tenth of the loans in the survey) for most of its correspondent loans. Other companies used it only in isolated instances. Using this method, the percentage rate is constant for a specified number of years, then changes. For example, the rate might be .25 per cent for the first three years and .125 per cent thereafter.[8]

[8] In order to make service fees on correspondent loans with variable formulas comparable to those with constant service fee percentages, it was necessary to convert the former into a constant average percentage for the estimated life of the loan. This was done by assuming that the loan would be outstanding for one-half its contract maturity. Then the total dollar amount of service fee required for that period (based on the formula) was divided by the sum of outstanding loan balances (taken at the middle of each year) for the half-life of the loan.

The average service fee for correspondent loans declined from nearly .40 per cent in 1954 to about .25 per cent in 1963 and 1965 (see Table 3-3). In all four quarters, the average service fee varied inversely with loan amount. In 1965, for example, the average service fee was .33 per cent for loans under $100,000. The fee declined steadily as loan size increased, being .04 per cent for loans of $10 million and over. The larger average loan size in the later two quarters only partially explains the lower average service fees in those periods, however. Service fees also declined within loan size categories.

LOAN AMOUNT. Loans included in the survey ranged in size from under $25,000 to over $25 million. Table 3-4 indicates that more of the larger loans were made in 1963 and 1965 than in the other two quarters. In 1954 and 1959, around three-fourths of the loans were under $250,000; in 1963 and 1965, this proportion was less than one-half. About one-sixth of the loans made in 1963 and 1965 were for $1 million or more as compared to slightly over one-twentieth in the two earlier periods.

The large size of some income property loans limits the kinds and numbers of institutions able to make the loans. This is borne out to some extent by the present study. The five smallest companies in the survey, each with assets of less than $2 billion (see Appendix A), made only 4 per cent of the loans for $1 million or more in the four quarters. But these same five companies made 15 per cent of the total number of loans during the four quarters.

The large loans accounted for a great share of the total dollar amounts loaned. In 1963 and 1965, loans of $1 million or more accounted for one-sixth of the number of loans but for about two-thirds of all dollars loaned. Even in the earlier two quarters when large loans were relatively less numerous, loans of $1 million and above (about one-twentieth of the number of loans) constituted about half of the dollar amounts.

Loan Size and Other Loan Characteristics. In this paper, loan size is used to cross classify many other loan characteristics to which it appears to be closely related. (The relationship of loan size to service fee has already been considered.) In part this relation may reflect the fact that the size of loan acts as a proxy for the size and financial strength of the borrowers.

Loan size varied directly with the length of time between the authorization and the closing of loans. Data on all loans in this study were obtained as of the date of loan authorization (when funds were committed

TABLE 3-3. Average Contract Interest Rates, Service Fees, and Net Increase Rates of Direct and Correspondent Loans by Loan Amount and Quarter

Loan Amount ($000)	Direct (contract rate)				Correspondent											
	3rd Qtr. 1954	4th Qtr. 1959	3rd Qtr. 1963	1st Qtr. 1965	3rd Quarter 1954			4th Quarter 1959			3rd Quarter 1963			1st Quarter 1965		
					Contract Rate	Service Fee	Net Rate	Contract Rate	Service Fee	Net Rate	Contract Rate	Service Fee	Net Rate	Contract Rate	Service Fee	Net Rate
Under 100	4.81	6.09	5.84	5.85	4.87	.44	4.42	6.18	.38	5.80	5.97	.35	5.62	6.04	.33	5.71
100–249	4.57	6.09	5.74	5.77	4.76	.35	4.40	6.18	.33	5.86	5.93	.27	5.67	5.98	.28	5.70
250–499	4.50	6.07	5.83	5.76	4.59	.29	4.29	6.14	.26	5.88	5.96	.24	5.72	6.03	.26	5.77
500–749	4.40	6.15	5.83	5.88	4.75	.24	4.51	6.18	.23	5.96	5.98	.21	5.77	5.96	.22	5.74
750–999	4.25 a	6.20	5.75	5.83	4.63 a	.28 a	4.34 a	6.19	.21	5.99	5.92	.17	5.76	5.92	.19	5.73
1,000–1,999	4.28	6.25	5.75	5.89	4.75 a	.25 a	4.50 a	6.07	.20	5.87	5.92	.16	5.76	5.92	.16	5.75
2,000–4,999	4.25	6.14	5.82	5.83	4.50	.16	4.34	6.13	.19	5.94	5.83	.10	5.73	5.89	.12	5.77
5,000–9,999	4.41	6.00 a	5.50	5.75	4.56 a	.13 a	4.43 a	6.00 a	.08 a	5.92 a	5.71	.08	5.63	5.82	.08	5.74
10,000 and over	4.50	6.25 a	5.75 a	5.67	–	0	–	–	0	–	–	0	–	5.38 a	.04 a	5.34 a
All loans	4.64	6.10	5.79	5.81	4.79	.39	4.41	6.17	.33	5.85	5.94	.24	5.70	5.98	.25	5.73

NOTE: Direct loans are those serviced (and usually originated) by the lender. Correspondent loans are originated and serviced by a correspondent (usually a mortgage company). Net rates of correspondent loans are calculated by subtracting service fees from contract rates. Variable balance and variable time service fees have been converted to a constant per cent per year, as described in footnote 8, and included in this table. Subgroups may not add exactly to totals because of rounding.

a Fewer than five loans.

TABLE 3-4. Number of Loans and Total Dollars Loaned by Loan Amount and Quarter

Loan Amount ($000)	3rd Quarter 1954		4th Quarter 1959		3rd Quarter 1963		1st Quarter 1965	
	Number	Total Dollars ($000,000)	Number	Total Dollars ($000,000)	Number	Total Dollars ($000,000)	Number	Total Dollars ($000,000)
Under 100	262	12	304	17	173	11	166	11
100–249	146	22	226	34	237	39	267	45
250–499	44	15	99	33	157	56	177	60
500–749	19	11	39	23	78	46	93	56
750–999	7	6	14	12	52	43	39	34
1,000–1,999	12	16	19	27	76	98	81	109
2,000–4,999	15	39	15	39	38	110	53	150
5,000–9,999	5	33	2	13	13	85	12	74
10,000 and over	1	10	2	28	3	48	7	105
All loans	511	166	720	225	827	535	895	643

Loan Amount ($000)	Loans (per cent)	Dollars (per cent)	Loans (per cent)	Dollars (per cent)	Loans (per cent)	Dollars (per cent)	Loans (per cent)	Dollars (per cent)
Under 100	51.0	7.5	42.2	7.6	20.9	2.0	18.5	1.7
100–249	28.4	13.4	31.4	15.2	28.6	7.2	29.8	6.9
250–499	8.6	9.2	13.8	14.6	19.0	10.4	20.0	9.4
500–749	3.7	6.7	5.4	10.1	9.4	8.6	10.4	8.7
750–999	1.4	3.5	1.9	5.2	6.3	8.1	4.4	5.2
1,000–1,999	2.3	9.9	2.6	11.8	9.2	18.3	9.1	17.0
2,000–4,999	2.9	23.8	2.1	17.4	4.6	20.5	5.9	23.3
5,000–9,999	1.0	19.9	0.3	5.8	1.6	15.9	1.3	11.5
10,000 and over	0.2	6.0	0.3	12.2	0.4	9.0	0.8	16.4
All loans	100.0	100.0	100.0	100.0	100.0	100.0	100.0	100.0

NOTE: Subgroups may not add exactly to totals because of rounding.

TABLE 3-5. Number of Months Loan Authorizations Were Outstanding

Number of Months Between Authorization and Closing	3rd Quarter 1954			4th Quarter 1959		
	Number	Per Cent	Average Amount ($000)	Number	Per Cent	Average Amount ($000)
Authorized and closed same month	17	5.6	132	18	4.4	181
1–3 months	140	46.5	187	96	23.3	202
4–6 months	49	16.3	149	60	14.6	187
7–9 months	26	8.6	212	77	18.7	143
10–12 months	17	5.6	251	69	16.7	229
13–18 months	18	6.0	922	42	10.2	476
Over 18 months	11	3.7	1,150	20	4.9	621
Authorization expired	23	7.6	265	30	7.3	284
All loans	301	100.0		412	100.0	

NOTE: Percentages may not add exactly to 100 because of rounding.

for a particular loan) and not as of the date of loan closing (when funds were paid out to borrowers).[9] This dating distinction is important because characteristics of mortgage loans at the time of closing reflect the market conditions of an earlier time, which varies depending on the time lag between authorization and closing.[10]

The length of time between the authorization date and the closing date for the loans in this survey ranged from less than one month to over eighteen months (see Table 3-5). Authorization periods were usually longer for loans in 1959 than in 1954. During 1959, just over one-fourth of the loans were closed within three months of authorization; nearly one-half were closed between seven and eighteen months after authorization. In 1954, over one-half of the loans were closed within three months of their authorization date. Table 3-5 also shows that larger loans tend to have longer authorization periods than shorter ones. In 1954, for example, the average size of a loan with an authori-

[9] Some loans included in the survey were authorized but, for a variety of reasons, were never closed. These loans are labeled "Authorization expired" in Table 3-5. They constituted between 7 and 8 per cent of the loans authorized in 1954 and 1959, the only periods in the present study for which this information is available.

[10] For a more comprehensive discussion of the advantages of data based on the authorization date see Jack M. Guttentag, "Mortgage Interest Rates: Trends and Structure," in *Conference on Savings and Residential Financing, 1964 Proceedings*, pp. 130–131.

zation period of over one year was about $1 million. But the average size of a loan with an authorization period under one year was less than $200,000.

Other characteristics affected by loan size will be discussed below. Since larger loans carry more liberal nonrate terms (as the subsequent discussion will show), interest rates might have been expected to vary with loan size as well. As Table 3-3 indicates, however, no such relationship prevailed. The level of interest rates seemed to be largely independent of loan size.

MATURITY. Holding other loan terms constant, the maturity of an amortized loan determines the rate at which the principal must be repaid, hence, the amount still outstanding at any time after closing. The longer the maturity, the lower will be the periodic payments toward principal and interest required to service the loan. This means that with a longer maturity, any income from property operations will more likely be sufficient to cover debt payments. That, in turn, reduces the likelihood of delinquency or default. With longer maturities, however, a greater amount of the original loan will be outstanding at any time after closing; hence the risk of loss is greater should delinquency or default occur.

Average loan maturity increased from a little over fifteen years in 1954 to nearly twenty years in 1965. This change appears to represent a secular lengthening of maturities over the period. Like interest rates,

TABLE 3-6. Frequency Distribution of Loan Maturities by Quarter

Maturity (years)	3rd Quarter 1954		4th Quarter 1959		3rd Quarter 1963		1st Quarter 1965	
	Number	Per Cent	Number	Per Cent	Number	Per Cent	Number	Per Cent
10.0 and under	101	19.8	62	8.6	27	3.3	21	2.3
10.1–14.9	42	8.2	50	6.9	26	3.1	21	2.3
15.0	185	36.2	213	29.6	147	17.8	141	15.8
15.1–19.9	54	10.6	38	5.3	44	5.3	71	7.9
20.0	107	20.9	328	45.6	436	52.7	398	44.5
20.1–24.9	13	2.5	23	2.9	104	12.6	170	19.0
25.0	6	1.2	6	0.8	31	3.7	54	6.0
Over 25.0	3	0.6	0	0	12	1.4	19	2.1
All loans	511	100.0	720	100.0	827	100.0	895	100.0

NOTE: Percentages may not add exactly to 100 because of rounding.

loan maturities show a tendency to cluster at particular levels. In the later three quarters, nearly one-half of the loans were made with maturities of twenty years. In 1954, fifteen years was the most common maturity with over one-third of the loans at that figure (see Table 3-6).

Average maturities were longer on larger loans than on smaller ones in all four quarters (see Table 3-7). The average maturity in 1965 was seventeen years for loans under $100,000; it was over twenty-five years for loans of $10 million or more.

TABLE 3-7. Average Loan Maturities by Loan Amount and Quarter (*years*)

Loan Amount ($000)	3rd Quarter 1954	4th Quarter 1959	3rd Quarter 1963	1st Quarter 1965
Under 100	14.4	16.4	17.0	17.0
100–249	15.2	17.2	18.2	18.8
250–499	16.7	17.4	19.3	19.8
500–749	18.1	18.3	19.7	19.8
750–999	20.6	17.3	20.1	21.1
1,000–1,999	18.9	18.8	20.9	21.8
2,000–4,999	18.9	20.0	22.5	22.6
5,000–9,999	19.0	20.2 [a]	24.0	23.2
10,000 and over	26.3 [a]	22.5 [a]	25.1 [a]	26.6
All loans	15.3	17.0	19.0	19.5

[a] Fewer than five loans.

Per Cent-Constant Ratio. If a loan is fully amortizing with uniform payments, its maturity and interest rate determine the amount of required debt payments per dollar loaned. Per cent constant (sometimes called annual constant) is a ratio used by borrowers and lenders to indicate the size of annual debt payments in relation to the loan amount.[11] As Table 3-8 shows, per cent constant varies directly with changes in interest rates and inversely with changes in maturities.

[11] Per cent constant equals

$$12\left[\frac{i}{1 - \dfrac{1}{(1 + i)^n}}\right]$$

where i is interest rate per month and n is maturity in months. The formula assumes fully amortizing, uniform monthly payments loans. Another way to derive per cent constant is to divide the annual debt payment by the original loan amount.

Borrowers on income properties often prefer a combination of interest rate and maturity which gives them the smallest possible per cent constant.

TABLE 3-8. Per Cent-Constant Ratios for Selected Contract Interest Rates and Maturities (*per cent*)

Maturity (years)	Contract Interest Rate			
	4.5 Per Cent	5 Per Cent	5.5 Per Cent	6 Per Cent
10	12.4	12.7	13.0	13.3
15	9.2	9.5	9.8	10.1
20	7.6	7.9	8.3	8.6
25	6.7	7.0	7.4	7.7
30	6.1	6.4	6.8	7.2

SOURCE: Adapted from *Monthly Payment Direct Reduction Loan Amortization Schedules,* 9th ed., Boston, 1958.

Differences in the level of per cent-constant ratios during the four quarters are explained by changes in average interest rates and maturities. The per cent constant averaged 9.6 in both 1954 and 1959

TABLE 3-9. Average Per Cent-Constant Ratios by Loan Amount and Quarter (*per cent*)

Loan Amount ($000)	3rd Quarter 1954	4th Quarter 1959	3rd Quarter 1963	1st Quarter 1965
Under 100	10.0	9.8	9.7	9.7
100–249	9.4	9.6	9.2	9.0
250–499	8.9	9.5	8.8	8.7
500–749	8.4	9.2	8.7	8.6
750–999	7.8	9.5	8.4	8.4
1,000–1,999	7.9 [a]	9.5	8.4	8.1
2,000–4,999	12.2 [a]	8.4	7.8	7.9
5,000–9,999	7.5 [a]	–	7.7	7.6
10,000 and over	6.5 [a]	–	7.5 [a]	7.0 [a]
All loans	9.6	9.6	9.0	8.8

NOTE: Includes only fully amortizing, uniform payment loans.
[a] Fewer than five loans.

(see Table 3-9) despite the fact that interest rates were much higher in 1959. This was because the average maturity had lengthened between the two dates. In 1963 and 1965 when interest rates were only slightly below the 1959 high, however, the average per cent constant was substantially lower than in the other two quarters because maturities had continued to lengthen.

Table 3-9 also indicates that per cent constant was smaller for larger loans. This reflected the relation between maturity and loan amount mentioned above. It meant that per dollar of loan, principal was repaid more slowly on larger loans.

LOAN-VALUE RATIO. The size of loan-value ratios on life insurance company mortgage loans is limited by state statutory regulations. Although each life insurance company is "domiciled" or chartered in a particular state, the company may obtain licenses to do business in other states. (Several companies in the survey are licensed to do business in every state. The other companies are licensed in most states.) The question remains unresolved as to which state's investment regulations apply when a company domiciled in one state makes a loan in another state.[12]

As a general rule, the companies in the survey were limited to loan-value ratios of two-thirds for most of the loans they made in the 1954, 1959, and 1963 quarters. By 1965, most companies could make 75 per cent loans in most states.

Loan-value ratios in this study were calculated by dividing the loan amount by the appraised value of the property as determined by the lending company. The average loan-value ratio increased over the period studied, going from 60 percent in 1954 to almost 69 per cent in 1965 (see Table 3-10). Loan-value ratios seemed to be larger for the larger loans.

LOAN REPAYMENT PROVISIONS. All loan contracts contain conditions for the repayment of principal. The amortization provision controls the rate at which regular repayments of principal are made. The prepayment provision controls repayments of principal at a rate faster than the regular schedule.

Loan Amortization Arrangements. Nearly 90 percent of the loans

---

[12] See the discussion of this problem in *Life Insurance Companies As Financial Institutions,* a monograph prepared for the Commission on Money and Credit by the Life Insurance Association of America, Englewood Cliffs, N.J., 1962, pp. 75–94, 110–113, 148–150.

TABLE 3-10. Average Loan-Value Ratio by Loan Amount and Quarter (*per cent*)

Loan Amount ($000)	3rd Quarter 1954	4th Quarter 1959	3rd Quarter 1963	1st Quarter 1965
Under 100	59.2	62.3	63.9	67.4
100–249	59.8	63.9	65.5	68.7
250–499	59.4	62.3	66.1	68.4
500–749	60.3	62.8	66.4	70.2
750–999	67.0	59.7	67.3	70.3
1,000–1,999	66.6	62.4	66.4	68.4
2,000–4,999	66.6	63.2	68.8	70.7
5,000–9,999	64.8	69.7 [a]	66.5	71.7
10,000 and over	66.7 [a]	70.6 [a]	71.6 [a]	77.0
All loans	60.0	62.9	65.7	68.8

[a] Fewer than five loans.

included in the survey were fully amortizing (see Table 3-11).[13] Most of these loans required monthly payments of equal size, although quarterly payments were made in some instances.[14] A substantially smaller proportion of loans was fully amortizing in 1954 than in the other quarters. This was particularly true for loans of $1 million and over, as Table 3-11 indicates. In 1954, only 29 percent of these large loans were fully amortizing, compared with between 75 and 80 per cent in the later periods. Loans of under $1 million were also more likely to be fully amortizing in the later three quarters, although the difference was not so great as for the larger loans.

A secular shift in the proportion of loans fully amortizing, par-

[13] That is, periodic payments made by borrowers to lenders include both principal and interest, and when the loan matures the principal will have been fully repaid.

[14] The frequency (monthly, quarterly, annual) of loan repayments was not recorded in the survey. In calculating some of the ratios examined in this paper (such as per cent constant and average service fee for loans using the variable formulas) it was necessary to make an assumption regarding repayment frequency. Since most loans in the survey required monthly payments, the assumption was made for calculating purposes that all loans were amortized monthly. The difference between monthly and quarterly payments is small in terms of dollar amounts involved. In the case of a 6 per cent, 20-year, $1 million, fully amortizing loan with uniform payments, the annual debt payments (including principal and interest) would be $86,192 if payments were made quarterly and $85,968 if made monthly—a difference of $224. The difference occurs because quarterly-payment loans always have a larger amount outstanding; hence, interest payments are slightly larger.

TABLE 3-11. Number and Per Cent of Loans by Amortization Arrangements and Quarter

Amortization Category	3rd Quarter 1954		4th Quarter 1959		3rd Quarter 1963		1st Quarter 1965	
	Number	Per Cent	Number	Per Cent	Number	Per Cent	Number	Per Cent
Fully amortizing:								
Uniform payments	367	74.3	596	88.6	690	83.6	723	86.4
Irregular payments	22	4.5	15	2.2	38	4.6	32	3.8
Partially amortizing:								
Uniform payments	93	18.8	59	8.8	85	10.3	73	8.7
Irregular payments	12	2.4	3	0.4	12	1.5	9	1.2
All loans	494	100.0	673	100.0	825	100.0	837	100.0

	3rd Quarter 1954	4th Quarter 1959	3rd Quarter 1963	1st Quarter 1965
Per cent of loans under $1 million which are:				
Fully amortizing	82.1	91.7	90.4	92.3
Not fully amortizing	17.9	8.3	9.6	7.7
All	100.0	100.0	100.0	100.0
Percent of loans $1 million and over which are:				
Fully amortizing	29.0	75.7	76.7	80.9
Not fully amortizing	71.0	24.3	23.3	19.1
All	100.0	100.0	100.0	100.0

NOTE: Percentages may not add exactly to 100 because of rounding.

ticularly marked for large loans, apparently occurred between 1954 and 1959. An earlier NBER study suggests that such a shift had been occurring since the 1920's. Data from this study indicate that loans originated in the years prior to 1947 were even less likely to be fully amortizing than loans authorized in 1954. Of the conventional multifamily and nonresidential loans included in a sample of loans held by life insurance companies in 1947, some 34 per cent of the loans, but only about 19 per cent of the loan amounts outstanding, were fully amortizing, showing that larger loans were less likely to be fully amortizing.[15]

[15] J. E. Morton, *Urban Mortgage Lending: Comparative Markets and Experience,* Princeton for NBER, 1956, pp. 75, 150–151.

Prepayment of Loan Principal. Contracts of most loans in the survey contained conditions under which prepayment of loan principal could occur. In the absence of such an agreement in the contract, borrowers cannot make any prepayment without the lenders' consent.[16] In cases where prepayment was permitted, a penalty usually could be charged by the lender if the option was exercised.[17]

TABLE 3-12. Number of Years During Which No Principal Prepayment Was Permitted

Closed Period (years)	3rd Quarter 1954		4th Quarter 1959		3rd Quarter 1963		1st Quarter 1965	
	Number	Per Cent	Number	Per Cent	Number	Per Cent	Number	Per Cent
No closed period	254	68.3	239	43.8	312	43.6	306	39.3
1	57	15.3	20	3.7	93	13.0	128	16.4
2	5	1.3	3	0.5	6	0.8	3	0.4
3	10	2.7	24	4.4	31	4.3	20	2.6
4	1	0.3	1	0.2	2	0.3	3	0.4
5	38	10.2	197	36.1	188	26.3	207	26.6
6	1	0.3	1	0.2	2	0.3	2	0.3
7	0	–	19	3.5	21	2.9	51	6.5
8 and over	6	1.6	42	7.7	61	8.5	59	7.6
All loans	372	100.0	546	100.0	716	100.0	779	100.0

NOTE: Percentages may not add exactly to 100 because of rounding.

Prepayment of loan principal can be either partial or full. Partial prepayments are made whenever a borrower increases his periodic repayments of principal in excess of the required amount. Prepayment in full occurs if a borrower pays off his loan in one lump sum before maturity. This usually happens when a borrower refinances his loan while retaining possession of the property, or when he sells the property.[18] Prepayment arrangements followed a similar pattern for loans made by all fifteen companies. In each of the later three quarters, about six-tenths of all loans for which this kind of information was available had a "closed period" during which no prepayment of

[16] See Robert H. Pease and Lewis O. Kerwood (eds.), *Mortgage Banking*, 2nd ed., New York, 1965, pp. 25–26.
[17] The prepayment penalty is often waived if the borrower refinances with the same lender, or in case of sale, if the new owner arranges a loan with the original lender.
[18] See Hoagland and Stone, pp. 90–91, for a more complete discussion of loan prepayment.

TABLE 3-13. Per Cent Penalty for Prepayment in Full in Seventh Year

Penalty (per cent)	3rd Quarter 1954 Number	3rd Quarter 1954 Per Cent	4th Quarter 1959 Number	4th Quarter 1959 Per Cent	3rd Quarter 1963 Number	3rd Quarter 1963 Per Cent	1st Quarter 1965 Number	1st Quarter 1965 Per Cent
0	86	23.1	12	2.2	10	1.4	11	1.4
1	95	25.5	5	0.9	9	1.3	14	1.8
2	114	30.6	157	28.8	160	22.3	107	13.7
3	22	5.9	151	27.7	269	37.6	266	34.1
4	2	0.5	19	3.5	78	10.9	79	10.1
5	–	–	23	4.2	42	5.9	69	8.9
6	–	–	46	8.4	–	–	2	0.3
7	–	–	–	–	1	0.1	–	–
Prepayment in full not permitted in seventh year	53	14.2	133	24.4	147	20.5	231	29.7
All loans	372	100.0	546	100.0	716	100.0	779	100.0

NOTE: Percentages may not add exactly to 100 because of rounding.

The penalty ordinarily applies only to prepayments exceeding 10 to 20 per cent of outstanding principal.

TABLE 3-14. Number and Per Cent of Loans by Loan Amount and Liability of Borrower (*loan amounts in $000*)

	3rd Quarter 1954 Loan Amount Under 100	100– 499	500– 1999	2000 & Over	4th Quarter 1959 Loan Amount Under 100	100– 499	500– 1999	2000 & Over
Liable: Number of loans	167	95	13	5	191	181	36	4
Per Cent of loans	78.4	56.9	46.4	35.7	80.6	67.3	55.4	22 2
Not liable: Number of loans	46	72	15	9	46	88	29	14
Per Cent of loans	21.6	43.1	53.6	64.3	19.4	32.7	44.6	77.8
All loans	213	167	28	14	237	269	65	18

principal could be made. In these later periods, the closed period was five years or less on about nine-tenths of the loans containing such restrictions (see Table 3-12).

If a loan was not closed for any period or if the closed period had passed, most loan contracts permitted a percentage of the outstanding principal (usually 10 to 20 per cent), in addition to regular amortization payments, to be paid back each year without penalty. Also, if there were no closed period or if the closed period had passed, the borrower was permitted to prepay the loan in full, but only by paying a penalty calculated as a per cent of the outstanding loan balance. This per cent penalty became smaller each year; after about ten years had elapsed there was usually no penalty for prepayment.

In the present survey, a record was made of the per cent penalty in the seventh year of loan life. The figures in Table 3-13 indicate this penalty for prepayment of principal in excess of the 10 to 20 per cent which does not require a penalty. In the seventh year of loan life, between one-half and two-thirds of the loans authorized in the later three quarters had prepayment penalties of between 2 and 4 per cent. Tables 3-12 and 3-13 indicate that prepayment of loan principal was considerably less costly to borrowers in 1954 than in the other three periods.

BORROWER LIABILITY. Lenders look primarily to the size and certainty of the income stream in evaluating loans on income properties. However, they also carefully analyze the characteristics of the borrower

3rd Quarter 1963 Loan Amount				1st Quarter 1965 Loan Amount			
Under 100	100– 499	500– 1999	2000 & Over	Under 100	100– 499	500– 1999	2000 & Over
96	252	111	12	80	237	71	17
77.4	70.2	59.7	26.1	74.1	58.8	36.6	27.0
28	107	75	34	28	166	123	46
22.6	29.8	40.3	73.9	25.9	41.2	63.4	73.0
124	359	186	46	108	403	194	63

and usually make him liable on the note. In addition to when the borrower is specifically exempted from liability, he was not considered to be liable in this study if a special corporation had been set up to own the mortgaged property, which property was the corporation's only asset. This device was often resorted to even by parent manufacturing companies building new industrial plants or warehouses. In this study, the borrower was liable on about two-thirds of the loans for which this information was available.

Borrowers were more likely to be personally liable on small loans than on large ones as Table 3-14 shows. For example, in 1965 liability extended to nearly three-fourths of the loans under $100,000, but to just over one-fourth of the loans of $2 million and over.

It should be noted that even though a borrower is not liable, the lender is not indifferent to his identity and characteristics. If a lender has had prior dealings with a borrower, or if the latter is financially strong or has a reputation for developing successful projects, the lender will undoubtedly take this into account in evaluating the loan application.[19]

The importance of financial strength in obtaining large loans is shown in Table 3-15. This table includes only loans on which borrowers were

TABLE 3-15. Average Borrower Net Worth by Loan Amount and Quarter for Liable Borrowers (*$000*)

Loan Amount ($000)	3rd Quarter 1954	4th Quarter 1959	3rd Quarter 1963	1st Quarter 1965
Under 100	268	421	377	469
100–499	1,058	1,576	1,897	1,374
500–1,999	4,207	2,587	4,147	3,176
2,000 and over	5,014	23,229	14,141	19,700
All loans	747	1,217	2,177	2,290

liable and indicates a marked difference in average borrower net worth for large as opposed to small loans. For the later three quarters, average net worth of borrowers was between $14 million and $23 million for

[19] See *A Handbook for FHA Multifamily Projects,* Washington, D.C., Federal Housing Administration, 1965, pp. 288–290; Pease and Kerwood, pp. 235, 261; and Maisel, pp. 219–223. In discussing the importance of borrower characteristics, it is not clear if these authors refer to those who are or those who are not liable. It appears that much of what they say would be applicable in either case.

loans $2 million and over. For loans under $100,000, average net worth of borrowers was less than $500,000 in all four quarters.

Size and Certainty of Income

The terms of the loan transaction discussed above are all subject to bargaining between lenders and borrowers. Since some terms are more important to lenders and others are more important to borrowers, the bargaining could result in trade offs.[20]

The willingness of lenders to grant more liberal terms, or to trade off some terms against others, will also be influenced by the size and certainty of the income stream generated by the property securing the mortgage. But the lender can only assess the income stream; he cannot control it.

Information could not be obtained, in this survey, on all of the attributes of a property which a lender considers in evaluating the size and certainty of its income. For example, data were not available on the reliability of the expense prediction, the likelihood of competitive construction, the stability of the area in which the property was located, or the quality of property management.[21] Two of the property characteristics for which information could be obtained are discussed below.

PROPERTY TYPE. Lending on a variety of income properties (apartments, office buildings, shopping centers) involves differing degrees of risk. This is mainly because a more stable demand for services is generated by some types of properties than by others. As a result, some property types are more rapidly subject to obsolescence than others.

The characteristics of loans made on different property types reflect this difference in risk. Although the average loan terms for different properties shown in Table 3-16 vary from quarter to quarter,

---

[20] "One factor that makes bargaining possible is that certain conditions have different values to the borrower and the lender. Their tax situations may be entirely dissimilar. The length of their time horizons may differ radically. As an example, if a borrower is primarily interested in his cash flow rather than his accounting costs or eventual equity, he may find it well worthwhile to accept a higher interest rate in trade for lower amortization payments. The lender may be in exactly the opposite position. Thus a bargain becomes possible." Maisel, p. 343.

[21] *The Appraisal of Real Estate,* 4th ed., The American Institute of Real Estate Appraisers, Chicago, 1964, p. 281.

TABLE 3-16. Average Interest Rate, Loan-Value Ratio, and Maturity by Property Type and Quarter

Property Type	3rd Quarter 1954			4th Quarter 1959			3rd Quarter 1963			1st Quarter 1965		
	Interest Rate	Loan-Value Ratio	Maturity (years)	Interest Rate	Loan-Value Ratio	Maturity (years)	Interest Rate	Loan-Value Ratio	Maturity (years)	Interest Rate	Loan-Value Ratio	Maturity (years)
Elevator apartments	4.47	65.2	17.3	6.13	62.9	19.3	5.88	66.5	21.6	5.96	69.9	22.6
Nonelevator apartments	4.94	61.6	15.9	6.19	63.5	18.9	5.99	66.4	20.2	6.01	69.0	20.7
Hotels and motels	5.00	47.8	13.8	6.44	54.4	14.4	6.05	58.8	16.3	6.32	64.7	16.3
Retail stores	4.61	59.1	15.0	6.03	62.2	15.7	5.70	63.3	17.6	5.72	67.3	17.6
Shopping centers	4.70	60.7	18.5	6.17	61.0	18.4	5.81	65.5	20.2	5.77	69.7	21.5
Office buildings	4.53	61.0	15.4	6.08	63.4	15.4	5.78	66.1	18.4	5.80	71.2	19.2
Medical office buildings	4.82	60.8	14.7	6.14	62.6	16.2	5.81	68.6	18.8	5.90	70.5	17.9
Warehouses	4.65	61.7	15.0	6.05	65.8	14.8	5.79	67.7	16.6	5.81	69.7	18.0
Industrial properties	4.61	59.4	13.9	6.17	63.5	15.4	5.78	64.2	16.2	5.81	68.8	18.2
Misc. commercial properties	4.67	63.7	15.2	6.11	62.4	13.6	5.74	65.2	15.3	5.74	68.5	18.0
Institutional properties	4.62	38.2	14.5	6.18	44.1	16.3	5.86	53.3	19.0	6.10	56.5	16.9
All loans	4.72	60.0	15.3	6.14	62.9	17.0	5.88	65.7	19.0	5.91	68.8	19.5

the property types maintain roughly the same relative position with respect to the liberality and restrictiveness of terms. Hotels and motels, the demand for whose services is most uncertain,[22] had the most restrictive terms in all four quarters. Such properties as retail stores, shopping centers, office buildings, and warehouses had more liberal terms because of their stable stream of income.

LONG-TERM LEASES. In addition to a generally more stable demand for their services, the income of some properties is backed by tenants

TABLE 3-17. Number of Loans by Per Cent of Gross Income Accounted for by Long-Term Leases: First Quarter 1965

Property Type	Per Cent of Gross Income Backed by Long-Term Leases				
	0	1–49	50–99	100	Total
Elevator apartments	50	0	0	0	50
Nonelevator apartments	319	0	0	3 [a]	322
Hotels and motels	20	0	0	1 [a]	21
Retail stores	9	3	2	44	58
Shopping centers	1	5	15	2	23
Office buildings	29	12	9	52	102
Medical office buildings	6	1	2	4	13
Warehouses	8	0	8	53	69
Industrial properties	5	0	3	47	55
Miscellaneous commercial properties	7	1	0	24	32
Institutional properties	16	0	0	10	26
All loans	470	22	39	240	771

NOTE: Long-term leases are those whose duration is at least one-half the maturity of the loan.

[a] Since it is unlikely that tenants of these two types of properties would have a lease for at least half the loan maturity, a more probable explanation is that the loans were made to the owner of the fee simple who had leased the entire property to a third party to operate.

with long-term leases. In these cases, the credit rating of the tenants is as important to lenders as is that of the borrowers.[23] In the present

[22] For an extensive discussion of this point see Royal Shipp and Robert Moore Fisher, "The Postwar Boom in Hotels and Motels," a Federal Reserve Staff Economic Study (see *Federal Reserve Bulletin,* December 1965, p. 1703).

[23] See *The Appraisal of Real Estate,* pp. 246–247, for a discussion of the tenant characteristics in which lenders are interested.

study, information was obtained about the share of estimated gross income from the property that was backed by leases extending for at least one-half of the loan maturity.

As Table 3-17 shows, apartments seldom have any of their projected income backed by long-term leases although at the time the structure is completed, in the case of new properties, a good share of the project may have been rented to tenants with short-term leases. Hotels and motels, which in effect have occupants with one-day leases, are even more vulnerable to shifts in demand.[24] Small properties, usually with a single tenant, such as retail stores, warehouses, and industrial plants, had long-term leases accounting for 100 per cent of their income in most cases—nearly four-fifths in 1965. Most loans in the survey had either all or none of their estimated income backed by long-term leases. Only office buildings and shopping centers had an appreciable number of properties with long-term leases covering from 1 to 99 per cent of estimated gross income.

Leases have a substantial effect on interest rates as is shown by Table 3-18. Generally, interest rates on retail properties, office

TABLE 3-18. Average Interest Rates by Selected Property Type and Per Cent of Income Backed by Long-Term Leases

	Per Cent of Gross Income Backed by Long-Term Leases							
	3rd Quarter 1954		4th Quarter 1959		3rd Quarter 1963		1st Quarter 1965	
	0%	100%	0%	100%	0%	100%	0%	100%
Retail properties	4.70	4.52	6.14	6.03	5.83	5.62	5.84	5.66
Office buildings	4.73	4.46	6.14	6.07	5.85	5.55	5.94	5.72
Warehouses and industrial plants	4.73	4.60	6.12	6.11	5.82	5.75	5.82	5.77

NOTE: The property types included in this table are a combination of some of the types shown in Table 3-17 above. They are grouped this way to provide a contrast between loans with no income and those with 100 per cent of income backed by long-term leases.

buildings, and warehouses and industrial properties were higher in cases where long-term leases were absent than in cases where long-term leases accounted for all of the gross income.

[24] See Shipp and Fisher, p. 10.

Over-All Measures of Credit Risk

This section will discuss the debt coverage ratio and the capitalization rate. These two ratios seem to be useful as over-all measures of the credit risk of individual mortgages.

DEBT COVERAGE RATIO. In evaluating the income stream of a property, lenders are primarily concerned with its ability to service the mortgage.[25] The debt coverage ratio is one measure of a property's ability to produce sufficient income to service the mortgage loan. This ratio has been calculated here by dividing the estimated net income from the property (after operating expenses, property taxes, and a vacancy allowance but before depreciation, debt service payments, and income taxes) by the amount of the required debt payments, including principal and interest.[26] For example, a DCR of 1.00 indicates that after paying operating expenses and property taxes, the estimated income is just sufficient, on the average, to meet the debt payments.

Average DCR for all loans was higher in 1954 (1.57) than in the later periods, all of which were about the same (just over 1.40). In all of the quarters, from three-fourths to four-fifths of the loans had DCRs between 1.13 and 1.62 (see Table 3-19).

Although the net income figure used in calculating DCRs is presented as a constant amount per year for an indefinite period, the actual amount realized will usually fluctuate from year to year.[27] Debt coverage ratios are higher on loans for which the income stream is thought to be more variable. In other words, lenders adjust the size of DCR they require to account for the certainty of the income stream. Table 3-20 shows that the average DCRs are lower for loans with all of their estimated income assured by long-term leases.

[25] For a discussion of the problem of debt service, see Leo Grebler, *Experience in Urban Real Estate Investment,* New York, 1955, pp. 141–156.

[26] This ratio could only be derived for loans which were fully amortizing with uniform payments and for which the estimate for net income was available. The information was available for from 70 to 75 per cent of loans in the later three quarters and for around 50 per cent in 1954.

[27] See *ibid.,* pp. 150–156. The data presented by Grebler indicate that income available for debt service from particular income properties showed a great deal of variance during the period between 1920 and 1950. The average net income for the period was more than sufficient to meet debt charges in nearly every case studied. But the actual income was not sufficient to meet the debt service requirements for some particular year (or years) in every case. Grebler described the situation as being an ". . . inherent conflict between fixed debt charges and fluctuating net income." (P. 148.)

TABLE 3-19. Frequency Distribution of Debt Coverage Ratios

Debt Coverage Ratio	3rd Quarter 1954		4th Quarter 1959		3rd Quarter 1963		1st Quarter 1965	
	Number	Per Cent	Number	Per Cent	Number	Per Cent	Number	Per Cent
Under 1.00	10	4.2	13	2.6	6	1.0	5	0.8
1.00–1.12	32	13.5	36	7.2	40	6.9	63	9.6
1.13–1.24	25	10.5	68	13.7	63	10.8	77	11.7
1.25–1.37	37	15.6	166	33.4	156	26.8	179	27.2
1.38–1.49	30	12.7	72	14.5	151	25.9	169	25.6
1.50–1.62	28	11.8	65	13.1	97	16.7	86	13.1
1.63–1.74	22	9.3	22	4.4	28	4.8	28	4.2
1.75–1.99	19	8.0	29	5.8	21	3.6	33	5.0
2.00 and over	34	14.3	26	5.2	20	3.4	19	2.9
All loans	237	100.0	497	100.0	582	100.0	659	100.0

NOTE: Percentages may not add exactly to 100 because of rounding.

TABLE 3-20. Average Debt Coverage Ratios by Selected Property Type and Per Cent of Income Backed by Long-Term Leases

	Per Cent of Gross Income Backed by Long-Term Leases							
	3rd Quarter 1954		4th Quarter 1959		3rd Quarter 1963		1st Quarter 1965	
	0%	100%	0%	100%	0%	100%	0%	100%
Apartments	1.63	–	1.42	–	1.44	–	1.45	–
Retail properties	1.52	1.39	1.47	1.29	1.51	1.34	1.51	1.30
Office buildings	1.52	1.41	1.47	1.30	1.47	1.32	1.36	1.27
Warehouses and industrial plants	1.83	1.40	1.38	1.26	1.33	1.33	1.31	1.33
All loans	1.71	1.35	1.47	1.31	1.45	1.36	1.47	1.32

See note to Table 3-18.

CAPITALIZATION RATE. Much of the information available to lenders about the size and degree of certainty of the income stream of a property could not be obtained for a study such as this. It appears from the survey data that it may be possible to use the capitalization rate as a proxy for the characteristics for which information is not available. As the authors of a recent book said, the capitalization rate is determined by

TABLE 3-21. Average Capitalization Rates by Property Type and Quarter

	3rd Quarter 1954	4th Quarter 1959	3rd Quarter 1963	1st Quarter 1965
Elevator apartments	7.5	8.6	8.1	8.2
Nonelevator apartments	8.5	8.1	8.1	8.3
Hotels and motels	13.1	12.0	12.6	12.3
Retail stores	8.0	8.1	8.1	7.9
Shopping centers	7.4	8.2	8.1	8.1
Office buildings	7.5	8.5	8.3	8.2
Medical office buildings	8.9	9.3	7.9	8.7
Warehouses	8.0	8.5	8.1	8.3
Industrial properties	8.5	8.5	8.6	8.6
Miscellaneous commercial properties	8.4	9.0	8.3	8.0
Institutional properties	9.1	10.5	10.2	9.5
All loans	8.3	8.5	8.2	8.4

the characteristics of the property to be appraised. . . . In this respect it also measures the quantity, quality, and possible duration of the income stream. . . . It will probably be difficult to find any single property that combines all the most desirable features of an ideal investment, that is, absolute security of principal, ready marketability, adequacy and certainty of returns, good location, tax free income, good financing, probability of capital appreciation, etc. However, as the particular type of property approaches most closely these favorable features, the rate of capitalization will be lower.[28]

The capitalization rate used in this study was calculated by dividing estimated net income from the property by the property value. This is usually referred to as the "over-all" capitalization rate. It assumes that the property will not increase or decrease in value during the time the loan is outstanding.[29]

Capitalization rates were relatively constant for the four quarters studied. The average for 1963 was 8.2 per cent and for 1959 was 8.5 per cent with the other two quarters within that narrow range (see Table 3-21). Rates for most property types also varied within a relatively

[28] S. A. Kahn, F. E. Case, and A. Schimmel, *Real Estate Appraisal and Investment,* New York, 1963, pp. 122–123.

[29] See *The Appraisal of Real Estate,* p. 274. For a method of adjusting capitalization rates for the effect of appreciation or depreciation in the value of the property, see L. W. Elwood, *Elwood Tables for Real Estate Appraising and Financing,* New Jersey, 1959, pp. 191–204.

TABLE 3-22. Average Interest Rate, Maturity, Loan-Value Ratio, and Debt Coverage Ratio by Capitalization Rate

Capitalization Rate (per cent)	3rd Quarter 1954				4th Quarter 1959				3rd Quarter 1963				1st Quarter 1965			
	Interest Rate	Maturity	Loan-Value Ratio	DCR	Interest Rate	Maturity	Loan-Value Ratio	DCR	Interest Rate	Maturity	Loan-Value Ratio	DCR	Interest Rate	Maturity	Loan-Value Ratio	DCR
Under 7.1	4.55	16.4	61.9	1.24	6.04	17.5	61.4	1.14	5.63	19.4	66.8	1.10	5.66	21.3	68.7	1.14
7.1–7.6	4.59	16.0	67.4	1.25	6.10	18.9	65.8	1.29	5.89	20.2	67.5	1.30	5.79	20.5	70.9	1.26
7.7–8.0	4.71	14.7	60.0	1.49	6.13	17.3	63.8	1.34	5.84	19.8	66.6	1.39	5.87	20.3	69.8	1.33
8.1–8.4	4.66	15.1	55.7	1.70	6.13	16.4	63.3	1.33	5.84	19.2	65.7	1.45	5.90	19.9	69.8	1.39
8.5–9.0	4.72	15.0	59.2	1.59	6.18	16.4	61.8	1.45	5.94	18.7	65.2	1.49	5.98	19.5	68.0	1.47
9.1–9.9	4.82	14.7	56.1	1.77	6.29	15.8	61.5	1.52	5.99	16.2	61.8	1.59	5.97	18.2	65.7	1.60
10.0 and over	4.89	14.2	55.4	2.36	6.29	14.2	57.2	2.02	6.05	16.6	61.9	1.97	6.12	16.2	67.8	1.87
All loans (including those for which capitalization rate was not available)	4.72	15.3	60.0	1.57	6.14	17.0	62.9	1.43	5.88	19.0	65.7	1.43	5.91	19.5	68.8	1.41

small range. The major exceptions were institutional properties and hotels and motels, which had rates considerably above the other property types in all four quarters.

Table 3-22 indicates that capitalization rates are related to other loan characteristics. Loans whose property income streams are capitalized at low rates have lower interest rates, lower debt coverage ratios, higher loan-value ratios, and longer maturities. Thus, viewing the capitalization rate as a summary measure of credit risk, these relationships show that lenders "reward" low risk borrowers with liberal terms and low interest rates.

Appendix A

Life Insurance Companies Included in NBER Survey, Ranked by Asset Size (*$000,000*)

Company	Total Assets End of 1966	Mortgage Loans Owned End of 1966
1. Prudential	23,512	8,836
2. Metropolitan	23,595	9,993
3. Equitable	12,576	5,515
4. New York Life	9,169	2,583
5. John Hancock	8,380	2,805
6. Connecticut General	3,635	1,413
7. Mutual of New York	3,318	842
8. Mutual Benefit	2,257	1,050
9. Connecticut Mutual	2,250	855
10. Penn Mutual	2,203	758
11. National Life and Accident (Nashville)	1,374	475
12. Phoenix Mutual	1,184	453
13. National Life (Montpelier)	1,178	583
14. Provident Mutual	1,038	373
15. Fidelity Mutual	488	134
Total — 15 companies	96,157	36,688
Total of all U.S. life insurance companies	167,022	64,609
Per cent of total held by 15 companies	57.6%	56.8%

SOURCE: *Moody's Bank and Finance Manual,* New York, 1967, and *Life Insurance Fact Book,* New York, Institute of Life Insurance, 1967.

Appendix B

EXPLANATION OF PROPERTY TYPES IN THE STUDY

1. Elevator apartment—multifamily residential project of five or more units with at least one elevator. Includes only conventionally financed properties.
2. Nonelevator apartment—same as above with no elevators.
3. Hotels and motels.
4. Retail stores—includes bakeries, barber shops, beauty parlors, dress shops, drug stores, showrooms, supermarkets, delicatessens, department stores, and all other retail stores and shops.
5. Shopping centers—must have five or more stores.
6. Office buildings—includes regular office buildings, loft buildings, bank buildings, savings and loan association buildings, and life insurance company buildings.
7. Medical office buildings—includes office buildings occupied solely by doctors and dentists, and clinics.
8. Warehouses—in addition to regular warehouses, includes industrial grain elevators and storage silos.
9. Industrial properties—includes production and assembly buildings in all manufacturing industries as well as dry cleaning plants, laundries, and miscellaneous light manufacturing buildings.
10. Miscellaneous commercial properties—this category includes types for which there were not sufficient loans in any period to justify a separate category. These are post office buildings, garages, service stations, restaurants, bowling alleys, and other miscellaneous commercial properties.
11. Institutional properties—religious properties such as churches, Sunday schools, tabernacles, synagogues, convents, monasteries, theological seminaries, funeral parlors, crematories, mausoleums, mission houses; educational properties such as elementary and secondary schools, college buildings, libraries and museums, fine arts buildings; hospitals including infirmaries, sanatoriums, nurseries and nursing homes, institutions for the elderly; and social and recreational properties such as assembly buildings, auditoriums, community houses, golf and country clubhouses, athletic and social clubs, lodges, theaters, music conservatories, radio broadcasting studios, gymnasiums, indoor stadiums, indoor arenas, indoor coliseums, indoor courts, indoor swimming pools, locker buildings, YMCA buildings, bathhouses at beaches, billiard rooms, dance halls, indoor rinks, exhibit buildings, and other social and recreational buildings.

4

A Study of Liquidity Premiums on Federal and Municipal Government Securities

Phillip Cagan

A rate premium on long- relative to short-term securities of comparable quality may be due to transaction costs, expectations of a rise in rates, or the greater "liquidity" of short-term securities. Recent studies have helped to clarify the nature and magnitude of these influences. An important study by Kessel[1] shows that U.S. long-term bond yields typically exceed bill rates by more than the difference in transaction costs plus any differential attributable to expectations. The premium apparently reflects the greater liquidity of short securities, that is, their greater marketability at relatively stable prices, a characteristic of financial instruments which declines as term to maturity increases. Liquidity provides a nonpecuniary return that substitutes in part for interest payments and accounts for the higher interest rate on longer-term securities. The premium on the higher yielding security measures the marginal advantage of holding the more liquid security.

NOTE: Conversations with Stanley Diller on earlier drafts of this paper have helped greatly to clarify the argument. I also received useful comments from Jack Guttentag and Geoffrey H. Moore of the National Bureau and from Herschel Grossman, Reuben Kessel, and Burton G. Malkiel.

I wish to thank also Josephine Trubek, who collected the data and supervised the initial, exploratory computations, and Jae Won Lee, who helped in the final stages of the research.

[1] Reuben Kessel, *The Cyclical Behavior of the Term Structure of Interest Rates,* NBER Occasional Paper 91, New York, 1965.

Such a premium is analytically distinct from yield differentials due to expectations of changes in rates and to risk of borrower default. This study examines the changes in liquidity premiums over long and short periods and tests two theories of their behavior. To abstract from default risk, the data pertain to U.S. securities and municipal bonds of uniform quality. Allowing for expectations is more difficult, and the analysis explores various ways of removing their effects.

Average Liquidity Premiums Over Business Cycles

A curve showing yields by term to maturity incorporates the cyclical influence of expectations. Investors will ordinarily expect short-term rates to rise during business expansions and to fall during business contractions.[2] An expected rise in rates would make long rates higher than short rates in anticipation of greater capital losses on the longer maturities, thus contributing to an upward sloping yield curve, and conversely for an expected fall in rates. These varying expectations over a cycle will tend to cancel out in an average curve for each full cycle. Given that expansions are usually much longer than contractions, it is not clear that an unweighted average of monthly data is best. It may be better to give each stage rather than each month of the business cycle an equal weight, in order to approximate a yield curve for which expectations forecast no cyclical change in rates. If investors expect the cyclical movement of rates to proceed more rapidly in business contractions than it does in expansions, such stage averages overweight contraction periods, when rates are generally expected to fall, and so make the estimated slope of the yield curve, if anything, too flat. An unweighted monthly average, in contrast, probably makes the slope too steep. Neither the weighted nor the unweighted cycle average, however, eliminate any expected secular trend in rates; the upward trend in rates during the 1950's, if expected, could have added an upward. tilt to the curve throughout that decade. Trend is discussed subsequently.

Chart 4-1 presents yield curves which, to eliminate most of the cyclical effects of expectations, are averages of National Bureau reference stages. There are nine stages in reference cycles. The initial

---

[2] See my study of "Changes in the Cyclical Behavior of Interest Rates," *Review of Economics and Statistics,* August 1966, reprinted as NBER Occasional Paper 100. There have been changes in the timing and amplitude of interest rates, but their conformity to reference cycles has always been high.

and terminal trough stages are averages of data for the three months surrounding the two trough months, and the peak stage for the three months surrounding the peak month. The period of expansion is divided equally into three stages, as is the contraction period. These nine

CHART 4-1. Yield Curves of U.S. and Municipal Securities, Reference Cycle Averages

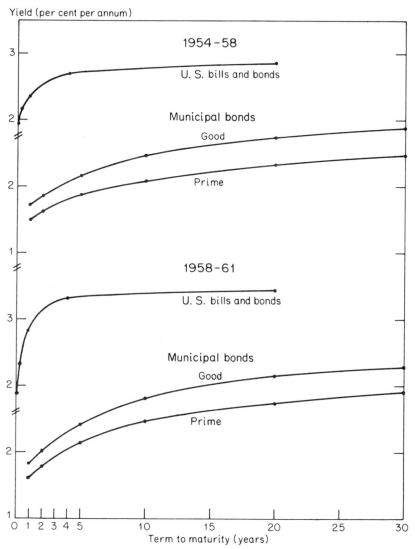

stage averages are then averaged with equal weight except for the initial and terminal trough stages, each of which receives one-half weight. The curves in the chart are for U.S. and municipal securities in the 1954–58 and 1958–61 cycles. The municipal series is composed of new issue yields in two quality groups.[3] Most of the series underlying the chart begin after World War II and do not allow comparisons with earlier decades.

The curves exhibit a strong upward slope, somewhat greater for the later cycle than for the earlier one. For U.S. securities, the upward slope tapers off rapidly in the maturity segment of one week to about two or three years. The slope for municipals starts out smaller, judging by the one- to two-year maturities, but declines more gradually. The slope is somewhat greater for good than for prime municipals.[4] The stage averages, as noted, probably even understate the degree of upward slope. The characteristic upward slope of government yields is well known and has been widely commented on; the results presented here quantify this general impression and extend it to municipal securities.

How much of the upward slope reflects transaction costs or expected trends, and how much liquidity premiums? Brokerage costs for the purchase and sale of Treasury bills (the spread between dealer bid and ask prices) vary, but the range seldom exceeds 4 to 20 cents per $1,000 security on maturities of three months or less, while the comparable cost for long-term U.S. bonds is about $2.50.[5] The implication for the yield differential depends upon the holding period between purchase and sale. (A new issue acquired from the Treasury and held to maturity involves no brokerage costs.) In purchasing a bond from brokers and selling back after three months, the brokerage cost is

[3] For U.S. securities, market yields on one-week bills (kindly supplied by Jacob Michaelsen from data he obtained from the first Boston Corporation for his "The Term Structure of Interest Rates and Holding-Period Yields on Government Securities," *Journal of Finance,* Sept. 1965, pp. 444–463), three- and nine- to twelve-month bills and three- to five-year bonds (*Federal Reserve Bulletin*), twenty-year bonds (Morgan Guarantee Company). For municipal securities, new issues (Salomon Brothers and Hutzler, *An Analytical Record of Representative Municipal Yield Scales by Quality and Maturity 1950–June 1965,* n.d.).

[4] Possibly because, in addition to relative differences in marketability, the risk of default increases more with maturity on the lower than on the higher grade bonds. See R. E. Johnson, "Term Structures of Corporate Bond Yields as a Function of Risk of Default," *Journal of Finance,* May 1967, pp. 313–345.

[5] Reuben Kessel, "Market Segmentation in the Treasury Bill Market," May 9, 1967, dittoed; and Allan H. Meltzer and Gert von der Linde, *A Study of the Dealer Market for Federal Government Securities,* Joint Economic Committee, 1960, pp. 111–112.

100 basis points (that is, 1 per cent per annum), a sizable amount when compared with the zero cost for bills held for a full term. Between three-month bills and twenty-year U.S. bonds, the premium (Chart 4-1) was 69 points in 1954–58 and 113 points in 1958–61. We cannot take the 100-point figure, however, as the relevant difference in transaction costs. Bonds are typically held much longer than three months, and the difference in transaction costs between bonds of any two maturities is small. If transaction costs accounted for the upward slopes, the differential between one- and thirty-year municipal yields should be quite small; in fact, it exceeds the differential between bills and twenty-year U.S. bonds. Transaction costs appear far from sufficient, therefore, to account for the actual slope of these yield curves, even though we cannot assign an exact figure to such costs without knowing the average length of holding periods.

What about trend? Three-month bill rates rose 128 basis points from their average monthly level during the 1949–54 cycle to that during the 1958–61 cycle, or (dividing by the interval between the reference peaks taken as the cycle midpoints) rose 17.1 basis points per year. Suppose that investors had anticipated the actual trend and assumed it would continue for several decades. The market would have required that the yield curve rise by 8.5 points per year of term to maturity,[6] and so could have accounted for more than the entire upward slope in

[6] A long rate can be expressed as a geometric average of the current short rate and the expected (forward) short rates for each subsequent period to maturity (ignoring coupon payments and liquidity premiums). If these expected short rates rise by a trend factor,

$$(1 + R_n)^n = (1 + R_1)(1 + r_2 + T)(1 + r_3 + 2T)(1 + r_4 + 3T) \ldots (1 + r_n + [n-1]T),$$

where R_n and R_1 are the current yields to maturity on maturities of n and 1 periods, r_i the 1 period rate in the ith period ahead expected now *exclusive of trend,* and T the expected increase in rates per period.

An arithmetic approximation, ignoring the compounding of interest, gives

$$R_n = \frac{R_1 + \sum_2^n r_i + \sum_1^n (i-1)T}{n}.$$

If investors expect no changes, aside from trend, all r_i equal R_1, and the expression reduces to

$$R_n = R_1 + \frac{n-1}{2} T.$$

The term structure then rises (approximately) linearly with a slope of $T/2$. From ten- to twenty-year bonds, it would rise $(\frac{19}{2} - \frac{9}{2})$ 17.1 = 85.5 basis points. (Incorporating the higher-order terms ignored in the approximation produces a curve in which the slope is not constant but increases with maturity.)

Chart 4-1 beyond a certain point. On the 1958–61 yield curves, a slope of 8.5 points per year occurs at a maturity of only about three years for U.S. securities and only about seven years for municipals.

Judging by the long end of the curve, the actual trend was considerably underestimated. If investors expected a trend to continue for two decades, we can measure the expected trend by the average differential between ten- and twenty-year prime municipals, assuming a negligible liquidity premium between them. The figure is about 25 basis points per decade. Adjusting the short maturities for that estimate of expected trend still leaves a steep slope at the very short end of the curve. (The slope, as noted, tapers off more rapidly for U.S. securities than it does for municipals.) Whatever adjustments for expected trend should be made, it cannot explain a yield curve with a tapering slope, unless investors expect the upward movement to taper off.[7]

The sharp rise at the lower end of the yield curves is more plausibly explained by liquidity premiums. Such premiums are consistent with the traditional theory of liquidity preference, which posits a widespread demand in the economy for the stable market value of liquid assets. For example, federal and municipal bonds, as they age to within several years of maturity, become especially attractive to commercial banks and other financial intermediaries as secondary reserves, and short-term Treasury bills and certificates appeal to corporate treasurers as investment outlets for funds needed on short notice. To be sure, some institutions with long-term obligations, such as life insurance companies and pension funds, desire a predictable income more than stable capital value. A desire to hedge against the risk of changes in interest rates by matching the maturity of acquired assets with the maturity of given liabilities makes long-term securities the preferred investment for these institutions. The evidence of yield curves, however, implies that the demand for liquidity is large relative to the total market supply of short-term securities.

The demand for liquid assets relative to total financial assets is not infinitely elastic; it declines with respect to the price paid for liquidity, that is, the lower pecuniary yield on liquid assets. Given

---

[7] A trend expected to terminate in a certain number of years could produce such a curve, but the same expectation would produce a flatter curve in the next cycle, not a steeper one as we observe, unless the expected terminal date of the trend was progressively moved forward in time. By such *ad hoc* assumptions, of course, any yield curve can be "explained."

a downward sloping demand curve, the price paid for liquidity declines with increases in the supply of such assets. If borrowers of funds were indifferent to the maturity of the securities they issued, liquidity premiums could not exist. Short-term securities would then be issued to take advantage of the lower yield until they saturated the market's preference for short securities and eliminated the differential yield relative to long debt. The existence of liquidity premiums therefore implies that the supply is not infinitely elastic at the same yield as prevails on long-term bonds. Most borrowers prefer to issue long-term debt; this is certainly true of state and municipal governments and most business corporations. Their desire to hedge leads to long-term financing of long-lived physical assets. The federal government also limits the issue of short securities according to the goals of debt management. One implication of a less than infinitely elastic demand for liquidity and supply of short liquid assets is that an exogenous shift in the supply curve of one class of short securities affects the liquidity premiums on all. As a case in point, commercial banks have in recent years taken advantage of increases allowed in the deposit rate ceiling to issue marketable certificates of deposit in large volume. These are good substitutes for Treasury bills and add to the total supply of liquid assets. It is plausible that their expanded issue during the early 1960's made the yield curve flatter than it would otherwise have been.[8]

Accepting the evidence of Chart 4-1 that liquidity premiums exist, we may ask whether the premiums vary over time and if so why, the two questions examined in the following sections.

Fluctuations in Liquidity Premiums

EVIDENCE OF FLUCTUATIONS. Chart 4-2 shows reference cycle patterns of the differential yield between long- and short-term U.S. securities. This series has no adjustment for expectations, which must therefore be taken into account. Cyclical fluctuations in the differential display an inverse conformity to business activity, though often during contractions there was no increase, only a slackening in the rate of decline. The trough generally came at stage V, though sometimes, as

---

[8] F. Modigliani and R. Sutch ("Innovations in Interest Rate Policy," *American Economic Review*, May 1966, pp. 195–196) argue that CDs enhance the ability of commercial banks to arbitrage the yield differential between long and short rates, a similar point to that made here.

CHART 4-2. Reference Cycle Patterns of Yield Differential Between U.S. Bonds and Certificates or Bills, 1921–67

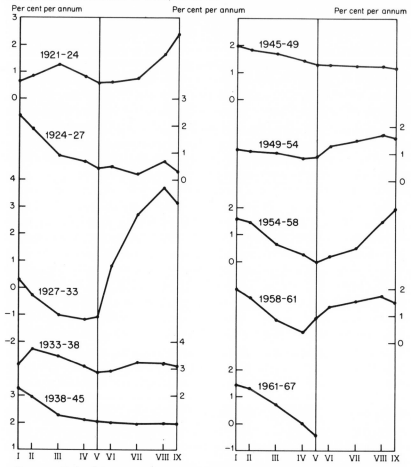

SOURCE: *Federal Reserve Bulletin.* Long-term U.S. bond series; and three- to six-month Treasury certificates through 1930, spliced to three-month bills thereafter.

in the 1958–61 cycle, at stage IV. The pattern for 1961–67 shows a large decline in the differential during that period (these stages were computed on the basis of a hypothetical business peak in December 1967). The individual bond and bill rates composing the differential have positive conformity to business cycles and similar timing, but the short rate has the larger amplitude, which accounts for the inverse conformity of the differential. The inverse conformity may be attributed, at least in part, to anticipations of cyclical fluctuations in the level of rates. During the later stages of business expansion, interest rates rise to heights which investors feel cannot last; hence long rates do not rise as sharply as do short rates in the expansion phase, and the differential gradually declines. During business contractions when rates fall, investors form the opposite expectation which causes the differential to rise. If investors anticipated cyclical turning points in rates perfectly, the differential would turn ahead of business, contrary to its actual timing. But the absence of leading turns in the differential yield does not mean that it is not affected by expectations. They may not be so precise. Vague expectations of cyclical movements, with a belief that turning points will occur but no clear idea of when, could produce the observed inverse pattern.

If we could adjust for expectations, therefore, the resulting differential might have any pattern. The behavior of the adjusted pattern is important, because the two leading explanations of the premium have opposite implications about the cyclical pattern. The next subsection discusses these explanations, after which additional evidence is examined.

TWO THEORIES OF FLUCTUATIONS IN LIQUIDITY PREMIUMS. The preference of most investors for short securities, giving rise to liquidity premiums, can be attributed to the relatively stable market prices of such securities. There is little disagreement that the existence of liquidity premiums reflects an aversion to the risks of capital losses due to changes in interest rates. The question of how the premiums fluctuate over time, however, is not settled. One theory views short securities as partial substitutes for money balances, performing to a degree the same functions, at least in large portfolios. These securities provide a nonpecuniary return, representing the value of the services they perform as substitutes for money holdings. On the margin this nonpecuniary return equals the liquidity premium. Another theory is that investors believe that interest rates tend to return to "normal" levels. Given an aversion to the risk of capital losses on long-term securities, these securities will carry a yield premium depending upon the relation of current yields to what is considered normal. This theory can be distinguished from the standard expectations hypothesis that expected holding-period yields are equal for all maturities.

These two theories of liquidity premiums, developed further below, are the leading interpretations in the literature.[9] While not incompatible with each other, they give opposite implications for the behavior of liquidity premiums, which allows us to test them against the data.

Short Securities As Substitutes for Money. Investors are presumed to equate the marginal returns from the various financial assets in their portfolios. If short securities are closer substitutes for money than are long securities — which seems plausible though there is little direct evidence on the question — the slope of the yield curve is affected by a change in its average level. Suppose the entire yield curve rises because of a shift in the demand or supply of loanable funds. The foregone interest income in holding money is higher, and the public attempts to exchange part of its money balances for securities. For a time this prevents yields from rising as much as they otherwise would. Moreover, because investors prefer short to long securities as substitutes for money, they favor shorts in the exchange, which prevents the yield on shorts from rising as much as that on longs. Hence the premium on longs over shorts increases (aside from any effects of expectations) as a result of a rise in the entire yield curve, and the converse is true for a decline.

On the margin investors will adjust their portfolios so that the marginal services of liquidity just compensate for differences in pecuniary yields. The pecuniary yield differential, apart from differences due to expected changes in interest rates, therefore measures the nonpecuniary services of the lower yielding security. This equality allows us to relate yield differentials to the marginal differences in liquidity. Suppose a security of term n, because of its services as a liquid asset, allows a person to reduce his average money holdings by ΔM_n. We may then define $S_n = \Delta M_n / P_n$, where P_n is the purchase price of the security. S_n measures the fractional amount by which the security substitutes for money. No longer wanting to hold as much money as before, investors can purchase nonliquid bonds or nonfinancial assets. If r_M is the nonpecuniary return to money balances, the total return

[9] On the money-substitute theory, see Kessel, *Cyclical Behavior*, p. 25, and Cagan, "A Partial Reconciliation Between Two Views of Debt Management," *Journal of Political Economy*, December 1966, pp. 624–628. On risk aversion and normal rates, see F. de Leeuw, "A Model of Financial Behavior" in Duesenberry *et al.*, *Brookings Quarterly Econometric Model of the United States Economy*, Chicago, 1965, Chap. 13; J. Van Horne, "Interest-Rate Risk and the Term Structure of Interest Rates," *Journal of Political Economy*, August 1965, 344–351; Modigliani and Sutch, *ibid.*; and B. G. Malkiel, *The Term Structure of Interest Rates*, Princeton, N.J., 1966, pp. 59–65. On normality in expectations, see S. Diller, "Extrapolations, Anticipations and the Term Structure of Interest Rates," forthcoming NBER study.

on the security of term n is

$$R_n + S_n r_M, \tag{1}$$

where R_n is the pecuniary return on the security and $S_n r_M$ the non-pecuniary return from its services as a money substitute. If, on the margin, an investor finds two securities the same except for differences in maturity (abstracting from expected changes in rates), the total returns will be equal. For example, indifference between thirteen-week bills and twenty-year bond implies

$$R_{13w} + S_{13w} r_M = R_{20y} + S_{20y} r_M. \tag{2}$$

This is an equilibrium condition attained through appropriate changes in market yields.

If money holdings are in equilibrium with respect to long-term bonds, we have, for example, $r_M = R_{20y} + S_{20y} r_M.$[10] There appears to be little error in assuming that S_{20y} is a relatively small fraction of unity; hence $r_m \simeq R_{20y}.$ Then the measured liquidity premium, based on (2), is

$$R_{20y} - R_{13w} = S_{13w} R_{20y}. \tag{3}$$

If S_{13w}, which represents the marginal substitutability of thirteen-week bills for money, is constant, the differential yield between the long and short securities (abstracting from expected changes in rates) varies directly with the level of long-term rates.[11]

The values of S may not, of course, remain constant. Aside from shifts in preferences for liquidity, we may expect relative supplies to alter to some extent the marginal services of liquidity. When the relative supply of short securities increases, their marginal substitutability for money diminishes, signified by a decline in the values of S. An

---

[10] This treats any pecuniary return to money holdings as negligible.

[11] At the short end of the yield curve, indifference between one- and thirteen-week securities implies

$$R_{13w} + S_{13w} r_M = R_{1w} + S_{1w} r_M.$$

The measured liquidity premium is

$$R_{13w} - R_{1w} = r_M (S_{1w} - S_{13w}).$$

Setting $r_M = R_{20y}$ and using $R_{20y} = R_{13w}/(1 - S_{13w})$ from (3), we have

$$R_{13w} - R_{1w} = R_{13w}(S_{1w} - S_{13w})/(1 - S_{13w}).$$

Similarly, the liquidity premium between any two securities depends upon the level of the rates (here represented by the longer of the two) and their relative liquidity.

increased supply of any one substitute for money reduces the marginal substitutability for money of all of them, but not by the same proportion; a change in supply of one substitute affects its own marginal liquidity the most. Hence an increased supply of thirteen-week bills would reduce its liquidity premium relative to other securities. This will be manifested in a reduced yield differential relative to longer-term securities and an increased differential relative to shorter-term securities. The effect is to tilt the entire yield curve of U.S. securities toward the horizontal, and at the same time to produce a peak at the thirteen-week maturity. The change is analogous to pulling a loose string lying on top of the previously existing yield curve and fastened to it at the longest maturity, as in Figure 4-1. An increase in the relative supply of a given maturity swings and bends the curve, equivalent to pulling the string upward at that point. (This analogy ignores the possibility that an increase in supply of securities relative to the money stock may temporarily raise the yield on even the longest maturity, if it too is a partial substitute for money.) Given an upward sloping curve to begin with, the transformation makes the slope more horizontal and slightly peaked at the point of pull. For a decrease in supply, the effect is just the reverse. In the following weeks, the new supply approaches maturity, of course; if no further changes in the relative supplies occur, the point of pull on the string would slide down the curve toward a zero maturity and then disappear.

Different implications follow from the often stated view that the market demand for securities is divided into separate compartments. If the demands for different maturities are independent, an increased supply of thirteen-week bills would raise their yield relative to both longer and shorter securities equally, producing a hump just in that section of the curve. The effect of supply on liquidity premiums presented above, however, assumes that liquidity is a property shared by all maturities in varying degree. Consequently, a change in relative supply affects differential yields all along the curve; the slope of the entire curve changes.

The "Normal" Level of Interest Rates and Risk of Capital Loss. A belief that interest rates sooner or later gravitate toward a "normal" level provides an explanation of the fluctuations in liquidity premiums which contains different implications. (Some of the studies cited in footnote 9 claim to find evidence of such an attitude by investors in the behavior of interest rates.) Given a preference for short over long securities to avoid unanticipated capital losses, the belief in a return to normal levels can produce variations in liquidity premiums. Like the first theory, this effect relies on a preference for the stability of capital

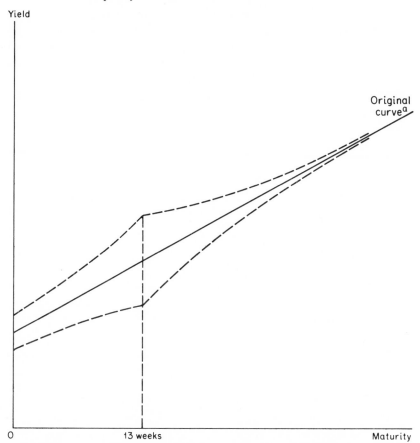

Yield

O   13 weeks   Maturity

[a] Original curve is drawn as a straight line for graphic simplicity only.

FIGURE 4-1. Hypothetical Effect on Yield Curve of Change in Relative Supply of Thirteen-Week Securities

value, but it disregards any difference between long and short securities as substitutes for money while at the same time implying variations in premiums opposite to the first theory. The second theory is implicit in much recent literature and may be formulated as follows.

Investors' expectations of the short-term rate can be viewed as a probability distribution of the possible rates, as illustrated in Figure 4-2. The illustration is shown there as symmetrical, but it need not be. The unweighted mean of the distribution is "the" expected short rate for a future date. Current yields on longer-term securities reflect the short rates expected in coming periods. If there is no liquidity premium,

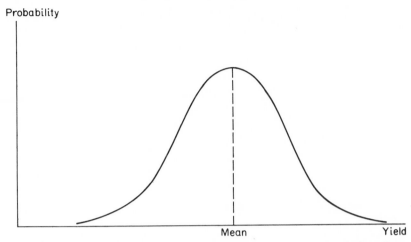

FIGURE 4-2. Investors' Probability Distribution of the Expected Short Rate

security prices will be adjusted to make the expected yields over any given period, composed of coupon payments and expected changes in price, equal on comparable securities of varying maturities. If the mean expected short rate for a later date turns out to be correct, the actual return on longer securities over the period will be as expected; the coupon payments plus price changes will provide the same return (aside from any liquidity premium) on all maturities. If the short rate turns out to be higher than the mean of the distribution, the yield to maturity on longer-term securities will then also be higher than expected, produced by an unanticipated decline in their market prices and resulting in a capital loss over the period. Conversely, if the short rate turns out to be lower than the mean, holders of longer-term securities will receive an unanticipated capital gain over the period.

A preference for stability of principal implies an asymmetrical view of price changes: A potential capital gain does not offset an equal potential loss. We can imagine that investors attach weights to the probabilities according to the importance of *avoiding* particular outcomes. Rates higher than the mean value will receive progressively greater weight, in reflection of their undesirability, since it is the higher than expected rates which produce unanticipated capital losses. The weighting pattern attaches a lower importance to potential rates below the mean expected value. The *weighted* mean value of the distribution will thus be pulled to the right, leading to a demand for higher yields on longer-term securities to partially compensate for the risk of capital loss. The amount of compensation will depend upon the probability of various rates and the capital loss each rate would produce for a security of given maturity, as well as the weighting pattern which quantifies the aversion to risk. (The relative supply of short securities would also be relevant, because the willingness to accept lower yields on short securities to avoid the risk of capital loss will diminish as the average maturity of an investor's total portfolio declines.) Since the amplitude of fluctuation in security prices is known to increase with term to maturity,[12] the risk of capital losses increases correspondingly. Insistence by investors on receiving compensation for such risk can account for liquidity premiums on long relative to short securities. Such a premium, increasing with term to maturity, modifies the "pure" expectations hypothesis (that investors adjust security prices to make expected returns equal regardless of maturity).

This explanation of liquidity premiums, though it says nothing about short securities as substitutes for money, shares with the first theory an assumption of risk aversion. But the two theories may have different implications about fluctuations in the premiums. If the shape of the probability distribution (as well as the weighting pattern) does not change over time, the compensation demanded by investors for incurring risk will remain the same. Premiums will be constant over time. If, on the other hand, the shape of the distribution varies systematically over business cycles, cyclical fluctuations in liquidity premiums will occur. One kind of variation, based on expectations of a return to normal levels, implies a certain skewness of the distribution.

Suppose that, as is often contended, investors have in mind a "normal" level of interest rates toward which they expect actual rates to gravitate in the long run; that level would indicate the likely direction of any large change in rates. The probability distribution of expected rates would then be skewed toward the normal level. When the mean expected rate is well above normal, investors would not rule out a large decline in the rate toward or beyond the normal level. The probability distribution is then skewed to the left, as in the top panel of Figure 4-3. Conversely, when the mean expectation is below normal, the distribution is skewed to the right, as in the bottom panel. The shaded areas of the distributions represent short rates above the mean expectation. If any one of those short rates turned out to be the actual future rate, unanticipated capital losses occur on longer-term securities. Actual rates below the mean produce unanticipated gains. If investors weight the probabilities to reflect an aversion to risk of capital losses, the weighted

[12] This is not a mathematical necessity but has generally been true.

mean expectation would, as noted above, lie to the right of the unweighted mean, giving rise to a liquidity premium (larger for securities
of longer term) to partially compensate for the risk of capital loss. As
the expected level of short-term rates fluctuates, therefore, liquidity
premiums move inversely, being larger for a given maturity when expected rates are low relative to the normal level than when they are
relatively high.[13]

It seems reasonable to suppose that the level of rates at any time
considered to be normal reflects past experience, can be approximated
by an average of past rates, and does not change greatly over the duration of a business cycle. In contrast, the rates expected for periods
immediately ahead will ordinarily not differ greatly from current actual
rates because it is difficult to foresee sizable short-run changes in
rates. Consequently, the difference between the expected short rate
and the normal level will vary similarly to actual short rates, and to
actual long rates too, since cyclical fluctuations in long and short
rates are highly correlated. For practical purposes, therefore, the
foregoing theory implies an inverse dependence of liquidity premiums on the level of interest rates, the opposite of the relation implied
by the money-substitute theory discussed previously.

Similarities and Differences Between the Two Theories. Let us
summarize the two theories in terms of an investor's behavior. When
interest rates are low, we might imagine him to demand relatively large
money balances because the cost of holding money is low, in terms of
the foregone interest earnings on financial assets. According to the
first theory, the marginal value attached to the liquidity provided by
short-term assets is then also low, and for that reason he is willing to
purchase short securities only if their yield is not too far below the
return on long securities. Liquidity premiums are then comparatively
small.

---

[13] A recent study finds that expectations of near-term rates are skewed in the direction
of recent changes in rates—that is, investors expect that any unusually large changes in
rates are more likely to reinforce recent changes than to reverse them (see Edward J.
Kane and Burton G. Malkiel, "The Term Structure of Interest Rates: An Analysis of a
Survey of Interest-Rate Expectations," *Review of Economics and Statistics,* August
1967, pp. 343–355, esp. p. 349).

With risk aversion, such skewness of near-term expectations would be positively correlated with current or recent changes in rates. This relationship was not tested in the
subsequent statistical analysis. As explained below, our estimates of the liquidity
premium are *negatively* correlated with changes in rates chiefly because of errors in expectations. There is no way to test for a positive effect of changes in the rates while, at
the same time, holding the errors in expectations constant.

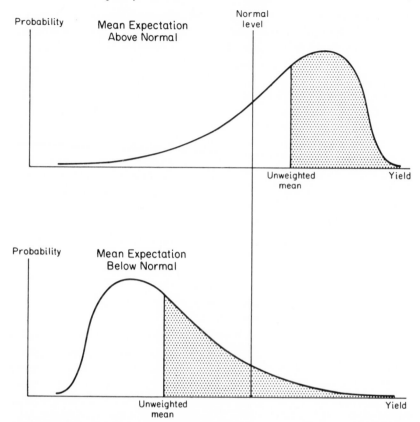

FIGURE 4-3. Investors' Probability Distribution of the Expected Short Rate in Relation to the Expected "Normal" Level

At the same time, his expectations may alert him to an impending rise in short-term rates toward normal levels, and he will acquire long-term securities only if they carry a higher current yield in reflection of a later rise in short rates. (Such expectational effects, though they do not produce a premium, are compatible with any theory of liquidity premiums.) Furthermore, according to the second theory he wants to avoid the risk of capital losses even at the expense of giving up what he considers an equal chance of capital gains. Due to the lingering recollection of the normal level of rates, he regards the currently low short rate as temporary, and his probability distribution of expected rates is skewed toward a return to the higher, normal level. Thus he regards an extra large capital loss on long securities as more probable than an extra large gain even though the expected dollar values of gains and losses are equal, and he avoids long securities unless they carry an extra premium yield. Liquidity premiums are then comparatively large. When interest rates are high, these considerations apply in reverse.

Both theories therefore help to explain the existence of liquidity premiums, but the fluctuations they imply in the premiums are opposite in direction—the first positively associated with the level of rates, the second associated inversely. They might both be valid descriptions of behavior for different groups of investors, or even perhaps as two influences on the same investors. Whether the fluctuations they produce in liquidity premiums cancel each other out or one of the two generally prevails can only be determined empirically.

Either of the two theories can explain the "humped" yield curve often observed in periods of tight credit. At such times the curve slopes upward at the lower end and downward at the longer end, forming a hump usually in the range of the two- to five-year maturities. When explained by expectations alone, such a curve implies that investors anticipate a rise in short-term rates for the next year or two, and thereafter a decline. Yet the short rates of such periods seldom remain high more than a few months, and it seems unlikely that investors would consistently misjudge actual developments. A more appealing explanation of the hump, as Kessel has emphasized,[14] is to combine liquidity premiums and expectations that rates will decline shortly. The premiums contribute to an upward slope in the yield curve, and the expectations to a downward slope. If the slope due to liquidity premiums tapers off sharply for maturities beyond a year or two, a combination of the two effects can produce the observed humped curve.

The occurrence of these curves in times of tight credit indicates that liquidity premiums impart a strong upward slope to the yield curve especially when the level of rates is high. This seems to suggest that the premiums vary directly with the level of rates, but such evidence is not inconsistent with an inverse variation, so long as the level of rates at such times is not so high that the risk of capital loss becomes negligible and the premium, due to that risk, falls to zero.

The inverse conformity to business cycles of the U.S. bond-bill rate differential (Chart 4-2) seems to support the second theory of liquidity premiums. The differential is lowest near business peaks when the level of rates tends to be highest, as that theory predicts.

---

[14] *Cyclical Behavior,* Chap. 4.

But that evidence is relevant only if expectations play a negligible part in the fluctuations, which seems most unlikely. Near business peaks, investors who are alert to business prospects will expect rates to decline sooner or later, and they will push long rates down close to current short rates. (That effect does not require any skewness in the probability distribution of expected rates or an aversion to capital losses.) Consequently, whether liquidity premiums vary directly or inversely with the level of rates, or change at all, is not implied by such cyclical movements in the long-short differential. Those movements can be said to suggest that investors expect unusually high or low short-term rates to return to normal levels.[15] But if we also want to distinguish between the two theories of liquidity premiums, it is necessary to isolate the effect of expectations.

Tests of the Two Theories

In his study, Kessel concluded that liquidity premiums fluctuate positively with the level of interest rates, based on data for the short end of the yield curve in the post-World War II period. He found that the premium on eight-week bill rates relative to four-week rates, adjusted for expectations,[16] had a positive correlation with the level of four-week rates from October 1949 to February 1961, and that the adjusted premium on six-month rates relative to three-month rates also exhibited a positive correlation with the level of three-month rates from January 1959 to February 1961.

To estimate liquidity premiums, Kessel compared the yields on two securities of different maturity for the same periods. This eliminates the effects of expectations, because as noted the market adjusts prices so that expected holding-period yields (aside from liquidity and risk premiums) on different securities will be the same. The yield differential then reflects influences other than anticipated changes in rates. The yield period he selected for comparison was the period to maturity of the longer security. With maturities of three months and one year, for example, the yield to maturity on the one-year security is compared with the total return from investing in the three-month security, then

---

[15] That is the explanation for those movements given by B. G. Malkiel, *The Term Structure*, Chap. 4. He does not distinguish between such expectations and fluctuations in the liquidity premium.

[16] *Cyclical Behavior*, p. 26. Kessel measured the premium by the difference between the forward rate and the corresponding future spot rate, which allows for expectations.

upon its maturity reinvesting the proceeds three more times in successive three-month issues, thus keeping the funds invested for a full year. Such comparisons are only feasible, however, for fairly short maturities. (Kessel used this procedure in the results just cited for maturities of eight weeks and six months.) For bonds, the procedure introduces statistical difficulties. It would involve, for example, comparing the yields on five-year bonds and three-month bills over a holding period of five years; that is, each observation of their differential yield would pertain to a five-year period. Whether or not overlapping periods are used, such long intervals render time-series analysis quite impractical, as well as involve large errors in investors' expectations because of the long lead time.

An alternative procedure, used here, is to calculate yields on all securities for the same holding period of some short duration, regardless of their individual maturities, which eliminates the necessity of comparisons for widely separate dates. The holding-period yields of long-term securities still involve large errors in expectations—the problem cannot be avoided. But these errors can be taken into account to some extent, so that estimates of premiums at the long end of the yield curve adjusted for expectations appear feasible for time-series analysis.

ESTIMATING LIQUIDITY PREMIUMS BY DIFFERENCES BETWEEN HOLD-ING-PERIOD YIELDS. Holding-period yields measure the rate of return on a security purchased at the beginning of a given period and sold at the end, which ordinarily will not coincide with the term to maturity. The data presented below are one-week holding-period yields on Treasury securities.[17] No special appropriateness can be claimed for the one-week period. Other periods, while worth experimenting with, would probably give similar results.

The one-week holding-period yield on a security of maturity n at

---

[17] Ideally we want to use the holding period for which the error variance of expectations is lowest, which seems most likely to be the actual period over which investors plan to hold. Some speculation in bills may occur on a daily or weekly basis, while bond investors may purchase to hold for months, quarters, or years. Actual holding periods for which investors form expectations and make comparisons among securities probably differ widely among investors and over time. Data on average holding periods are not available, moreover, which makes the one-week period somewhat arbitrary. Yet if expectations equalize yields for periods of one week or less, the equality will carry over to longer periods as well. Errors of forecast may or may not be larger for longer periods; it depends upon whether public anticipations are more accurate for short- or long-run changes in rates.

time t, $H_{n,t}$, expressed as an annual rate with continuous compounding, is

$$H_{n,t} = 52 \log_e \frac{(P_{n-1,t+1} + C_{n,t})}{P_{n,t}} \qquad (4)$$

where $P_{n,t}$ is the price of a security at the beginning of week t with n weeks to maturity (disregarding buying and selling costs); and $C_{n,t}$ is the coupon payment, if any, on that security at the end of the week.[18] The expectations theory, altered to allow for liquidity premiums, assumes that

$$H_{n,t} = E_t - L_{n,t} + \xi_{n,t}, \qquad (5)$$

where E_t is the expected total yield during week t, the same for all maturities; $L_{n,t}$ is the known nonpecuniary yield during week t due to liquidity services from a security with n weeks to maturity ($E - L$ is the expected pecuniary yield); and $\xi_{n,t}$ is the error of expected pecuniary yield for this security in week t. All yields are expressed as annual rates. For any two maturities n and m, $n > m$:

$$H_{n,t} - H_{m,t} = L_{m,t} - L_{n,t} + \xi_{n,t} - \xi_{m,t}, \qquad (6)$$

where the error terms are assumed to have zero means. Hence, as an approximation, for sufficiently large T,[19]

$$\sum_{t=1}^{T} \frac{(H_{n,t} - H_{m,t})}{T} = \bar{L}_m - \bar{L}_n > 0. \qquad (7)$$

This is the measure of liquidity premiums used here. T is thirteen weeks.

The error term ξ can be quite large at times. Although the difference between the errors, $\xi_{n,t} - \xi_{m,t}$, will be much smaller than either one separately owing to positive correlation, the difference may still be large at times, because unanticipated changes in rates usually have a

---

[18] The formula follows from the properties of exponential growth. If $\frac{P_T}{P_0}$, the growth in a price from 0 to T, equals e^{rT}, r is the constant exponential rate of growth. Hence

$$r = \frac{1}{T} \log_e \left(\frac{P_T}{P_0} \right).$$

[19] Since n and m do not change over time in (7), the average value of $H_{n,t}$ for a period of n weeks is *not* the same as $R_{n,t}$, the yield on holding the same security to maturity. Eq. (7) is based on selling each week a $n - 1$ week bill and replacing it with an n week bill. See the Appendix to this chapter for further discussion of measuring liquidity premiums.

greater affect on the prices of securities with longer maturities. The possibility of large errors means that fluctuations in measured liquidity premiums must be interpreted with some caution.

Chart 4-3 presents one-week holding period yields of one- to thirteen-week Treasury bills for various reference stages and their average for two full cycles,[20] showing in detail the steepest part of the yield curve — the short end. These curves are not smooth, no doubt mainly as a result of unanticipated changes in actual yields, but generally they rise up to the seven- to eight-week maturities. The data are averages of bid and ask prices and so do not allow for transaction costs in the form of dealer spreads. The spread is usually the smallest on newly issued thirteen-week bills and nearby maturities than on others, which may help explain why the curve levels off from the seven- to thirteen-week maturities. In any event, the over-all upward slope of these curves can be interpreted as evidence of liquidity premiums, since investors presumably adjust prices so that expected holding-period yields (apart from premiums) are equal on all maturities.

There is also evidence of cyclical fluctuations in the premiums; the peak stages (V) appear to have steeper slopes than do the trough stages (I and IX). This is brought out more clearly by Chart 4-4, which presents the quarterly differences between the thirteen- and one-week yields for the period 1951–65 (top panel), and some other related series discussed later. Reference contractions are shaded. (Differences between twelve- and two-week yields, not presented, exhibit similar movements.) The thirteen- and one-week yield differential fluctuated during this period generally in the same direction as business activity, though not consistently from quarter to quarter. The high point came considerably after the 1957 reference peak, for example, and the decline following the 1960 peak was slower and more prolonged than any previous one.

Much of the fluctuation in the differential appears to reflect errors in expectations, and to be negatively correlated with changes in the three-month bill rate (second panel). This suggests that the error terms in (6) are inversely associated with changes in interest rates, because

---

[20] Most of these data were kindly supplied to me by Jacob Michaelsen from his study. His compilation, from The First Boston Corporation, begins with 1951, ends with 1962, and is for Friday closing prices. The data were extended by the National Bureau back to 1948 and forward to 1965 and are for Tuesday prices from the quotation sheets kindly made available by the New York government securities department of Merrill Lynch. The difference in the day of the week should not make any difference for present purposes. The basic data are averages of bid and ask prices, except for the maturity value of one-week bills which was taken to be par.

CHART 4-3. Yield Curve of Treasury Bills, One-Week Holding-Period, Reference Stages and Cycle Averages

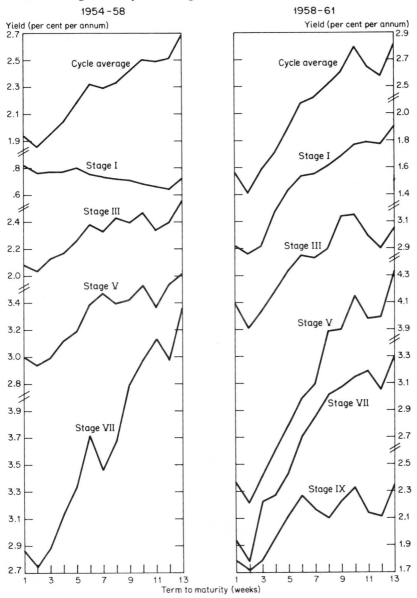

SOURCE: See footnote 20.

CHART 4-4. Estimated Liquidity Premium on Treasury Bills, Change, Level, and Deviation of Three-Month Rate, and Relative Supply, Quarterly, 1951–65

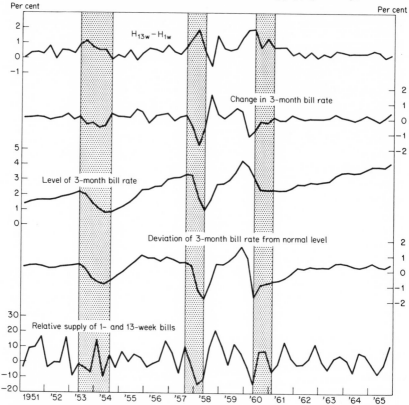

NOTE: Shaded areas represent reference cycle contractions.
SOURCE: See Table 4-1; data not seasonally adjusted.

changes in the level of rates, if not fully anticipated, produce greater capital gains and losses on long than on short maturities. This causes the difference between the error terms to duplicate their individual movements. Why should errors in expectations be negatively correlated with *changes* in rates? An obvious answer is "inertia" of expectations—a tendency of some investors to expect future rates to be the same as current ones. As a simple formulation of this interpretation, let us suppose that some constant fraction α of the market demand for securities is based on the expectation of no change in rates and the remainder is based on an expectation having a prediction error

ϵ with zero mean.[21] Then, assuming the Ls involve no error, the error terms in (6) are

$$\xi_{n,t} - \xi_{m,t} = \alpha[H_{n,t} - H_{n,t-1} - (H_{m,t} - H_{m,t-1})] + (1 - \alpha)(\epsilon_{n,t} - \epsilon_{m,t})$$

$$= \alpha[f(-\Delta R_t)] + (1 - \alpha)\,\epsilon_t. \tag{8}$$

The first term on the right is simply the difference between the changes in holding-period yields for the two maturities, which for $n > m$ is a negative function of the change in level of interest rates. The exact relationship depends upon the maturity of the securities, but we can treat it as approximately proportional to the negative of the change in the three-month bill rate. The second term is the prediction error, assumed independent of the level of rates. We may substitute (8) into (6) with a view to improving the estimate of liquidity premiums. The change in the bill rate will account for part of the errors in expectations and allow a better estimate of the effects of other variables on liquidity premiums.[22] If α is not constant, the estimates may be biased, though

[21] A more sophisticated hypothesis would be that expectations are formed from an autoregressive scheme of past rates plus an autonomous component with a mean error of zero.

[22] In *The Behavior of Interest Rates: A Progress Report,* NBER, New York, 1966, Appendix to Chapter 7, Joseph Conard questioned Kessel's empirical findings on the grounds that the liquidity premium is spuriously correlated with changes in the level of rates. Kessel's measure of the premium is the difference between the forward rate and the relevant future actual rate. Conard's point is that the forward rate, because of "inertia" in the formation of expectations, generally differs very little from the current actual rate; consequently, this measure of the liquidity premium approximates the current minus the future actual rate, which is the negative of the change in the rate. Then, if there is a tendency for the change in the rate over any period to be negatively correlated with the level of the rate at the beginning of the period, as is not unlikely because of cyclical fluctuations and as Conard presented evidence to confirm, one has identified a source of spurious correlation between the premium and the level of the rate to account for at least part of Kessel's results. In an unpublished work Kessel tested this interpretation by running regressions with the current spot rate in place of the forward rate in the estimate of the liquidity premium. On Conard's interpretation, these regressions should have higher correlation coefficients. Kessel finds higher coefficients using the forward rates, supporting the validity of his interpretation of the correlations.

The difference in holding-period yields used here as a measure of the liquidity premium is also negatively correlated with changes in the rate for a related reason: Unanticipated changes in the level of rates have an effect on the price of securities which increases with the length of maturity, and hence affect differences in holding-period yields. By holding the change in rates constant, we remove spurious correlation of the kind Conard attributed to Kessel's results and absorb part of the errors of expectations as well.

perhaps not seriously. For the tentative results derived below, such bias will be ignored.

MULTIPLE REGRESSIONS. The two theories of liquidity premiums discussed above imply certain testable relations among the variables. The relevant variables are depicted in Chart 4-4 for comparison with the differential holding-period yields between thirteen- and one-week bills. The cost of holding money is represented by the three-month bill rate — it should by the first theory relate positively to the differential. The relative supply is represented by the average difference between the amounts of one- and thirteen-week bills held by the public, expressed as a percentage of total bills held — it should by either theory relate negatively to the differential. The risk of capital losses is represented by the deviation of the three-month bill rate from normal levels estimated by a weighted average of the past nine quarters, the weights declining linearly [23] — it should by the second theory relate negatively to the differential. Multiple regressions of these variables, including the change in the three-month bill rate to represent errors of expectation, as in (8) are presented in Table 4-1.

The change in rates is highly correlated (negatively) with the difference in holding-period yields, as was evident in the chart. The level of bill rates is also significant, and has a positive regression coefficient consistent with the money-substitute theory. By this estimate, the premium increases 15 basis points for each 1 percentage point rise in the level of rates.[24]

The relative supply is not significant, however, and has a positive coefficient, inconsistent with both theories. Changes in this variable — the supply of one-week bills minus the supply of thirteen-week bills — should affect the premium inversely, since a relative rise in the supply of one-week bills can be expected to bring their yield closer to the thirteen-week rate, reducing the differential. To be sure, we may not have measured the relative supply properly. Other very short-term

---

[23] That is, normal level $= \sum_{i=1}^{9} \frac{10-i}{45} R_{t-i}$, as a rough approximation.

[24] Kessel (*Cyclical Behavior*, p. 26) found increases of 22 and 45 basis points in his two regressions, which, as noted, covered shorter periods and estimated liquidity premiums differently.

The regression results reflect the fact that thirteen-week yields fluctuate with greater amplitude than do one-week yields. The money-substitute theory is an acceptable explanation only if there is no inherent tendency of an institutional character for the cyclical amplitude of bill yields to increase with term to maturity. In particular, any cyclical variations in relative dealer spreads are ignored here.

TABLE 4-1. Multiple Regressions of Difference Between Holding-Period Yields for Thirteen- and One-Week Bills on Change, Level, and Deviation of Three-Month Rate, and Relative Supply, Quarterly, 1951–65

Equa-tion Number	Regression Coefficient (and *t* value)				Multiple Corre-lation Coeffi-cient
	Change in Rate	Level of Rate	Relative Supply	Deviation of Rate from "Normal"	
1	−.71 (6.8)	.15 (2.9)			.69
2	−.81 (6.8)	.15 (2.9)	.01 (1.6)		.70
3	−.84 (6.8)	.12 (1.8)	.01 (1.5)	.09 (0.9)	.71

SOURCE: Holding-period yields, see footnote 20. Bill rate, *Federal Reserve Bulletin*. Relative supply based on Treasury bills held by the public, *Monthly Treasury Bulletin*. Data not seasonally adjusted.

NOTE: Dependent variable is $H_{13w} - H_{1w}$, as defined by eq. (4), quarterly average of weekly yields, per cent per annum. The constant terms are not shown. Independent variables are:

Change in rate: change over the quarter in three-month bill rate, per cent per annum.

Level of rate: three-month bill rate, quarterly average of monthly data, per cent per annum.

Relative supply: difference between one- and thirteen-week bills held by the public, quarterly average of weekly data, as percentage of midquarter total bills held [actually, the numerator was estimated by the quarterly change in total bills held divided by 13, $(TB_{13} - TB_0)/13$, which approximates for each quarter the average of weekly differences:

$$\sum_{t=1}^{13} \frac{(B_t^1 - B_t^{13})}{13} = \frac{\sum_{n=1}^{13} B_{13}^n - \sum_{n=1}^{13} B_1^n}{13} = \frac{TB_{13} - TB_1}{13},$$

where B^n is bills of maturity n outstanding in week t and TB_t is total bills outstanding in week t].

Deviation from normal: three-month bill rate minus weighted average of past rates for nine quarters, linearly declining weights (see footnote 22), per cent per annum. Quarterly data are averages of monthly rates.

Signs of *t* values have been dropped. At .05 level of significance, $t > 2.0$.

bills are close substitutes for the one-week bills, and thirteen-week bills are substitutable with longer-term bills. It is not clear how to treat substitutes in measuring the relative supply. In addition, appreciable bunching in the maturity distribution of bills is fairly infrequent, occurring temporarily only when the rate of new issues is suddenly changed; consequently, relative supplies may not have affected the premiums between the bill yields sufficiently to register in these regressions.

The deviations of the rate from normal levels have a low and insignificant coefficient. This variable and the level of the rate have similar movements apart from trends.[25] Each correlates positively with the premium, even when the other is held constant, though the rate level has the stronger association. The deviations should affect the premium negatively, since a fall in rates below what is considered the normal level increases the risk of capital loss and requires as compensation a yield which is higher on longer than on shorter maturities. On this evidence, changes in the premium at the short end of the yield curve do not support the second theory.

Examining the long end of the yield curve is more relevant than the short end to theories of liquidity premiums. The relevant series are shown in Chart 4-5. The top series is the difference between holding-period yields on two and a half-year bonds and thirteen-week bills. Corresponding differentials using bills and five-, seven and a half-, and ten-year bonds (not shown) have similar movements. These data, compiled by Michaelson (see footnote 20) through 1962, were not extended. For ease of comparison the change and level of the rate and its deviations from normal are the same series as in Chart 4-4, based on the three-month bill rate. It would perhaps be better (see footnote 11) to compare the premium on bonds relative to bills with the level of the bond instead of the bill rate, but any mismatching on that score does not appear serious, since movements in bond and bill rates are similar.

The relative supply variable is necessarily different here, however. According to the money-substitute theory of liquidity premiums, bills are used as a substitute for money balances, while bonds serve that purpose only to a very limited extent. The marginal substitutability of bills for money depends upon the supply of bills relative to money.

---

[25] The simple correlation between these two variables for the period covered in Table 4-1 is +.58. Lengthening the weighted average which estimates the normal level of the rate (footnote 23) would increase this correlation.

Multicollinearity between the change in rates and the deviations from normal may have turned a negative coefficient for the latter into a positive one. The correlation coefficient between the two is +.35. However, the simple correlation between the deviations and the differential is virtually zero.

Multicollinearity can also result from common cyclical fluctuations. We can hold common cyclical fluctuations in the variables constant by means of dummy variables. A separate dummy variable can be added to represent each of the stages of reference cycles in business activity. When that was done, the coefficient of the deviations variable became negative, but again it remained low and insignificant while the significance of the rate level was increased.

CHART 4-5. Estimated Liquidity Premium on Treasury Bonds, Change, Level, and Deviation of Three-Month Rate, and Relative Supply, Quarterly, 1951–62

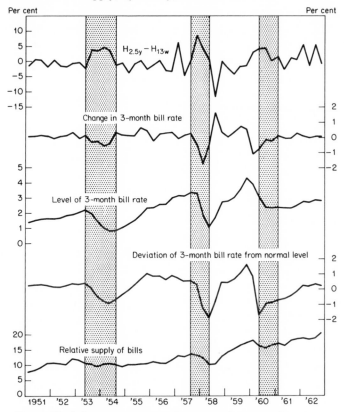

NOTE: Shaded areas represent reference cycle contractions.
SOURCE: See Table 4-2; data not seasonally adjusted.

The chart therefore shows the ratio of bills (and CDs [26]) to the money stock outside commercial banks. It might be preferable to use instead the ratio pertaining to business and financial institutions, which hold most outstanding bills, but such data were not readily available.

[26] The statistical analysis implicitly assumes that the pecuniary yield on money is zero. With the rise of time deposit rates toward the end of the 1950's and expansion of certificates of deposit, this assumption was no longer valid. CDs were therefore treated as a substitute for bills, and were included in total bills outstanding and excluded from the money stock. Nevertheless, CDs were not quantitatively important until after 1962.

The ratio of bills to bonds outstanding is also relevant to the second theory, since a

The bond-bill differential in the chart naturally shows much greater volatility than the corresponding differential in Chart 4-4 (note that the scale is compressed here). Unanticipated changes in rates affect holding-period yields more for longer maturities. The bond-bill differential is subject to frequent and substantial errors of expectations, and some allowance for these errors seems necessary to improve the estimates of the premium. As before, we may use (the negative of) changes in the three-month rate as an index of the direction and magnitude of the errors.

Table 4-2 presents multiple regressions of the differential on the other variables in Chart 4-5. The bottom three regressions use longer-term bonds for the differential rate. The results, though generally in the same direction as in Table 4-1, are materially weaker. Changes in the rate are inversely related to the bond-bill differential, reflecting unanticipated capital losses on bonds when rates rise and unanticipated gains when rates fall. The other variables are all positively related, but none are significant. Since the relative supply and the deviations from normal are supposed to have negative coefficients but have positive ones here, we may tentatively conclude that these variables do not have the effects implied by the theory, or at least were not important in the period covered. The main qualification is that the supply variable may as before fail to include relevant substitutes for bills, and thus may be misspecified.

The level of the rate has a positive effect consistent with the money-substitute theory, and, though not significant as in Table 4-1, the coefficient has a reasonable magnitude. The coefficients for the level of the rate in Table 4-2 provide estimates of the marginal substitutability of bills for money balances. If we assume that ten-year bonds have negligible liquidity, then, as in eq. (2), $R_{13w} + S_{13w}R_{10y} = R_{10y}$. The regression may be written as

$$R_{10y} - R_{13w} = 1.2\,R_{13w}.$$

Hence

$$S_{13w}R_{10y} = 1.2\,R_{13w} = 1.2(R_{10y} - S_{13w}R_{10y}),$$

and

$$S_{13w} = \frac{1.2}{2.2} = .5;$$

rise in the ratio helps to satisfy the preference for bills and leads to a smaller differential. What total quantity of bonds should be used in the denominator, however, appears arbitrary. Yet, such a ratio, however defined, might behave similarly to the ratio of bills to money stock used here.

TABLE 4-2. Multiple Regressions of Difference Between Holding-Period Yields for Various Bonds and Thirteen-Week Bills on Change, Level, and Deviation of Three-Month Rate, and Relative Supply, Quarterly, 1951–62

Maturity of Bond in Dependent Variable (years)	Regression Coefficient (and t value)				Multiple Corre- lation Coeffi- cient
	Change in Rate	Level of Rate	Relative Supply	Deviation of Rate from "Normal"	
2.5	−4.7 (5.9)	.51 (1.1)			.66
	−4.6 (5.7)	.06 (0.1)	.16 (1.0)		.67
	−4.8 (5.7)			.38 (0.6)	.66
5	−9.6 (5.6)	1.0 (0.9)			.64
7.5	−12.2 (5.7)	1.3 (1.0)			.65
10	−11.8 (5.0)	1.2 (0.9)			.60

SOURCE: Same as for Table 4-1. Money stock, M. Friedman and A. Schwartz, *A Monetary History of the United States, 1867–1960*, Princeton for NBER, 1963, Table A1, extended and revised. Negotiable CDs of $100,000 or more, weekly reporting banks, from Federal Reserve Bank of St. Louis, *Review*, August 1965, Chart 1, with logarithmic interpolation.

NOTE: The dependent variable for the first regression is $H_{2.5y} - H_{13w}$, as defined by eq. (4), per cent per annum, and similarly for the others with longer bond maturities. Independent variables are the same as for Table 4-1, except for relative supply, which is total Treasury bills held by the public as a percentage of the money stock (adjusted for CDs – see footnote 26). The constant terms are not shown.

Signs of t values have been dropped. At .05 level of significance, $t > 2.0$.

that is, the liquidity premium for the given supply makes the bill yield on the average one-half the bond yield.[27]

The failure of the level of the rate to achieve statistical significance in Table 4-2 may be due to the volatility of the bond-bill differential and the failure of changes in the rate to account adequately for errors of expectations. Whether a more reliable method of adjusting for the errors would alter these results is not known. By all indications, the

[27] The liquidity premium measured from the slope of the yield curve for 1954–58 in Chart 4-1 is

$$1 - R_{13w}/R_{10y} = .22.$$

This is an alternative estimate of S_{13w}. Aside from the periods covered, the two estimates should differ only in that the method of holding expectations constant is not the same, and the measurement from the yield curve (based on a cycle average) assumes that the relation between the premium and the level of the rate is log linear and goes through the origin, while the regression assumes arithmetic linearity and does not require the constant term to be zero.

money-substitute theory outperforms the theory based on normal rates and risk aversion. The first is strongly supported by the regressions for the short end of the yield curve. Its importance to the premium between bonds and bills, though suggested by the results here, remains tentative.

Summary and Conclusions

The yields of U.S. and municipal securities, plotted by maturity, have an upward slope which appears *not* to reflect differences in transaction costs or expectations. The slope represents a lower pecuniary yield on the shorter-term securities apparently due to the greater stability of their market prices. This "liquidity" premium can be observed on U.S. securities back, at least, to 1920 when Treasury certificates were first traded.

Two theories were examined to explain short-run fluctuations in the premium. The first theory views the premium as reflecting the greater substitutability of short-term securities for money balances. When an expansion, say, in business conditions raises the level of interest rates, money becomes comparatively more expensive to hold, and it is exchanged for new securities and other assets until the marginal value of the services from the remaining money balances rises to equal the foregone return available on nonliquid long-term bonds or on capital goods. In exchanging money for other assets, the more liquid short-term securities are preferred. Short-term yields are therefore held down relative to long-term yields; although interest rates as a whole rise, the differential yields between short and long securities widen. Conversely, in a business contraction producing a decline in interest rates, the differential narrows. This increase in slope of the yield curve when the level rises, and decrease in slope when the level falls, occurs independently of any expectation of changes in rates.

The second theory views liquidity premiums as resulting from a general belief that interest rates gravitate toward the "normal" level expected to prevail over the long run and from an aversion to the risk of capital losses on long securities. If we take an average of past yields to reflect what appears to investors as normal at any time, we should find a higher yield on long relative to short securities when interest rates are relatively low, because long securities are then especially subject to capital losses; and conversely when rates are high. This implies an inverse relationship, opposite to the first theory. A test of these theories requires data on yield differentials from which the effects of expected changes in rates have somehow been eliminated.

Investors are presumed to bid bond prices up or down until, taking account of expected capital gains or losses, the expected returns on all options are equally attractive. On the average, therefore, returns from all investments are supposed to be equal over a given period except for errors in expectations and any liquidity premiums. If the errors tend to cancel out, the premiums can be estimated by the difference between the actual returns on two optional investments. The usual method has been to compare the yield to maturity of one security with the accumulated yield from successive reinvestments in a shorter-term security; for example, the yield to maturity on a six-month bill compared with the total return on two successive three-month bills. For bonds with maturities of several years or more, however, the method becomes impractical since the period covered by each comparison is as long as the maturity of the bond. Hence an estimate of the premium on two and a half-year bonds (say) gives one observation every two and one-half years; if we permit overlapping comparisons, the observations are then serially dependent and unfit for time-series analysis. To avoid such disadvantages, this study has used one-week holding-period yields, which compare the returns on buying two securities and selling both after one week regardless of their maturity. This provides one observation per week (though the statistical analysis used quarterly averages). The main drawback of this method is that unanticipated changes in interest rates produce large discrepancies between realized and expected holding-period yields on bonds. These errors in expectations are incorporated into the estimates of the liquidity premium and obscure the analysis. We attempted to account for these errors by adding changes in the market bill rate as an independent variable to the regressions. The volatility of holding-period differentials nevertheless remains troublesome, and it should be profitable in future research on liquidity premiums to explore other methods of dealing with the errors in expectations.

Although limited and necessarily tentative, the results give no support to a theory of liquidity premiums based on normal rates and favor instead the money-substitute theory. The deviations of interest rates from the normal level, representing the risk of capital loss, has the wrong sign (and is not significant) for regressions covering both the short and long ends of the yield curve. The level of interest rates does have a correct and significant positive correlation with the estimated premium on thirteen-week bills relative to one-week ones, as Kessel also found for slightly longer maturities. For the premium on bonds relative to bills, the regression coefficient of the rate level is again positive though not significant. It is unclear whether the lack of statistical significance here indicates no relation or simply our failure to measure it properly, perhaps because errors in expectations were not adequately eliminated. In any event, the size of its regression coefficient appears reasonable, suggesting that during the 1950's a $1000 Treasury bill substituted on the margin for about $500 of money balances.

Although the relative supply of money substitutes should also affect the liquidity premium, the supply variable is insignificant in the regressions. This is not, however, a conclusive test of the importance of the supply. Most changes in the distribution of Treasury bills seem too small to have measureable effects on premiums between the very short maturities. And supply effects on the bond-bill premium may not be adequately represented by changes in the ratio of Treasury bills to the money stock, as is used here. What to include in the total supply of substitutes cannot be settled theoretically but requires further empirical study. Developments during the early 1960's, when the sharp growth of certificates of deposit accompanied a decline in the bond-bill premium, suggest that supply effects may be important.

Supply effects on liquidity premiums have acquired a practical importance in recent years because of the Federal Reserve's "operation twist"—an effort during the early 1960's to raise short-term interest rates relative to long-term rates. The purpose was to alleviate the adverse U.S. balance of payments by attracting capital funds from abroad for domestic investment in short-term securities, while at the same time to reduce domestic unemployment by keeping long-term rates low enough to encourage investment expenditures. The twofold policy required a reduction in the differential between short- and long-term rates. Based on subsequent events, the policy appeared to reduce the differential, though only somewhat more than had occurred in the two previous business expansions (Chart 4-2). Whether the reduction reflected Federal Reserve market operations at all is subject to question. By the money-substitute theory, the policy required an increase in the supply of bills relative to the money stock or a decline in bond yields. But neither change appears to have been large enough to account for the decline that occurred in the differential. That is why one looks for alternative explanations such as the increased issue of CDs.

While we are not yet able to measure liquidity premiums accurately or to understand fully the causes of fluctuations, recent developments in the technique of measurement, reviewed and extended here, hold out the promise of answering such questions by quantitative analysis.

Appendix

A COMPARISON OF TWO ESTIMATES OF LIQUIDITY PREMIUMS: HOLDING-PERIOD YIELDS AND YIELDS TO MATURITY

A holding-period yield which happens to coincide with the period to maturity of a security equals the yield to maturity; otherwise the two are different. When the yields contain liquidity premiums, there are also conceptual differences in measurement of the premium. Although for most practical purposes these differences do not appear important, they should be made explicit. A simple example will help to clarify the two definitions of the premium.

Let us compare four- and eight-week bills, and suppose we calculate a holding-period yield of four weeks. That yield for four-week bills is simply their yield to maturity, $R_{4,t}$ (all yields expressed at an *annual* rate). The eight-week bill, with maturity value $P_{0,t+8}$, can be purchased at the price $P_{8,t} = P_{0,t+8}/(1 + R_{8,t})^{8/52}$, and sold in four weeks at the price then of four-week bills: $P_{4,t+4} = P_{0,t+8}/(1 + R_{4,t+4})^{4/52}$. Hence the first four-week holding-period yield on eight-week bills, at an annual rate, is

$$H_{8,t} = \left(\frac{P_{4,t+4}}{P_{8,t}}\right)^{13} - 1 = \left[\frac{(1 + R_{8,t})^{8/52}}{(1 + R_{4,t+4})^{4/52}}\right]^{13}. \tag{A1}$$

The estimate of $L_{4,t} - L_{8,t}$ by eq. (6) is therefore

$$H_{8,t} - H_{4,t} = \frac{(1 + R_{8,t})^2}{(1 + R_{4,t+4})} - 1 - R_{4,t}, \tag{A2}$$

which by an arithmetic approximation equals

$$2R_{8,t} - R_{4,t+4} - R_{4,t}. \tag{A3}$$

As originally defined by Hicks in *Value and Capital,* liquidity premiums attach to forward rates. An estimate of the premium is the forward rate minus the actual future rate. For eight- and four-week rates, we have

$$_4F_{4,t} - R_{4,t+4} = L_{4,t+4} - L_{8,t}, \tag{A4}$$

where $_4F_{4,t}$ is the forward rate at time t on a four-week security beginning in four weeks, which covers eight weeks of time. The four-week forward rate, at an annual rate, is

$$_4F_{4,t} = \left[\frac{(1 + R_{8,t})^{8/52}}{(1 + R_{4,t})^{4/52}}\right]^{13} - 1. \tag{A5}$$

The arithmetic approximation to (A5) is

$$2R_{8,t} - R_{4,t} - R_{4,t+4}, \tag{A6}$$

the same as for holding-period yields in (A3), though conceptually the pre-mium estimated there is $L_{4,t} - L_{8,t}$, not $L_{4,t+4} - L_{8,t}$ as here. This equivalence of formulas, of course, holds only if the term of the predicted rate equals the length of the holding period. With a shorter holding period, there is no equiv-alent formula using forward rates and no equivalent estimate of liquidity premiums pertaining to the same time period.

In fact, since forward rates are defined in terms of yields to maturity, the liquidity premiums estimated from them are an average for a series of holding periods. Consider the premium attached to $R_{n,t}$ as implied by the slope of the yield curves in Chart 4-1. Its relation to $L_{n,t}$ used in eqs. (3)–(7) may be de-rived as follows.

Express $R_{n,t}$ as a geometric average of successive holding-period yields (footnote 6),

$$(1 + R_{n,t})^n = (1 + H_{n,t})(1 + H_{n-1,t+1}) \ldots (1 + H_{1,t+n}),$$

or by the arithmetic approximation,

$$R_{n,t} = \frac{\sum_{i=0}^{n-1} H_{n-i,t+1}}{n}.$$

By (5), this may be written, ignoring the error terms,

$$R_{n,t} = \frac{\sum_{i=0}^{n-1} E_{t+i} - \sum_{i=0}^{n-1} L_{n-i,t+i}}{n}.$$

For an average yield curve, let us assume that interest rates are expected to remain the same (that is, the Es for all periods are equal) and that L_n expected at t is the same for all time periods. Then, for any two successive maturities and all t,

$$R_n - R_{n-1} = -\frac{1}{n}\left(L_n - \frac{\sum_1^{n-1} L_i}{n-1}\right).$$

By holding-period yields, the corresponding premium is

$$H_{n,t} - H_{n-1,t} = L_{n-1,t} - L_{n,t}.$$

It seems unlikely that these differences in the measurement of liquidity premiums have much practical importance, however.

5

The Yield Spread Between

New and Seasoned Corporate Bonds,

1952–63   *Joseph W. Conard and Mark W. Frankena*

I. Introduction and Summary of Findings

Recorded data indicate that in the period since the 1951 Accord there has generally been a substantial excess of yields on new corporate bond issues offered to the market above the average yield on ap-

NOTE: We are indebted to many people for their aid in providing data and suggestions for this study. We especially want to thank Sidney Homer of Salomon Brothers and Hutzler, who provided us with hypotheses to test, much of the basic data, and invaluable information without which the study would not have been possible. Also, we thank Moody's Investors Service for permitting us to use their series and to work with the data underlying their published series. Mortimer Kaplan of the Federal Housing Administration has likewise been generous in providing data underlying his *Journal of Finance* article of March 1962, and William H. White of the International Monetary Fund has kindly sent us some of his unpublished material in addition to providing useful suggestions and criticisms. Ronald Bodkin of the University of Western Ontario, Jacob Mincer of the National Bureau of Economic Research, and Robert Summers of the University of Pennsylvania have given needed advice on statistical procedures, and Geoffrey H. Moore of the National Bureau and Roger F. Murray of the Teachers Insurance and Annuity Association discussed many of our problems with us. Eleanor Barr's assistance in collecting data, carrying out statistical tests, and preparing charts in the early stages of this study was invaluable.

An article prepared by William H. White in 1957 and published in the March 1962 *Staff Papers* of the IMF, after our hypotheses were formulated and testing had been begun but before the initial draft of this study was completed, suggested several general conclusions that are strikingly similar to ours. Since our work and his were independent up to that stage and used somewhat different procedures — White concentrating on cross sections rather than time series — this seems to lend substantial support to many of the conclusions reached.

parently comparable bonds already outstanding.[1] The average new-seasoned yield spread as recorded by Moody's for Aa corporate bonds for the period from 1952 through 1963 was 16.7 basis points. During extended periods in this interval appreciably higher returns could be earned on new Aa corporates than on seasoned A-rated bonds, and on occasion the new Aa's yielded more than seasoned Baa's. Yet, the size of the new-seasoned yield spread is extremely variable, and on some occasions new issues sold below the average yield on seasoned bonds with the same quality rating.

There are a number of reasons for special interest in the determinants of the yield spread between newly issued and seasoned bonds. Lending institutions are concerned with the spread as an indication of profit opportunities. Economists are mainly interested in the implications yield spreads may have for the efficiency of capital markets and perhaps for the effectiveness and incidence of monetary policy. Monetary policy can affect economic activity through new issue yields (the "cost of funds effect") or through seasoned yields (the "availability" or "lock-in" effect). The behavior of spreads could shed light on the relative importance of these channels.

This study is an attempt to explain those yield spreads. Three major hypotheses were tested: (1) The spreads reflect differences between the yield-determining characteristics of the bonds used in the new and seasoned yield averages. (2) The spreads are a result of the under-writers' pricing policies and arise out of their attempt to minimize the risk of capital losses on new issues. (3) The spreads are due to transaction costs and imperfections in the capital market which cause yields in the seasoned market to lag behind those in the new issue market.

Our major efforts were devoted to studying the behavior of new-seasoned yield spreads for Aa corporate bonds. The analysis included series prepared by Moody's Investors Service, The Bankers Trust Company, Mortimer Kaplan of the Federal Housing Administration, and Sidney Homer of Salomon Brothers and Hutzler.

A major conclusion of this study is that differences between the average coupon rate on the bonds used in the new issue and seasoned issue series accounted for roughly half the recorded new-seasoned yield spread. Over the 1952–63 period as a whole, it was found that the average coupon rate on the new issues exceeded that on seasoned

---

[1] The term "seasoned" will be used to indicate bonds which have been outstanding for a period of months or years. The yield spread is measured as the yield on newly issued bonds minus the yield on seasoned bonds; hence, it is positive when the former is greater than the latter.

issues by .70 per cent in the Moody series and 1.29 per cent in the Homer series. Bonds with higher coupon rates carry higher yields because the danger that they will be called for refunding is greater and the possibility of capital gains is more limited at times of declining interest rates. Nevertheless, even after adjustment for coupon rate, it was found that the average new-seasoned yield spread was approximately 9 basis points in both the Moody and the Homer series.

The bonds in the new issue and seasoned issue series also differed with respect to other yield-determining characteristics, such as industrial classification, term to maturity, average length of refunding deferment, and sinking fund provisions. These variables appear to have relatively little effect on yield spreads, however. The spread on individual new issues tends to disappear within two or three months after the issue is released from syndicate price-maintenance agreements, indicating that the spread remaining after correction for coupon rate differences is not due to systematic differences in other yield-determining characteristics.

Using series which were specially constructed so that coupon rate was held constant, it was found by multiple regression analysis that the change in new issue yields for each of the twelve months preceding the month of the observation explained 60 to 70 per cent of the remaining variance in yield spread.[2] It was also found that the greater was the rise in yields, particularly in the recent past, the larger was the spread. This influence of the change-in-yield variables is consistent with either the hypothesis concerning underwriters' pricing policies or that concerning market imperfections, or a combination of the two.

According to the former hypothesis, if underwriters anticipate a rise in yields and a fall in bond prices, they will be reluctant to hold new issues for fear of suffering capital losses. In order to assure that new issues would sell quickly, underwriters could be expected to increase their yield, thus increasing the new-seasoned yield spread. If rising yields in the recent past generate a fear on the part of underwriters that yields will continue to rise in the near future, the expectation may cause new-seasoned spreads to increase. This would explain the positive correlation of the change-in-yield variables with the spread. It follows that the explanatory power of the change-in-yield variables might be interpreted as support for the hypothesis that the new issue spread remaining after correction for coupon differences is due to the pricing policies of the underwriters distributing new issues.

[2] See the text, Section IV, for an explanation of our reservations on this finding.

The hypothesis that spreads are the result of market imperfections provides an alternative explanation for the effect of the change-in-yield variables on the yield spread. If forces determining interest rates operate more directly and immediately on yields in the new issue market and if yields in the seasoned market adjust to their equilibrium level only with a lag, rising new issue yields in the past would then lead to an increase in yield spreads because of the failure of yields in the seasoned market to adjust immediately to the new higher levels.

Both of the above hypotheses are supported by other types of evidence. Institutional evidence and the tendency for the yield spread of individual bonds to be eliminated two or three months after they have been issued both support the capital-market imperfections hypothesis. Also, in months when new issue yields fell but remained above outstanding yields, the latter more often than not rose, suggesting a lagged response. Finally, the correlation between changes in seasoned yields in a given month and changes in new issue yields in the previous month was high, while the correlation between changes in new issue yields in a given month and changes in seasoned yields in the previous month was negligible.

On the other hand, there is evidence that underwriters underprice new issues, at least during periods of rising yields. Yields on recent issues often decline after the issues have been released from syndicate even when new issue yields are rising. If new-seasoned yield spreads were due entirely to the lagging of the seasoned market, the yields on actively traded, recent new issues should rise along with the yields on current new issues. Our conclusion, therefore, is that both the hypothesis concerning the pricing policy of underwriters and that concerning market imperfections are important in explaining the new-seasoned yield spread.

Several variables besides coupon difference and past changes in yields were tested in the regression equations. It was hypothesized that because of underwriting risks, the new-seasoned yield spread would increase if there was a larger volume of new issues competing for investment funds. This hypothesis received moderate but not conclusive statistical support when we used the volume of corporate securities issued during the three months preceding the observation of yield spread as the independent variable.

It was also hypothesized that when new issues have been selling slowly, underwriters would guard against a further inventory build-up by bidding lower for new issues to permit their distribution at attractive prices below those on comparable seasoned issues. This would suggest that the new-seasoned yield spread would be positively correlated with the proportion of slow-moving new issues in the recent past. However, no statistical support was found for this hypothesis.

The hypothesis that a tight money market would increase the cost and difficulty of underwriting new issues and, hence, contribute to a new-seasoned yield spread suggested use of the Treasury bill rate as an explanatory variable. Again, this hypothesis received no statistical support.

II. The Yield Spread Between New and Seasoned Corporate Bonds, 1952–63

DESCRIPTION OF THE PROBLEM. Chart 5-1 shows the Moody series for yields on new and seasoned Aa corporate bonds for the period from 1952 through 1963. It is apparent at once that the spread between these series is often substantial. In June 1957 it equaled 90 basis points, which was almost one-fourth of the yield on the seasoned issues. In every month from April 1956 through December 1957, the investor could have obtained a higher yield on new Aa corporates than on seasoned A-rated corporates; his average gain, in addition to securing the higher grade bond, would have been 33.5 basis points. Yet in 1962–63 the average spread for the Moody series was negative, reaching a low of −19 basis points. These dates have obviously been selected to emphasize the extremes to which the spread between new and seasoned issue yields as recorded by Moody's has moved. Yet the spread between new and seasoned yields on Moody's Aa corporates averaged a substantial 16.7 basis points even for the full period from 1952 through 1963, despite periods of negative spread.

The major purpose of this study was to discover and analyze the determinants of this yield spread. We first attempt to discover factors, such as differences between the bonds used in the two series or the existence of uncertainty and risk in the underwriting process, which could explain the existence of the substantial new-seasoned yield spread without implying market imperfections. We then examine the extent to which this spread is due to imperfections or frictions which could restrict the flow of funds to the most profitable channels. A study of the spread between the yields on new and seasoned issues, and particularly changes in the spread, leads inevitably to a consideration of some of the differences between the markets for new and seasoned bonds.

CHART 5-1. Moody New and Seasoned Aa Corporate Bond Yields and Yield Spreads

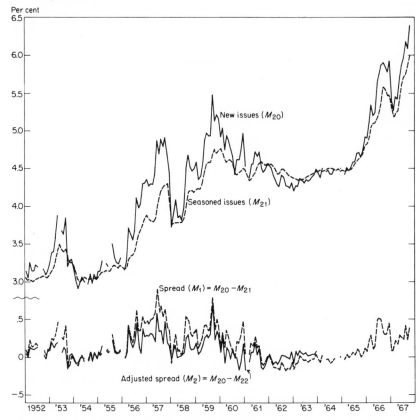

NOTE: M_{22} is yield on seasoned issues with coupon rate equal to that on new issues.

DESCRIPTION OF THE DATA. Most of our work covers the 1952–63 period, although some of the tests use data through 1966. It begins after the 1951 Accord when Federal Reserve support of long-term government bond prices was discontinued. The study uses five different series for the yields on new issues, three series for the yields on seasoned issues, and modifications of two of the seasoned issue series. The yield spreads for which an explanation was sought were measured as the difference between an appropriate combination of one of the new issue and one of the seasoned issue yield series. Our method was primarily multiple regression analysis in which the variable to be explained was the new-seasoned yield spread.

Because the series are quite different in their manner of construction and because each has certain advantages and disadvantages, a description of the data and some of the problems they present is necessary before going on to the statistical tests. The shortcomings of the series stem primarily from a lack of homogeneity in the bonds used to derive the new and seasoned yield averages. As a result, the size and variation in the new-seasoned yield spread between any two of the series may be influenced in part by differences or changes in the bonds represented in the averages. For each new issue series, we describe the seasoned issue series which was used with it to derive the new-seasoned yield spread.

The Appendix explains the symbols used for the variables in the multiple regressions, giving an exact definition of each of the series and listing the data sources. The actual yield series and much of the other data used in the study are shown in the Appendix.

Moody's Aa Corporate Yield Series. Moody's Investors Service has compiled monthly series for the average yields on both new and seasoned bonds by quality rating for the period since January 1951.[3] The averages are based on individual public utility, industrial, and railroad bonds. Convertible bonds, issues with warrants, serial bonds, equipment trust certificates, and the obligations of finance, real estate, steamship, and foreign companies are excluded. The series are broken down by quality rating for bonds rated from Aaa to Baa. This study made use of the Aa series, which has a more uniform quality than the series for bonds with lower ratings and a larger number of new issues than the series for Aaa bonds.

The series for new issues is a monthly average of offering yields, weighted by the size of the issue, and includes all newly issued corporates as described above regardless of size of issue and call price or refunding provisions. The number of new issues included in the Moody average, as in all of the new issue averages, was very small; there are eight months during the 136-month period from 1952 to 1963 when no Aa bonds were issued and twenty-six months when only a single issue was offered.

Moody's series for seasoned Aa corporate yields is normally based on about ten industrials, ten utilities, and a half-dozen rails. Yields are monthly averages of daily quotations obtained from dealers and are

---

[3] Published in *Moody's Bond Survey,* February 9, 1959, and subsequent issues, usually the first weekly edition of each month.

computed on the basis of a price midway between the bid and asked quotations.[4]

Because our study indicated that a large part of the new-seasoned yield spread was caused by differences in the average coupon rate of the bonds in the two yield series, we constructed a special monthly series for the yield of seasoned bonds with coupon rate equal to the average coupon rate of new issues for the month. The new-seasoned yield spread measured as the excess of new issue yields over yields in this series is therefore free of the influence of differences in coupon rate; we refer to it as the new-seasoned yield spread corrected for coupon.

This series was constructed on the basis of the yields on the individual bonds in Moody's series for seasoned Aa corporates. Since there were a number of months in which there were no seasoned bonds in Moody's average with a coupon rate equal to the average on new issues for the month, a linear interpolation or extrapolation of yields at available coupon rates was used. When the procedure required only interpolation between actual observations, it presented no real problem. However, at times when new issue yields were reaching unprecedented peaks and, hence, new issues had very high coupon rates, there were no seasoned bonds with comparable or higher coupon rates, making it necessary to extend the estimates beyond the range of actual observations. Such extrapolation had to be employed in 39 of the 136 months during 1952–63.

Bankers Trust Company Grade 2 Public Utility Yield Series. The Bankers Trust Company compiles a monthly series for new "Grade 2"[5] public utility bonds which differs in several respects from the Moody series. The average is based on the yields at which Grade 2 utility bonds are *successfully placed* (rather than offered) during the month. The series thus tends to be somewhat higher than if it were based solely on offering yields. For an issue to be included at the offering yield, at least 90 per cent of the issue must have been placed at the offering yield in the month in question. Issues which were initially offered in the previous month but which did not sell at that time may be included in the average for the current month. If a syndi-

---

[4] A spot check by Andrew Brimmer covering the 112 issues used in all Moody indexes of seasoned issues in September 1958 indicated average differentials of about 9 basis points between the yields calculated from the bid and asked prices. Andrew F. Brimmer, "Credit Conditions and Price Determination in the Corporate Bond Market," *The Journal of Finance,* September 1960, p. 363.

[5] Grade 2 is approximately equivalent to Moody Aa.

cate terminates before 90 per cent of the issue has been placed, the yield used is calculated from the mean between the bid and asked prices at the time the syndicate terminates. The averages are based on the yields of individual bond issues weighted by the size of the issue.

Some of the circumstances which may cause a modification of this basic approach for the calculation of the averages are: (1) When no Grade 2 issues are offered during the month, an estimate of the yield is made. (2) When there are not enough offerings of Grade 2 bonds over the whole month to reflect a representative cross section of yields, an adjustment in the average yield may be made. (3) When there is a distortion of traditional relations, e.g., Grade 2 yields lower than Grade 1 yields, an adjustment is made. (4) Telephone bonds are included when their yields are at the level of Grade 2 yields, despite the fact that telephone bonds are rated Grade 1.

The seasoned issue series used along with the Bankers Trust new issue series is Moody's Aa public utility series, which is basically the same as the Moody's Aa series described above except that it covers only the ten public utility issues, excluding the industrials and rails.

Kaplan Recently Issued Aa Corporate Yield Series. In contrast to the Moody series which is based on unadjusted offering yields, and the Bankers Trust series which is based on offering yields but with an upward adjustment for issues that do not sell well, the series compiled by Mortimer Kaplan of the Federal Housing Administration [6] is designed to measure market yields to investors on recent issues *after* they have been released from price-maintenance agreements among members of the underwriting syndicate and are actively traded in a free market. Weekly yield series are compiled for each quality rating by averaging the yields to maturity for recently issued corporate bonds (excluding obligations of finance companies and convertible bonds). This is done by using the mean of the bid and asked quotations for each Friday as reported in the *Commercial and Financial Chronicle*. For Aa issues the average number of bonds used was six, each bond was used for an average of eight weeks after being released from syndicate, and the average maturity of the bonds used was thirty years. We converted Kaplan's weekly Aa series into a monthly series by taking an unweighted average of the yields for each Friday in the calendar month.

[6] Mortimer Kaplan, "Yields on Recently Issued Corporate Bonds: A New Index," *The Journal of Finance*, March 1962, pp. 81–109, and supplementary data supplied directly to us.

The seasoned issue yield series used with the Kaplan recent issue series was Moody's series for seasoned Aa corporates, described above.

Homer Aa Public Utility Yield Series. The fourth series used was constructed by Sidney Homer of Salomon Brothers and Hutzler.[7] The yields are Homer's estimates of the going rate for new callable Aa utilities as of the first day of each month. (The other three series discussed above include bonds with call deferments, generally of five years.) The yields are derived, in most cases, directly from the offering yield on the new callable Aa utility issue offered closest to the first of the month; most of the bonds used were issued within a week either way of that date. Where no callable Aa utility issue was offered close enough to the first of the month, the yield is derived by interpolation between the yields of the last bond issued in the previous month and the first bond of the current month, or by an upward adjustment of the yield on an Aaa issue or a bond with a refunding deferment. Some slight upward adjustments in new issue yields were made to correct for issues which did not sell well, on the assumption that their offering yields did not accurately reflect market conditions. This, however, was done only if the issue was not offered within a week of the first of the month.

The seasoned issue series used with the Homer new issue series was based on six to eight callable Aa and Aaa public utility bonds with coupon rates of $2\frac{3}{4}$ and $2\frac{7}{8}$ per cent. Like the new issue series, the seasoned series pertains to the first of the month. The yields were calculated from the asked price listed on the daily dealer quotation sheets of Salomon Brothers and Hutzler and The First Boston Corporation. The series used was constructed by Sidney Homer for 1952 through 1956 and by Frankena for 1957 through 1963.[8]

As in the case of the Moody series, we also constructed a monthly series covering Aaa and Aa callable seasoned public utility bonds with coupon rate equal to that on new issues. This series was designed to be used with the Homer new issue series in order to derive a second measure of the new-seasoned yield spread, one which was free of the influence of differences in coupon rates between the two series. The series for 1952–56 was constructed by Homer and ourselves while the

---

[7] "An Analytic Record of Yields and Yield Spreads," available from Salomon Brothers and Hutzler, Wall Street, New York.

[8] Homer's series is in "An Analytic Record of Yields and Yield Spreads," *ibid.*, and Frankena's is in his paper "The Influence of Call Provisions and Coupon Rate on the Yields of Corporate Bonds," NBER, (forthcoming).

series for 1957–63 was prepared by Frankena.[9] As in the case of the Moody series, a linear interpolation and extrapolation was used when there was no observation for a seasoned bond with a coupon rate equal to that on new issues. However, such interpolation and extrapolation was required less frequently in the case of the Homer-Frankena series because the combined number of bonds used in their series for seasoned yields was larger and covered a wider range of coupon rates than was the case for the Moody series for seasoned Aa corporates.[10]

Cohan Aa Utility Thirty-Year Mortgage Bonds. The fifth new issue series used was a quarterly series constructed by Avery B. Cohan.[11] After running multiple regressions for a series of cross sections during the period from 1935 through 1958, Cohan concluded that five variables in addition to the date of offering significantly affected new issue yields: quality rating, industrial classification, maturity, type of bond, and type of transaction with the underwriter. Holding all five of these variables constant, Cohan constructed quarterly series by quality rating covering new public utility thirty-year mortgage bonds bought by underwriters in competitive bidding.

The Cohan series was not used in the multiple regressions but was compared to other new issue series which do not hold the above five factors constant.

BOND CHARACTERISTICS WHICH INFLUENCE YIELDS. For a number of reasons each of the series discussed above may misstate the "true" new-seasoned yield spread, i.e., the spread between bonds which are identical except for the length of time they have been outstanding. In part this is unavoidable because the number of new corporate issues each month is too small to permit the construction of a monthly series for new issues which is homogeneous from month to month or identical to seasoned issues in all important respects.

Other studies have indicated that certain characteristics of bonds may have a significant influence on yields, at least in some periods. Those are chiefly quality-rating, industrial classification, term to maturity, type of bond (mortgage bond, debenture, collateral trust

---

[9] *Ibid.*

[10] There were eighteen months when extrapolation was used in the Homer-Frankena series and thirty-nine in the Moody series.

[11] Avery B. Cohan, "Yields on New Underwritten Corporate Bonds, 1935–1958," *The Journal of Finance,* December 1962, p. 585 *ff.,* and supplementary data supplied directly to us.

Essays on Interest Rates

bond, etc.), type of transaction with underwriter (whether the sale of an issue was negotiated between underwriters and the issuer or was by public sealed bidding), period of refunding deferment, coupon rate, call price, size of issue, and sinking fund provision.

Not all of these characteristics could be held constant in this study at the same time. Consequently, some of the average spread could be due to systematic differences between the bonds used in the new and seasoned issue series, and some of the variability in the size of the spread could be due to random changes in the characteristics of the bonds used. However, by using four different series and modifications of two of them, the most important of these characteristics could be held constant for one or another of the series. Table 5-1 provides a summary of the yield-determining characteristics which are held strictly constant in each of the five new issue series used.

TABLE 5-1. Yield-Determining Characteristics Held Constant in the New Issue Series

Yield-Determining Characteristic	Moody (1)	Bankers Trust (2)	Kaplan (3)	Homer (4)	Cohan (5)
Quality rating	X	X	X	X	X
Industrial classification		X		X	X
Term to maturity					X
Type of bond					X
Type of transaction with the underwriter					X
Callability				X	
Coupon rate					
Call price					
Size of issue					
Sinking fund provision					

The same characteristics are held constant in the seasoned series corresponding to the first four new issue series, except that the type of transaction with the underwriter is not relevant and quality is not held strictly constant in the Homer-Frankena series, which includes Aa and Aaa rated bonds. The characteristics checked in Table 5-1 are thus not responsible for any of the new-seasoned yield spread, except possibly for some spread caused by quality-rating differences in the Homer-

Frankena series. In addition, for the modified Moody and Homer-Frankena series, the effect of the coupon rate on the spread is eliminated because the new issue and seasoned issue series carry the same coupon rate.

Quality rating was held constant in all series except the one for seasoned yields constructed by Homer and Frankena, where Aaa rated bonds were used along with Aa rated bonds. There was generally no very noticeable yield difference between callable Aa's and Aaa's with the same coupon rate. Also, telephone bonds were rated Aa until the late 1950's, when they were raised to Aaa.[12]

Industrial classification was not held constant by the Moody or Kaplan series, which include industrials, utilities, and rails, but it was by the Bankers Trust and Homer series, which used only public utilities.

Maturity was held strictly constant only in the Cohan series, but the bonds covered by all the series were relatively long-term. In Moody's seasoned series maturity was held within the range of twenty-five to twenty-nine years during the 1950's (the range during 1960–63 was not examined). In the Homer-Frankena seasoned series, maturities declined steadily from 1952 to 1963; the lack, in this period, of new bonds having coupons of $2\frac{3}{4}$–$2\frac{7}{8}$ per cent prevented the replacement of older bonds in the average with newer ones having longer maturities. By 1963, some of the bonds in this average had a maturity of only sixteen years. In the Homer-Frankena "current coupon rate" series maturity could be held roughly constant on seasoned bonds because more recently issued bonds were available to replace the older ones. Average maturity varied much more within all the new issue series, except Cohan's, than it did in the seasoned series because of the smaller number of bonds in the new issue series. For the Kaplan series average maturity varied between about twenty-five and thirty-seven years during the period from 1951 to 1960.

There is a fairly systematic tendency for the new issue series to have a longer average maturity than the seasoned issue series. The difference, however, is generally not more than a few years, and the relevant sector of the yield curve is typically fairly flat.[13] There is no reason

[12] It should be noted that part of the yield spread between the Moody series with different quality ratings was probably due to differences in the average refunding deferment on new issues and to differences in the average coupon rate on seasoned issues in the series; the lower quality series have a lower proportion of deferments and higher average coupon rates, which raise their yields.

[13] It should be noted that at least part of the observed slope of the corporate yield curve is due to systematic differences in the coupon rate of bonds of different maturities.

to believe that it plays any significant role in the new-seasoned yield spread.

In order to get a rough idea of how the new issue yield series is affected by the failure to hold constant industrial classification, term to maturity, type of bond, and type of transaction with the underwriter, we compared the Cohan series (which holds these four variables constant) with three other new issue Aa series which do not hold all of them constant. The other series were Moody's new issue public utility series, Moody's new issue corporate series, and Bankers Trust new issue utility series. Since the Cohan series is quarterly, we used quarterly averages for the other series. Table 5-2 presents the four quarterly series and the average difference between the Cohan series and the others. In only two quarters was the difference larger than 8 basis points. In the other quarters the differences were of the same order of magnitude as the differences between the Bankers Trust and Moody's corporate series, shown in the last column. It was concluded that variability in term to maturity, type of bond, and type of transaction did not systematically distort the new-seasoned yield spread in any serious way.

Some work by Frankena indicates that call protection in the form of refunding deferments significantly reduces yields on high coupon bonds. The reason is that such protection makes the bonds more attractive to investors.[14] Since low coupon bonds are unlikely to be called in any case, call restrictions do not influence low-coupon bond yields to the same degree. The Homer new issue series and the Homer-Frankena seasoned issue series exclude bonds with call deferments. For new issues included in the other three series, call deferments were more common and covered a longer period than in the seasoned issue series to which they were compared, thus reducing the new-seasoned yield spread. Call deferments came into common use only after 1957, however; by and large, it was only in 1959–61 that new issue coupons were high enough for the market to place any appreciable value on such protection. Our estimate is that in late 1959–61 the new issue series and hence the new-seasoned spreads (apart from Homer's) averaged about 5 basis points below what they would have been if only callable issues had been used.[15]

One of the findings of this study and an independent study by Wil-

---

[14] Frankena study.

[15] Frankena's study indicates that refunding deferments reduced yields on new issues by roughly 15 basis points relative to yields on comparable freely callable issues in this period and that about one-third of new issues had such call protection.

TABLE 5-2. Comparison of the Cohan Series With Three Other New Issue Yield Series

Quarter		Cohan Series	Moody Utility	Moody Corporate	Bankers Trust	Mean Differential Between Cohan Series and Other Series		Bankers Trust Less Moody Corporate
						Algebraic	Absolute	
1952	I	3.22		3.15	3.28	.5	6.5	13.0
	II	3.17		3.17	3.19	−1.0	1.0	2.0
	III	3.18		3.19	3.25	−4.0	4.0	6.0
	IV	3.13		3.13	3.22	−4.5	4.5	9.0
1953	I	3.35		3.34	3.34	1.0	1.0	0
	II	3.69		3.74	3.79	−7.5	7.5	5.0
	III	3.68		3.72	3.67	−1.5	2.5	−5.0
	IV	3.33		3.26	3.35	2.5	4.5	9.0
1954	I	3.06		3.04	3.09	−.5	2.5	5.0
	II	3.02		3.02	3.03	−.5	.5	1.0
	III	3.02		3.04	3.06	−3.0	3.0	2.0
	IV	3.03		3.03	3.05	−1.0	1.0	2.0
1955	I	3.15		3.19	3.19	−4.0	4.0	0
	II	3.23		3.22	3.24	.0	1.0	2.0
	III	3.32		3.41	3.37	−7.0	7.0	−4.0
	IV	3.30		3.27	3.30	1.5	1.5	3.0
1956	I	3.24	3.20	3.21	3.28	1.0	3.7	7.0
	II	3.58	3.63	3.63	3.60	−4.0	4.0	−3.0
	III	3.96	4.01	3.93	4.00	−2.0	4.0	7.0
	IV	4.25	4.25	4.21	4.27	.7	2.0	6.0
1957	I	4.37	4.36	4.31	4.36	2.7	2.7	5.0
	II	4.58	4.53	4.53	4.67	.3	6.3	14.0
	III	4.79	4.82	4.79	4.87	−3.7	3.7	8.0
	IV	4.72	4.71	4.68	4.73	1.3	2.0	5.0
1958	I	3.96	3.91	3.91	3.91	5.0	5.0	0
	II	3.87	3.86	3.85	3.93	−1.0	3.0	8.0
	III	4.18	4.29	4.39	4.40	−17.7	17.7	1.0
	IV	4.47	4.50	4.50	4.54	−4.3	4.3	4.0
1959	I	4.49	4.46	4.45	4.54	.7	4.0	9.0
	II	4.85	4.87	4.82	4.86	.0	2.0	4.0
	III	4.86	5.11	5.11	5.07	−23.7	23.7	−4.0
	IV	5.15	5.16	5.16	5.24	−3.7	3.7	8.0
1960	I	4.90	4.90	4.90	5.01	−3.7	3.7	11.0
	II	4.85	4.86	4.86	4.88	−1.7	1.7	2.0
	III	4.60	4.55	4.56	4.61	2.7	3.3	5.0
	IV	4.80	4.80	4.78	4.80	.7	.7	2.0

liam H. White [16] is that differences in coupon rate are responsible for a large part of the new-seasoned yield spread as measured by series like Moody's. This study takes account of coupon rate differences in two ways. First, the difference in average coupon rate between the new issue and seasoned issue series is used as an independent variable in explaining the new-seasoned yield spread. Second, as explained above, two additional seasoned issue series were constructed having the same coupon rate as those on the Moody and the Homer new issue series. The influence of the coupon rate on yield spreads is examined further in Section III.

Call price was not held constant in any of the series nor was it used as a variable in the multiple regressions. In general, new issues probably have more call protection in the form of higher call prices (although not in the form of coupon rates) than do seasoned issues, and, on this count, the new issues would tend to have lower yields. However, part of the impact of the call price on yields will be picked up by the coupon rate, which is positively correlated with the call price. This implies, of course, that the effect of the coupon rate on yields is underestimated when call price is not taken into account.

The size of the issue was not held constant in any of the series. However, all the series were dominated by issues with a principal of over $10 million, and we would not expect size variation to have any effect on yield.[17]

Some of the series, particularly those with industrials, include bonds with sinking funds. Sidney Homer informs us that if sinking funds accumulate more than 2–3 per cent of the issue per year, there will be a significant reduction in yield to maturity. This is due to the commitment of the borrowing company to repurchase a certain amount of the issue each year, which constitutes an additional source of demand for these bonds. Company treasurers may be most active in purchasing sinking fund issues when they can be obtained at bargain prices; and, in a thin market like that for seasoned corporate bonds, the result would be to reduce the yields on sinking fund issues. According to Homer, yield reductions of 10 to 50 basis points are not uncommon.

Two tests of this hypothesis failed to reveal any appreciable effect

[16] William H. White, "The Structure of the Bond Market and the Cyclical Variability of Interest Rates," *Staff Papers*, International Monetary Fund, March 1962.

[17] Avery Cohan found no statistically significant effect of size of issue on yield in the case of corporate bonds. Richard West concluded that "issue size has little, if any, influence on yield spreads" in the case of state and local government general obligation bonds. Richard West, "New Issue Concessions on Municipal Bonds: A Case of Monopsony Pricing," *The Journal of Business*, April 1965, p. 143.

of sinking funds on yields, but neither test was very powerful. Conard classified the bonds in the Moody Aa seasoned corporate series by industrial classification and coupon group, comparing the yields on sinking fund issues with other yields in each group, monthly from 1951 through 1961. There were no consistent differences in yield, but the number of observations was very small, and no distinction was made concerning the size of the sinking fund. The second test was by Avery Cohan.[18] Cohan's multiple regression analysis revealed sinking fund provisions to be a statistically significant influence on new issue yields in only one year (1943) between 1935 and 1958 — even then significant only at the 10 per cent level. However, this negative finding could be explained largely by the fact that the period he examined was primarily one of low interest rates, while the hypothesis suggests that sinking funds would have their greatest effect on yields when interest rates were high.

Because sizable sinking funds are common in industrials but rare in utilities, they may provide a source of heterogeneity in the Moody and Kaplan series but not in the Bankers Trust or Homer series.

In summary, a great many factors may influence corporate bond yields. Some of these factors, such as quality rating or industrial classification, are held constant in one or another of the statistical series used. Other factors (such as, maturity, size of issue, or sinking funds) are not held constant in the series but evidence of various types suggested that they were neither an important nor systematic influence on the yield spread. One factor, the coupon rate, is responsible for a large part of the yield spread and is treated explicitly in the analysis.

We ran a statistical test in Section IV to assure ourselves that the differences in the bonds included in the new issue and seasoned averages, which we dismissed as unimportant, were not — even in combination — responsible for any appreciable part of the yield spread remaining after taking account of coupon rate. The spread for individual new issues was recalculated one month after the offering, two months after, and so on. If the yield spread at the time of offering is due to differences in the yield-determining characteristics of the new and seasoned bonds, the spread should persist after the issue becomes seasoned. In fact, the differential tends to decline after the issue has been released from syndicate and is eliminated entirely in two or three months.

PROBLEMS IN THE CORRECT MEASUREMENT OF THE YIELD SPREAD. One problem involved in measuring the yield spread is that some new issues

[18] Cohan, *ibid.*

Essays on Interest Rates

are mispriced; for that reason their offering yields may not accurately reflect new issue yields. In order to estimate the significance of this problem, a series was constructed for "fast-moving" utility issues only. Fast-moving utility issues are defined as those no longer in syndicate on the first Monday after the date of their issue. In one test a regression was run between new-seasoned spreads and the level of yields, covering the period from 1951 to 1960, first using fast-moving utilities, then all utilities, for the measure of new issue yields. In a second test the correlation was between new-seasoned spreads and changes in the level of seasoned rates. Results are shown in the following table:

	Correlation Between Yield Spread and	
	Level of Yields	Change in Yields
Fast-moving securities	.597	.457
All securities	.526	.374

The fact that the correlation is improved in both cases when only fast-moving issues are used suggests, although it does not prove conclusively, that these issues may provide a better measure of new issue rates and permit the variables used in the regressions to explain more of the variance in new-seasoned spreads. This would not apply to the Bankers Trust and Kaplan series, however, since they are based on the market yields of the issues sold rather than the offering yields.

A second problem arises when measuring the yield spread of the Moody's series. Seasoned bonds in this series are calculated from a price midway between the bid and asked prices, whereas the Moody's and Bankers Trust new issue series which are used with the Moody's seasoned series are based on the asked price. This causes a downward bias in the spreads calculated from the Moody's and Bankers Trust new issue series. No such bias exists in the spread calculated from the Homer new issue series, since the seasoned series used with it is also on an asked price basis. Similarly the spread calculated from the Kaplan new issue series is not biased because both this series and the Moody's seasoned series used with it are calculated from the midpoint of bid and ask prices.

Brimmer found that in September 1958 the average difference between the yields calculated from the bid and asked prices for the bonds used in Moody's seasoned issue yield series was about 9 basis points. If this is typical it means that the bias in the spread calculated from

Moody's and Bankers Trust new issue series is about $4\frac{1}{2}$ basis points. We found that the bid-asked spreads between 1957 and 1964 on the daily public utility quotation sheets of Salomon Brothers and Hutzler and The First Boston Corporation were generally between $\frac{1}{2}$ and 2 points, which implied yield spreads of about 3 to 13 basis points and a bias of $1\frac{1}{2}$ to $6\frac{1}{2}$ basis points. Typical spreads differed between dealers and changed somewhat over time.[19] As we shall note below, however, there was no tendency for the bid-asked spread to change systematically with the direction of change of new issue yields.

A third measurement problem is that the offering yield on new issues may not fully reflect market conditions if changes occur in the underwriting spread, i.e., the difference between the new issue yield calculated from the price paid by the underwriter and the yield calculated from the offering price. A study of the behavior of the new-seasoned spread including the underwriting spread (M_4) suggested that this was not the case. We constructed a monthly series for the average underwriting spread on Aa corporate bonds, with spreads weighted by the size of the issue. The simple correlation between the underwriting spread and the new-seasoned spread was only .223. More important, the underwriting spread was small and relatively stable, averaging 4.4 basis points for the period from 1952 through 1963 with a standard deviation of only 1.4 basis points. Much of the variation was due to the fact that industrial bonds generally had a larger underwriting spread than did utilities and the proportion of industrial bonds varied between months.

A final measurement problem is that the prices on dealer quotation sheets for seasoned bonds may not reflect the current market if the bond is inactive. Thus, Sidney Homer notes that "the quotes on the great mass of seasoned issues are in their nature very different from the quotes on recent issues and revisions for seasoned issues are made more rarely."[20] Similarly, in the case of the bid-asked spread, "there is a good deal of difference between the actual bid-asked spread in the market for active utility bonds and the spread on most quotation sheets. Traders often make eighth and quarter point markets in active issues but quote them much wider on their sheets."[21] This can be viewed as a measurement problem or as an aspect of market behavior. It is discussed in the latter context in the next section.

---

[19] Spreads in the late 1950's were typically larger than those in the early 1960's, with few spreads being over 1 point in the period 1963–64.

[20] Sidney Homer, Letter to Mark W. Frankena, July 20, 1965.

[21] Sidney Homer, Letter to Mark W. Frankena, July 25, 1966.

III. Determinants of the New-Seasoned Yield Spread

HYPOTHESES. *Heterogeneity of Bonds: Differences in the Coupon Rate.* The only bond characteristic which is a consistently important cause of yield spreads between new and seasoned issues is the coupon rate.[22] During a period of generally rising rates, new issues will carry higher coupon rates than outstanding ones and issues with higher coupon rates carry higher yields. This is mainly because bonds with high coupon rates are more likely to be called for refunding at times of low new issue yields, and holders would have to reinvest at lower yields. Also, capital gains on high coupon bonds would be more limited in the event of a decline in yields.[23]

A borrowing company is normally able to call its bonds prior to maturity at a premium of a few points above par. Borrowers generally exercise this option at times of low new issue yields, when they can refund at a lower interest cost. Given the level of new issue yields, the primary determinants of the profitability of calling an outstanding issue are its call price and its coupon rate. The higher the coupon rate the greater is the current interest cost of the issue and the more profitable it would be to refund it at any given call price. The higher the call price the higher is the cost of call to the borrower and the less profitable refunding would be. In practice, when coupon rates on new issues increase, call prices are not increased enough to offset the greater profitability of calling the higher coupon issues. As a result, high coupon issues are more likely to be called than low coupon issues. The calling of high coupon bonds at a time of low new issue yields means a loss for the investing institution holding the bonds if it would otherwise have held them to maturity. This is because the funds repaid can be reinvested only at a lower yield, and reinvestment involves transaction costs.

High coupon bonds are also less advantageous to the investor because such bonds are less likely to generate capital gains when inter-

---

[22] However, because of the small number of new issues each month, other differences between the bonds in the series are no doubt the source of random fluctuations in the spread. Thus, it appears that the heterogeneity of bonds may explain some of the negative spreads remaining after the adjustment of the Moody series for differences in coupon rate; negative spreads are less common for the more homogeneous Homer series.

[23] The effect of the coupon rate on bond yields is the subject of a separate study by Frankena and the discussion here is based largely on that work. See Frankena's work. See Joseph W. Conard, *The Behavior of Interest Rates: A Progress Report,* New York, NBER, 1966, pp. 120–130, for a preliminary summary.

est rates fall. The market price of a bond cannot rise appreciably above the call price owing to the danger of call. As noted, the call prices on very high coupon bonds are at most only a few points higher than those on low coupon bonds. Because high coupon bonds must sell at a higher price than low coupon bonds in order to bear the same yield to maturity, the prices on the former are the first to reach the call price when market yields fall. As a result, capital gains on high coupon bonds are limited by their call price to a greater extent than are capital gains on low coupon bonds; for this reason the higher coupon bonds are less desirable. Yield differences resulting from differences in coupon rates are greatest when market yields are low, since in such circumstances the call price exercises the greatest constraint on the price of high coupon bonds. However, there is a very strong positive correlation between yields and coupon rates on individual bonds at all yield levels.

The influence of coupon rates on yields will give rise to a systematic positive new-seasoned yield spread when market yields are rising over an extended period and a negative spread when yields are falling. In times of high or rising new issue yields as in the late 1950's, seasoned bonds, issued in earlier years when new issue yields were lower, typically carry lower coupons than new issues, because of the practice of setting the coupon rate on new issues at a level approximately equal to their offering yields so that the bonds will sell near par. For this reason, the danger of call and the limitations on capital gains will be less on seasoned (i.e., low coupon) than on new (i.e., high coupon) issues, and the former will carry lower yields.[24] This is one reason the new-seasoned spreads in Charts 5-1 and 5-2 are greatest when new issue yields are high and rising.

Underwriting Risks. Another possible source of new-seasoned yield spreads is uncertainty and risk in the underwriting process. As with differences in coupon rates, this source of yield spread does not imply imperfections in the capital market. If underwriting syndicates offered new issues at yields exactly equal to those on comparable seasoned issues, there might be a lengthy period of distribution which would involve a high probability of capital loss or gain due to shifts in market conditions during the distribution period. Because they operate with a fairly thin capital position, underwriters' attitudes toward such gains and losses may be asymmetrical in the sense that they avoid exposing themselves to a risk of loss even though it is counterbalanced by an equal probability of gain. Furthermore, since their capital is limited, a

---

[24] White also reached this conclusion in his study, p. 126 *ff*.

CHART 5-2. Homer New Issue Aa and Homer-Frankena Seasoned Issue Aa-Aaa Utility Bond Yields and Yield Spreads

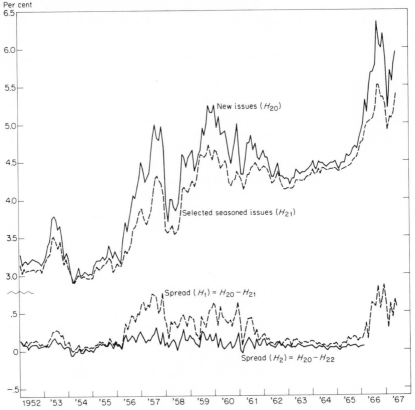

NOTE: H_{21} is yield on seasoned issues with coupon rate of $2\frac{3}{4}$–$2\frac{7}{8}$ per cent. H_{22} is yield on issues with coupon rate equal to that on new issues.

long distribution period reduces the number of issues they can underwrite. As a consequence, underwriters may bid low for new issues and, to assure rapid distribution, set yields higher than those on comparable seasoned issues.

This tendency to set relatively high yields on new issues might be accentuated if underwriters foresaw difficulties in distributing new issues, for example, if yields were expected to rise in the near future, or if the total volume of new issues to be marketed in the period were abnormally large, or if recent new issues had been selling slowly.

Other studies have indicated that expectations of yield change are based on an extrapolation of yield changes in the recent past.[25] This can be rationalized on the grounds that there is a strong cyclical pattern in interest rate series, which are based on business conditions and monetary and fiscal policy decisions, which are themselves related to business conditions. There is, of course, an opposite tendency, basic to the Keynesian "speculative motive" for holding cash balances: When yields have been rising for some time they may be viewed as high relative to some "normal" interest rate, and the market may therefore expect yields to fall back toward normal. However, the two forces are not mutually exclusive, since when yields are rising one may expect them to keep rising in the immediate future despite the expectation that over some longer period they will return to the "normal" level.[26]

In response to our inquiry on the tendency of underwriters to extrapolate recent yield charges, Sidney Homer writes that "there is no question that in bear bond markets underwriters are timid, bid low, and aim at immediate resale, whereas in rising markets or complacent markets (protracted stability) they bid high and are content with slow sale. This is why the spreads of the seasoned market narrow in good markets, widen in weak markets. It has indeed been occasionally true that new issue bids are dropped 2 to 4 points when dealers fear a further decline in the market. . . . Protracted discouragement is evident in the wide spreads of November 1957 and October 1959."[27]

The volume of new issues might also influence the bidding and pricing policies of underwriters. When the volume of new offerings rises, the market may become congested. The difficulty of selling new issues and the competition for buyers may force sellers to provide increasing yield advantages on new over seasoned issues.

Similarly, the speed with which recent new issues were sold might influence bidding and pricing by underwriters. If recent new issues have been moving very slowly and inventories are building up, underwriters might bid lower for additional issues and offer them at more attractive yields. However, we would expect both new issue volume and the rapidity with which recent issues have sold to be correlated with yield changes, so it is not altogether clear that either factor would

---

[25] See David Meiselman, *The Term Structure of Interest Rates,* Englewood, N.J., 1962, p. 18 and footnote.

[26] See Franco Modigliani and Richard Sutch, "Innovations in Interest Rate Policy," *American Economic Review, Papers and Proceedings,* May 1966, pp. 178–197, for a model which combines the extrapolative and regressive expectations hypotheses.

[27] Homer, July 20, 1965 Letter.

provide additional information after yield changes are taken into account.

Underwriters could also be influenced by the interest rates they pay on funds borrowed to carry new issues. Reliance on bank credit to finance bond inventories makes it more expensive and difficult in a tight money market for dealers to obtain funds for the purchase and distribution of newly issued securities. This might increase the pressure on underwriters to distribute new issues as rapidly as possible by pricing them attractively. Tightness in the money market might be measured by the level of short-term rates, the level of free reserves, or by the yield spread between long-term and short-term securities. The spread would be a rough measure of the cost to underwriters of carrying their inventories.[28]

One aspect of underwriting risks has not been considered thus far. Clearly underwriting risks are greatest on new issues, where the size of the inventories held is very large. But dealers who trade in seasoned bonds also assume a risk by holding an inventory and, by analogy to the argument concerning underwriting risks on new issues, might adjust the bid-asked price difference on seasoned bonds in response to the same factors which would make underwriters adjust their bids and offering prices on new issues.

Three spot checks were made to test the possibility that bid-asked spreads on seasoned bonds may be increased in periods of rising yields. Each check was a comparison of the bid-asked price spreads for all bonds common to the quotation sheets of a dealer on two different dates. One date in each comparison was in a period of rising yields and the other was in a period of falling yields.[29] We compared the bid-asked spreads on the quotation sheets of Salomon Brothers and Hutzler for August 1, 1957, a trading day in a period of rising yields, and January 2, 1958, a day in a period of falling yields. Out of 114 bonds common to the two sheets, 38 showed no change in bid-asked spread, 59 showed increases, and 17 showed decreases. The aggregate net change in the bid-asked spreads for all bonds taken together was an increase of $22\frac{1}{8}$ points — the equivalent of about 1 basis point in the average spread over the 114 issues.

Similarly, we compared the spreads on January 2, 1958, a day in a

---

[28] The cost is given by holding period yields, which equal yields to maturity only if interest rates do not change.

[29] The days chosen for this test were within broad cyclical phases of rise and decline in yields, and in each case were preceded by at least four consecutive weeks of rise or decline in weekly averages.

period of falling yields, and September 2, 1958, a day in a period of rising yields. Out of ninety-three bonds common to the two sheets, thirty-five showed no change in bid-asked spread, thirty-four showed increases, and twenty-four showed decreases. The aggregate net change in the bid-asked spreads was an increase of $4\frac{5}{8}$ points, the equivalent of less than 1 basis point in average spread.

Finally, we compared the bid-asked spreads on the quotation sheets of The First Boston Corporation for October 1, 1959, a day in a period of rising yields, and April 4, 1960, a day in a period of falling yields. Out of ninety-eight bonds common to the two sheets, forty showed no change in the size of the bid-asked spread, twenty-one showed increases, and thirty-seven showed decreases. The aggregate net change in the bid-asked spreads was a decrease of $11\frac{1}{8}$ points, again the equivalent of less than 1 basis point.

These spot checks show that bid-asked spreads do change, but the change is not related to the direction of change of yields, and the quantitative importance of the changes over any large sample of outstanding issues is very small. It appears that factors affecting underwriting risk would have a very small effect on the bid-ask spread on outstanding issues.

Imperfections in the Capital Markets: Lags in the Movement of Seasoned Yields. Finally, there are explanations for new-seasoned yield spreads which imply imperfections in the capital markets. As shall be noted later, spreads on individual new issues decline over a period of two or three months following the release of the issues from the syndicate. Neither of the two yield-spread hypotheses advanced above explains this finding. If yield spreads were based entirely on differences in the yield-determining characteristics of the bonds included in the averages, the spread on individual issues would have little tendency to decline after release from the syndicate. If yield spreads were based entirely on underwriting risk, on the other hand, market forces might be expected to eliminate yield spreads on individual issues in days instead of months.

For example, suppose a large volume of new issues forces new issue bond prices down and yields up. Why shouldn't holders of seasoned bonds immediately sell their holdings and shift into the more attractive new bonds, thereby reducing the price and increasing the yield on seasoned bonds? If holders of seasoned bonds are not fully aware of the current developments in the new issue market (which seems unlikely) or are not willing to take action, why do no arbitrageurs enter the market for new issues and immediately equalize rates on similar new and seasoned bonds? Evidently actions of these kinds do not occur, at least not on the scale necessary to eliminate yield differentials quickly. Finally, why would any investor acquire seasoned issues at yields which are less attractive than those currently available on new issues?

Holders of seasoned bonds may not switch into new issues with slightly higher yields because of the transaction costs involved in such an operation (e.g., the dealer's commission represented by the bid-asked spread); such behavior would not imply market imperfections.[30] It is clear, however, that transaction costs do not provide a full explanation of the failure of arbitrageurs to equalize new and seasoned yields, since new-seasoned spreads for bonds with the same coupon rate are often considerably greater than recorded bid-asked spreads. Many of the other explanations for the failure to make portfolio changes can be regarded as forms of market imperfection.

Another reason holders of seasoned bonds may not switch into new issues is simply that they are not in the business of day-to-day speculation. Institutions such as life insurance companies and pension funds invest for income and usually hold to maturity. Homer writes that "the giant funds, with a few exceptions, have felt themselves to be largely frozen into their bond portfolios. They consider that their investment activity must be confined largely to the investment of their huge annual flow of new money. This problem is so stupendous that there is little room left for portfolio changes. Perhaps many smaller funds have sacrificed the advantages given them by their smaller size and have followed a similar policy of ignoring desirable portfolio changes."[31]

Because bonds are carried and amortized on the basis of cost, investors may be discouraged from a profitable switch by the reluctance to acknowledge capital losses (the "locked-in" effect). Homer writes that "one of the most powerful forces preventing arbitrage is the fact that almost all institutions carry bonds at amortized cost and, when prices are low, they would realize an enormous loss by selling. My observation is that only a tiny percentage are willing to realize these

---

[30] As mentioned before, Brimmer found that in September 1958 the average differential between the yields calculated from the bid and asked prices for the bonds used in Moody's seasoned issue yield series was about 9 basis points, and our examination of the public utility quotation sheets of Salomon Brothers and Hutzler and The First Boston Corporation for the period 1957–64 indicates bid-asked yield differentials of about 3 to 13 basis points on individual long-term seasoned bonds.

[31] Sidney Homer, "A Dynamic Approach to Institutional Bond Investment," Salomon Brothers and Hutzler, New York, 1961, pp. 16–17.

losses. If they did it in a substantial way, capital would be entirely wiped out for many." [32]

Another limitation on switching is that institutional investors often work under restrictions such as requirements for committee authorization and a variety of inflexible conventions and procedures.

Investors may acquire seasoned issues at yields below those on new issues because of features of specific issues. All Aas are not perfect substitutes in the eyes of individual buyers. Either diversification or concentration may be sought, and these objectives may not be satisfied by the relatively few new issues available. Homer says that "a few institutions would even buy the higher priced issue just to round out their previous holding or because they had a committee authority in the old issue and not in the new," [33] or we may add in order to average down the cost of an issue being held. Certain buyers, including those buying for pension funds, show a preference for seasoned issues which have been tested by the market as opposed to apparently comparable new issues. The difference in the size of the transactions involved in the new and seasoned market no doubt plays a role as well.

The market for seasoned bonds, furthermore, may be so thin that the attempt to sell any sizable amount would immediately wipe out the yield differential by driving down prices of seasoned issues. Homer writes that "the secondary market for most corporate bonds is not good enough to permit the portfolio manager to make every block transaction (at the quoted price) that may appeal to him. My experience is that about three-fourths of the desired switches can be made at fair prices in a portfolio when the unit of holding is 50 bonds, about half when the unit is 100–200 bonds, and a third when the unit is 500–1000 bonds. . . . For funds with blocks of \$2–\$10 million, the market is rarely good enough to permit switches." [34] Hence, after deducting transaction costs, the gain from arbitrage might be too small to warrant the effort.

Buyers, it has been noted, may purchase seasoned bonds at yields below those available on new issues because of a preference for specific issues. At the same time, many quotations on seasoned issues may be nominal in the sense that no transactions actually occur at the quoted rates. Indeed, particularly for inactive securities, yields on dealer quotation sheets may not be revised rapidly enough to reflect the

---

[32] Sidney Homer, Letter to Mark W. Frankena, November 8, 1967.
[33] Homer, July 20, 1965 Letter.
[34] "A Dynamic Approach to Institutional Bond Investment," p. 16.

yields at which transactions would actually take place if they were made. It might be that quotations based on actual transactions in sizable amounts would not show such large spreads. Homer states:

Recent issues, if sizable, enjoy a very active market from the moment the syndicate price restrictions are removed; the turnover is sometimes enormous, especially if there is a market decline. Many temporary holders get in and out; markets are usually quoted at $\frac{1}{8}$ point spreads and are good for many million bonds either way. Furthermore, many dealers in the Street participate in these large recent issues and many speculators buy them for small near-term gains. During the first two or three hours after the syndicate price restrictions are removed, a large part of the total trading has usually been done. Thereafter, the volume will taper off sharply; but for a period up to, say, three months it will continue far larger than for seasoned issues. Around that point trading activity will die out, and the issue will take its place as just one more seasoned utility. Most Street traders will forget, most speculators will be out, and only a few people will remember that it exists. It follows that true dealer markets for recent substantial issues are much more active, and the quotes are much more sensitive and narrow, than for seasoned issues. Quotes on seasoned issues tend to lag quotes on recent issues, where all the business is being done. In other words, the traders will always be changing around the quotes on active issues, while they will sometimes delay for a few days changing their largely theoretical quotes on seasoned issues. I say "theoretical" only because they are not doing very much business in them and are estimating their quotes, in the absence of real buyers, from the yield book just so the yield will line up with that of other similar issues. Therefore, the quotes on the great mass of seasoned issues are in their nature very different from the quotes on recent issues and revisions for seasoned issues are made more rarely.[35]

Richard West has concluded that in the case of state and local government bonds quite a different type of market imperfection — namely, monopsony in the underwriting and distribution of securities —

---

[35] Homer, July 20, 1965 Letter. This conclusion should be compared with that of White who writes that "the available evidence shows an adequately large volume of transactions in seasoned bonds by professional investors (such as pension funds and the smaller life insurance companies for whom the market's size is adequate) so that the prices of many of the larger issues of seasoned bonds can be assumed to reflect fully the conditions on the broader, new issue market. And accurate, reliable prices of seasoned bonds could emerge even if only a very minor fraction of the outstanding amount were sold during a given year. This is made plausible (although not a certainty) by the homogeneity of the various bond issues and of investors' interest in them; these homogeneities should make most holders unwilling to make transactions at the market's equilibrium price but to make very large transactions at prices that diverge appreciably from that equilibrium." William H. White, pp. 136–137.

is responsible for part of the spread between new and seasoned yields. He argues that when only one underwriting bid is made for an issue the underwriting syndicate can buy a bond at a price below the competitive level. However, to maintain its monopsony status, the bidding syndicate must share its extra-normal returns with firms which would otherwise submit competing bids. This sharing is done by reoffering the bonds at prices below the competitive level and rationing their sale to those with whom the profits are to be shared. Thus, when there is only one underwriting bid, the yield spread between new issues and comparable seasoned bonds is relatively large. West found, however, that the influence of the number of bids on the yield spread in the state and local government bond market was limited to offerings that received only one or two bids.[36] Since the number of bids received for corporate bonds is normally between two and nine, it is unlikely that this type of market imperfection explains any of the corporate yield spread. In addition, West found a virtual disappearance of yield spreads for single bid issues only two days after reoffering, making it clear that the spreads are of a different sort from those on corporate bonds, which persist for two and three months.

FURTHER IMPLICATIONS OF THE HYPOTHESES. The different hypotheses advanced to explain the new-seasoned yield spread have quite different implications for the relationship between the new and seasoned issue markets. The hypothesis based on market imperfections implies that the forces determining interest rates operate most directly and immediately on new issue yields. The hypothesis which attempts to explain the spread in terms of the pricing policy of underwriters, in contrast, does not imply that either the market for new issues or that for seasoned issues is more sensitive to changes in market conditions (although it does suggest that new issue yields will be more volatile).[37] It implies only that underwriters' expectations about future

---

[36] West found that on the average a single bid raised the yield spread by 13 basis points and two bids raised it by 2 basis points, as compared to issues with more than two bids. West, p. 141.

[37] The fact that the new issue series is more erratic than the seasoned issue series may be due to three things: (1) the number of issues in the new issue series is often considerably smaller than the number in the seasoned series; (2) the large role of expectational forces in determining new issue yields due to the pricing policy of the underwriters; and (3) the possibility that market forces act more directly on new issue yields, with the seasoned issue series following a distributed lag adjustment to its equilibrium level.

conditions in these markets generally cause them to be more or less concerned about assuring a rapid distribution of their inventories of new issues.

The hypotheses we have presented are nevertheless complementary rather than contradictory explanations. Even if we accept the hypothesis concerning the pricing policies of underwriters, this hypothesis cannot explain a spread which persists for a number of weeks after the termination of the syndicate. In order to explain the persistence of the spread even on issues which are similar with respect to all yield-determining characteristics, we must allow for market frictions or imperfections.

IV. Statistical Tests

VARIABLES FOR MULTIPLE REGRESSION. Multiple regression analysis is the major analytical technique used in this part of the study. The technique involves the regression of a dependent variable, which in

TABLE 5-3. Independent Variables Suggested by Each of the Major Hypotheses

Independent Variable	Coupon Difference	Underwriting Risks	Market Imperfections
Coupon difference	+		
Change in the level of yields	−	+	+
Volume of new issues	+	+	
Level of long-term yields	−	+, −	
Ratio of slow-selling to total new issues		+	
Level of Treasury bill yields		+	

this section will always be the new-seasoned yield spread, on independent variables which the hypotheses suggest may explain the variations in the size of the dependent variable.[38] These variables are: (1) difference in coupon rate between new and outstanding issues; (2) changes in the level of yields; (3) volume of new issues; (4) level

---

[38] We have important reservations about some of the regressions run, but the results will be presented before discussing any problems of interpretation.

of long-term yields; (5) ratio of slow-selling to total new issues; and (6) level of Treasury bill yields.

Table 5-3 summarizes how each of various independent variables would be expected to influence the new-seasoned yield spread under each of the three major hypotheses regarding the cause of the yield spread. The direction of the influence is given by a plus or minus sign.

Because of intercorrelation among four of the independent variables (coupon difference, volume of new issues, level of yields, and bill rate), it was not advisable to include all of these variables in a single regression equation. For example, the level of yields and bill rates are both correlated with coupon differences. When either is added to a regression that already includes coupon difference, it takes a large negative coefficient and increases the coefficient of the coupon difference. In regressions run with data corrected for coupon, the yield level and bill rate do not show negative coefficients.[39] Similar problems pertain to the variable measuring the volume of new issues. Because of these statistical problems, the first set of regressions which will be presented include only the coupon difference and lagged yield changes as independent variables.

FINDINGS FROM FULL PERIOD REGRESSIONS. We begin with four regressions, one for each of the four monthly new issue series. All the regressions apply to the full period from 1952 through 1963, though the number of monthly observations varies as some of the series did not include observations of the new issue yield for every month. Table 5-4 summarizes the regression coefficients and their t-values when all variables are included in the regression, along with the F statistic for the addition of each variable to the preceding ones in the regression, and correlation coefficients.[40] The variable X_{10} stands for M_{10} in the case of the Moody regression, B_{10} in the Bankers Trust regression, K_{10} in the Kaplan regression, and H_{10} in the Homer regression. The same pattern follows for X_{30} through X_{41}. The subscript 1 denotes the

[39] The negative partial correlation of the level of yields and the yield spread in the regression with data uncorrected for coupon could be explained in part by the fact that the yield spread (due to any given difference in coupon rate) is lower when the level of yields is high. However, because of a high degree of multicollinearity between the difference in coupon rates and the level of interest rates, it seems probable that the correlation is essentially spurious. In any event, the regressions with data corrected for coupon are theoretically more satisfactory, and chief reliance is placed on them.

[40] An explanation of the statistical methodology used in this study is provided in any standard textbook of econometrics.

TABLE 5-4. Summary of Regressions for New-Seasoned Yield Spreads (X_1) Not Corrected for Coupon Differences (*by yield series*)

Independent Variable	Moody: M_1			Bankers Trust: B_1			Kaplan: K_1			Homer: H_1		
	b	t	F	b	t	F	b	t	F	b	t	F
X_{10} (coupon rate difference)	.284	11.34	243.38	.246	10.62	209.29	.287	15.17	232.94	.160	9.76	116.61
X_{30} (change in yields)	.492	8.94	45.95	.437	6.73	34.02	.384	4.35	24.59	.311	4.14	13.12
X_{31}	.265	4.62	8.79	.216	3.19	6.81	.084	0.91	1.44	.177	2.30	4.28
X_{32}	.167	2.93	3.02	.123	1.79	2.60	.055	0.60	0.95	.143	1.86	3.66
X_{33}	.147	2.61	2.32	.113	1.70	1.71	.121	1.38	1.89	.158	2.11	1.59
X_{34}	.145	2.69	2.99	.063	0.96	0.37	Not included			.084	1.13	0.65
X_{35}	.123	2.28	2.19	.072	1.02	0.35	"			.135	1.83	3.28
X_{36}	.127	2.36	2.77	.114	1.68	3.68	"			.157	2.14	4.93
X_{37}	.144	2.69	4.75	.151	2.27	4.48	"			.138	1.88	3.60
X_{38}	.107	1.98	2.02	.108	1.51	1.90	"			.105	1.41	1.56
X_{39}	.091	1.67	1.62	.114	1.72	3.03	"			.142	1.88	3.99
X_{40}	.093	1.74	2.34	.082	1.22	1.76	"			.112	1.48	4.04
X_{41}	.096	1.79	3.19	.080	1.22	1.48	"			.156	2.13	4.54
Constant	−.047			.017			−.060			.027		
Number of observations	121			127			144			144		
Mean of yield spread	.175			.231			.129			.251		
S.D. of yield spread	.235			.204			.175			.190		
Simple correlation coefficient of yield spread and X_{10}	.820			.791			.788			.672		
S.E. of estimate	.104			.104			.100			.124		
Multiple correlation coefficient	.910			.876			.829			.784		
F statistic of multiple correlation coefficient	39.40			28.74			60.65			15.94		

new-seasoned spread without correction for coupon, the subscript 10 denotes the coupon difference variable, and subscripts 30 through 41 denote changes in new issue yields. A full explanation of the symbols is provided in the Appendix.

Coupon Difference. Because of its importance in explaining yield spreads, the difference in coupon rate must enter the regression equation when the series used to calculate those spreads do not have the same coupon rate at each observation. The variable used here is the difference between the average coupon on the bonds in the two series, new issue minus seasoned. The hypothesis concerning the effect of coupon rates discussed above suggests a positive correlation between yield spread and coupon difference.

The hypothesis is borne out by the four regressions shown in Table 5-4, all of which show a very high simple correlation coefficient (.67 to .82) and high *t*-values for the *b*-coefficient in the multiple regression. Part of the statistical influence of the coupon rate is no doubt due to its correlation with other variables not included in the regression equation. The regression coefficient of the coupon difference is large in absolute terms, ranging from .25 to .29 in the first three regressions. This implies that a 10 basis point difference in coupon produces a 2 to 3 basis point difference in spread. The coefficient is somewhat smaller in the Homer regression because the coupon rate was substantially lower for the seasoned Homer series than for the seasoned series used in the other regressions; and the influence of a given amount of coupon difference is relatively small at low coupon levels.[41]

For a number of reasons, use of a coupon difference variable in a linear regression equation is a very imperfect way of accounting for the effect of the coupon rate. The coupon rate and other variables we wished to include in the regression are intercorrelated. The influence of coupon differences on yield spread is not linear, and the effect apparently changed over the period studied.[42] Moreover, there may be a reverse influence of yield spread on coupon difference, stemming from the practice of setting the coupon rate on new issues so that the issues will sell close to par.[43]

To deal with these problems, series of seasoned bond yields were constructed for use with the Moody and Homer new issue series which

[41] Frankena study.

[42] Frankena found a marked downward trend in the size of yield spreads due to coupon differences during the period.

[43] Because of this practice, the new issue coupon rate is an endogenous variable, and it follows that the difference in coupon rates is an endogenous variable.

carried the same coupon rate as the new issues in each month. In this way, the influence of coupon differences is eliminated from the new-seasoned spread, making the data more satisfactory for testing other explanations of the spread.

The extent to which the spread between new and seasoned issues is reduced by eliminating the effect of coupon differences is striking. Charts 5-1 and 5-2 show graphically the effect of this correction for the Moody and Homer series. The average new-seasoned spread for the period from 1952 through 1963 was 16.7 basis points for the basic Moody Aa corporate series when no adjustment was made for coupon differences. When the spread was measured as the difference between the new issue yield and the yield on seasoned bonds with the same coupon rate as the new issues, it averaged only 9.2 basis points. Similarly, for the Homer series, the average spread was 25.1 basis points using uncorrected series, but only 9.0 basis points when measured from the yield on seasoned bonds with coupon rates equal to those on new issues. Thus, equalization of the coupon rate eliminates more than two-fifths of the spread in the Moody series and more than three-fifths of the spread in the Homer series. The larger correction in the case of the Homer series is due to the lower coupon rate in the Homer seasoned series.

Changes in the Level of Yields. Both the hypothesis concerning underwriters' pricing policies and that concerning market imperfections suggest a positive correlation between past changes in the level of yields and the size of the new-seasoned yield spread.[44] If underwriters expect yields to continue rising, or if the seasoned market lags behind the market for new issues, the spread will increase when new issue yields rise.

The change-in-yield variables [45] were tested in the four initial regres-

---

[44] In the case of the regressions for the yield spread measured without correction for differences in coupon rate, there is another reason for a correlation (negative) of the spread with the change-in-yield variables: A given coupon difference will have somewhat less influence on yield spreads when yields are rising. Frankena found that yield spreads between bonds with different coupon rates were smaller in periods of rising yields. It was hypothesized that this occurred because the greater call protection and capital gains potential of lower coupon bonds were given a lower market value when bond prices were falling.

[45] These are defined in the Appendix. Variables X_{30} through X_{41} used in Tables 5-4 and 5-5 are one-month changes in new issue yields with lags of from one to twelve months preceding the observation to be explained. It may be noted that if only the market imperfections were involved, the model employed in this paper would be less plausible than a distributed lag model which assumed that the level of yields on seasoned issues would adjust to its equilibrium level according to a distributed lag process. For

TABLE 5-5. Summary of Regressions for New-Seasoned Yield Spreads Corrected for Coupon Differences

Independent Variable (changes in yield)	Moody: M_2			Homer: H_2		
	b	t	F	b	t	F
X_{30}	.524	11.81	56.42	.244	8.81	51.72
X_{31}	.287	6.18	11.09	.143	5.04	20.84
X_{32}	.228	4.92	7.43	.093	3.27	10.60
X_{33}	.220	4.77	8.52	.094	3.39	6.03
X_{34}	.224	5.02	12.38	.060	2.20	3.31
X_{35}	.184	4.14	9.16	.071	2.61	8.21
X_{36}	.160	3.57	6.49	.110	4.03	16.58
X_{37}	.178	3.98	8.57	.072	2.65	6.94
X_{38}	.197	4.43	11.97	.043	1.56	2.94
X_{39}	.140	3.09	6.17	.064	2.30	6.41
X_{40}	.120	2.68	5.37	.034	1.21	2.33
X_{41}	.143	3.17	10.07	.032	1.17	1.36
Constant	.070			.081		
Number of observations	121			144		
Mean of yield spread	.097			.090		
S.D. of yield spread	.154			.069		
S.E. of estimate	.089			.046		
Multiple correlation coefficient	.838			.772		
F statistic of multiple correlation coefficient	18.25			16.14		

NOTE: See Appendix for definition of symbols.

sions run for spreads not corrected for coupon differences and in the two regressions covering bonds with the same coupon rate (Table 5-5). In each of the six regressions, all twelve change-in-yield variables covering the year preceding the month of observation have positive regression coefficients.[46] Not all of the regression coefficients were

example, the one-month change in seasoned yields might equal a certain fraction of the difference between the equilibrium level of seasoned yields at the end of the month and actual levels of seasoned yields at the beginning of the month. This model would have different implications for yield spreads than would the model tested here, particularly at turning points.

[46] Only four change-in-yield variables were used in the Kaplan series, but when the variables for the change in Moody new issue yields (M_{30}–M_{41}) were used as independent variables with the Kaplan spread, all twelve had positive regression coefficients.

statistically significant individually, but the uniformly positive signs make them collectively more significant than is indicated by their individual *t*-values and *F* statistics.[47] A weighted average of changes in yields over the past year therefore appears to be a very significant variable. The weights show a clear tendency to decline as the lag becomes longer, particularly in the case of the Moody series. This is to be expected whether the change-in-yields variables are important because of their influence on underwriters' expectations or because of a lag in the adjustment of seasoned rates.

The twelve change-in-yield variables explain 70 per cent and 60 per cent, respectively, of the total variance in the Moody and Homer regressions for spreads corrected for coupon differences. In the equations for spreads uncorrected for coupon difference the change-in-yield variables increase the explained variance by a smaller percentage but a statistically significant amount.

This finding, however, is consistent with either hypothesis, the one concerning underwriting risks or that concerning imperfections in the capital market, or with both. (We will return later to the problem of differentiating between these hypotheses.) Part of the correlation of the change-in-yield variables with yield spread, furthermore, may be spurious. The observation for the level of new issue yields can be viewed as a random variable, the mean of a sample drawn from a theoretical population of new issue yields. Any random influence on the sample mean for the new issue yields, causing it to deviate from the population value, will result in a corresponding change in the recorded new-seasoned spread.[48] This would cause an upward bias in the coefficient of the change-in-yield variable for the month immediately prior to the observation (i.e., X_{30}) and also in the correlation coefficient. It would bias the other regression coefficients only if there is positive autocorrelation of the error terms in the regression equation. Unfortunately, there seems to be autocorrelation in our equations;[49] hence the possibility of bias extends to the change-in-yield variables of earlier periods as well.[50]

---

[47] The probability of a *t*-value greater than 1.64 would be .10, greater than 1.96 would be .05, and greater than 2.58 would be .01 if there were in fact no relation between the independent and dependent variables.

[48] An error of measurement or factors omitted from the regression which influence the new issue but not the seasoned market would lead to the same problem.

[49] The problem of autocorrelation will be discussed below.

[50] As a partial check on the severity of this problem, we tried a new specification, computing the change-in-yield variables from the yield on long-term governments rather than from the yield on corporate new issues. This reduces the spurious correlation between the yield spread and the change in yield in the preceding month. In applying this

Volume of New Issues. It was hypothesized above that the volume of new issues competing for investment funds might affect underwriting risk and, thereby, the size of the new-seasoned yield spread. This hypothesis received only moderate statistical support. Some measures of new issue volume were statistically significant when included in regressions along with the change-in-yield variables, but the levels of significance were not high enough, nor were the results consistent enough, to lend any certainty to the hypothesis.[51]

Among the different measures of volume tested in the study were (a) Aa corporate bonds, (b) Aaa through Baa corporate bonds, (c) all corporate bonds including both public offerings and private placements, (d) all corporate securities including both bonds and equities, (e) all corporate securities plus home mortgages, (f) all corporate plus two-thirds of state and local bonds,[52] (g) all corporates plus newly issued government bonds with maturities of fifteen years or more, and (h) all of these bonds. Simple and multiple regressions suggested that either all corporate bonds or all corporate securities including both bonds and equities were the best measures, although the results were not entirely consistent.[53]

In general, the best correlations were obtained using the volume for the month of the observation of yield spread plus the two months preceding. However, the best length of period varied from two to five months for different volume measures.

It seemed possible that the volume of new issues anticipated in the

procedure we employed a distributed lag technique developed by Shirley Almon after our other regressions were estimated (Shirley Almon, "The Distributed Lag Between Capital Appropriations and Expenditures," *Econometrica,* January 1965, pp. 178–181). This procedure generated a smoothly declining set of weights for the change-in-yield variables, and moderate reduction in the variance explained by these variables (from 70 and 60 per cent to 40 and 49 per cent in the Moody and Homer series, respectively). This change in procedure does not eliminate the possibility of bias, however, because changes in yields on governments in the month preceding the month of observation are correlated with changes in new issue yields, and may therefore be spuriously correlated with the yield spread.

[51] One problem caused by using new issue volume as an independent variable is that the volume is really endogenously determined. For this reason, the use of volume involves problems of simultaneous equations bias.

In his study of new-seasoned yield spreads for state and local government general obligation bonds, Richard West found that the regression coefficients for various measures of market volume (current or expected) and for dealer's inventories were not significantly different from zero.

[52] Two-thirds of the state and local issues were included on the basis that this might represent the long-term portion of the total.

[53] Deduction of new issues intended for refunding made no apparent improvement in the volume measures.

month following the observation for yield spread might also be relevant. Measures for the securities registered for issue in the succeeding month, for securities registered for issue in any future period including the next month, and for securities actually issued in the succeeding month, however, did not prove significant in any of the multiple regressions.

Tables 5-6 and 5-7 show the results of two regressions that generated relatively high t-values for volume as an independent variable.

TABLE 5-6. Summary of Regression for Moody New-Seasoned Yield Spreads Corrected for Coupon and Including Volume as an Independent Variable

Independent Variable	b	t	F
X_{30} (change in yield)	.515	12.08	56.88
X_{31}	.260	5.91	11.20
$X_{32} + X_{33}$	.222	6.69	16.66
$X_{34} + X_{35}$	.220	6.72	22.37
$X_{36} + X_{37}$	.163	5.05	16.05
$X_{38} + X_{39}$	.163	4.97	18.57
$X_{40} + X_{41}$	.134	4.25	16.09
V_{61} (volume)	.038	2.61	6.79
Constant	−.034		
Number of observations	122		
Mean of yield spread	.097		
S.D. of yield spread	.153		
S.E. of estimate	.085		
Multiple correlation coefficient	.845		
F statistic of multiple correlation coefficient	35.40		

NOTE: See Appendix for definition of symbols.

The equations used are for the Moody series with the same coupon rate for new and seasoned issues; change-in-yield variables are included in addition to volume.[54] The volume measure in Table 5-6 (V_{61}) covers new issues of corporate bonds and equities for the current and two preceding months, while volume in Table 5-7 (V_{62}) covers the same securities but includes three, rather than two, months

---

[54] In Table 5-6 the change-in-yield variables after the first one are each for two-month yield changes. This format was used at an earlier stage in the study, and does not significantly affect the regression.

TABLE 5-7. Summary of Regression for Moody New-Seasoned Yield Spread Corrected For Coupon and Including Level of Yields on Seasoned Bonds and Volume of New Issues as Independent Variables

Independent Variables	b	t
X_{30} (change in yield)	.518	11.77
X_{31}	.273	5.86
X_{32}	.223	4.86
X_{33}	.220	4.83
X_{34}	.231	5.22
X_{35}	.204	4.54
X_{36}	.169	3.81
X_{37}	.171	3.86
X_{38}	.193	4.39
X_{39}	.138	3.06
X_{40}	.115	2.60
X_{41}	.148	3.32
X_{21} (yield level)	−.015	−1.04
V_{62} (volume)	.028	2.10
Number of observations	121	
Mean of yield spread	.097	
S.D. of yield spread	.154	
S.E. of estimate	.088	
Multiple correlation coefficient	.846	
F statistic for over-all regression	19.01	

NOTE: See Appendix for definition of symbols.

prior to the current month. The t-value for volume is not quite as high when the level of yields is included in the regression, as in Table 5-7, but it is still significant at the .05 level. This overstates the true confidence level because a large number of volume measures were tried in order to find one with a t-value as high as this.[55]

In the Homer equation, the t-value for the best volume measure is 1.97 (Table 5-8).[56] However, addition of the level of seasoned yields

---

[55] This is true of all t-values for the volume variables.

[56] The volume measure in the Homer regressions, V_{52}, covers new corporate bonds only, for the three months preceding the observation of the yield spread. Since the Homer yield spreads apply to the first of the month while the Moody spreads are monthly averages, the time periods of the volume variables in the Moody and Homer regressions are approximately the same.

as an independent variable reduces it to .95, which is not statistically significant.[57]

Level of Yields. Charts 5-1 and 5-2 suggest that the yield spread is greatest when yields are high. For the most part, this is probably due to the correlation of yield levels with other factors affecting the spread, particularly with differences in coupon rates, which are larger when yield levels are higher.[58] Such an influence can be avoided by testing yield levels in the equations covering new and seasoned bonds with the same coupon rate.

The underwriting risk hypothesis indicates two reasons why the level of yields may be relevant. First, when yields are high the yield spread between long-term and short-term securities is small, or negative, making it more expensive to carry new issues (if holding periods yields are directly related to yields to maturity). Second, underwriters may fear that yields, which have climbed to high levels, may continue to rise.[59] Yet, the opposite reaction is often viewed as more plausible: When rates are high, dealers and investors may expect them to fall back toward "normal." The direction of influence is therefore not clear.

When the level of yields on seasoned bonds (unadjusted for coupon) is added to the Moody regression (adjusted for coupon) its coefficient is not significant (Table 5-7). In the Homer regression for spreads corrected for coupon, however, the level of yields on seasoned bonds with a coupon rate of $2\frac{3}{4}$ to $2\frac{7}{8}$ per cent is statistically significant at the .01 level in the multiple regression including the change-in-yield variables, whether or not volume is also included as an independent variable (Table 5-8). In the regression without a volume variable, the regression coefficient for the level of seasoned yields has a t-value of 3.57, and the F statistic for addition of the level of seasoned yields to the regression is 12.75. The addition of the level of yields increases the coefficient of multiple correlation from .772 to .795. The reason for the different results in the Moody and Homer regressions is not clear.

[57] The simple correlation coefficient of volume (V_{65}) and the level of yields (H_{21}) is .291.

[58] Partly offsetting this is the fact that the yield spread between bonds with the same coupon rates will be smaller the higher the general level of yields. The reason is that at a higher level of yields the risk of call and limited capital gains of the higher coupon bond appears smaller and hence the bond has a smaller risk premium. This relationship implies that the level of yields has a negative influence where coupon rates are held constant.

[59] William H. White study, p. 125.

TABLE 5-8. Summary of Regressions for Homer New-Seasoned Yield Spread Corrected for Coupon and Including Level of Yields on Seasoned Bonds With a Coupon Rate of $2\frac{3}{4}$–$2\frac{7}{8}$ Per Cent and Volume of New Issues as Independent Variables

Independent Variable	b	t	b	t	b	t
X_{30} (change in yields)	.243	9.12	.249	9.05	.246	9.17
X_{31}	.136	4.98	.140	4.98	.136	4.98
X_{32}	.087	3.21	.086	3.03	.086	3.16
X_{33}	.090	3.40	.093	3.38	.091	3.40
X_{34}	.053	2.01	.065	2.38	.053	2.02
X_{35}	.065	2.47	.080	2.92	.068	2.58
X_{36}	.105	4.04	.118	4.33	.111	4.15
X_{37}	.068	2.60	.078	2.89	.072	2.72
X_{38}	.040	1.53	.046	1.67	.043	1.63
X_{39}	.062	2.30	.064	2.33	.063	2.34
X_{40}	.034	1.26	.034	1.22	.034	1.28
X_{41}	.031	1.18	.034	1.27	.031	1.19
X_{21} (yield level)	.024	3.57			.021	2.97
V_{65} (volume)			.018	1.97	.0072	.95
Constant	−.007		.044		−.018	
Number of observations	144		144		144	
Mean of yield spread	.090		.090		.090	
S.D. of yield spread	.069		.069		.069	
S.E. of estimates	.044		.046		.044	
Multiple correlation coefficient	.795		.780		.797	
F statistic of over-all regression	15.98		14.41		16.03	

NOTE: See Appendix for definition of symbols.

Tightness in the Money Market. It was hypothesized that a tight money market could increase the cost and difficulty of underwriting new issues and, hence, contribute to a new-seasoned yield spread. To measure tightness in the money market, tests were performed using the level of free reserves, the yield spread between long-term and short-term issues, and the yield on newly issued three-month Treasury bills. On the basis of simple correlation coefficients, the bill rate was chosen as the best measure. However, in the multiple regressions covering the Moody and Homer series corrected for coupon differences, the regression coefficient for the bill rate was not significantly different from zero at even the .10 per cent level in either series, although it was positive in both.[60]

Ratio of Slow-Selling to Total New Issues. It was hypothesized that when new issues had been selling slowly in the recent past, underwriters would bid low enough for new issues to permit their distribution at prices below those on comparable seasoned issues. This would suggest that the new-seasoned yield spread would be positively correlated with the proportion of new issues which had moved slowly in the recent past. A new issue was defined as slow-selling if it was still in syndicate on the Monday following the date of issue. The ratio of such issues to total new issues of A, Aa and Aaa public utilities was calculated for the month preceding the observation of yield spreads, and separately for the month before that one. However, using either the Moody or Homer series corrected for coupon, the coefficients for the ratio of slow-selling to total new issues in each of the two preceding months were not statistically significant, even at the .10 level, in multiple regressions including the volume of new issues during the previous three months, the level of yields, and four variables measuring the change of yields during the previous twelve months.

Summary of Findings from Full Period Regressions. On the basis of the regressions run for the full period from 1952 through 1963, we can draw the following conclusions concerning the three major hypotheses which were being tested:

(1) Coupon differences between the bonds in the new issue and seasoned series explain a large part of the average level and the variance of the new-seasoned yield spread as it is usually recorded. Differences between the average coupon rates on the bonds used in the new issue and seasoned issue series accounted for an average of 41 and 62 per cent of the spread and for 57 and 87 per cent of the variance of the spread for the Moody and Homer series, respectively.

(2) A weighted average of changes in new issue yields over the preceding year has been found to be very important as an explanatory

---

[60] In a previously published summary of this study, the bill rate was included in the regression covering the Homer series corrected for coupon because its regression coefficient had a *t*-value of 2.69. However, subsequent changes in the other variables in the regression and extension of the time period covered by the regression sharply reduced the coefficient.

Using regression equations which included four rather than twelve separate variables to measure the change in new yields over the preceding twelve months and which included the volume of new corporate securities including equities issued in the current month and in the preceding one, the regression coefficient of the bill rate had *t*-values of .43 and 1.31, respectively, in the Moody and Homer regressions.

variable in the regressions for yield spread — accounting for between 60 and 70 per cent of the variance of the spread remaining after correction for coupon. This was suggested by the consistently positive and generally significant regression coefficients of the twelve lagged change-in-yield variables used in the regressions, both with and without correction for coupon. The results give strong support to either or both of two hypotheses. In the first, new-seasoned spreads increase when new issue yields have been rising, because underwriters are led to believe that the yields will continue to rise in the near future. Consequently, underwriters reduce their bids and offering prices on new issues to assure rapid distribution, which further causes new issue yields to exceed the yields on comparable seasoned issues. The second hypothesis is that new-seasoned spreads increase following a rise in new issue yields because yields on seasoned issues lag behind those on new issues. Thus, when new issue yields rise, the spread widens.

However, the multiple regressions give no basis for deciding between these two hypotheses, and there remains the problem of spurious correlation. As has already been seen, both hypotheses are supported by institutional considerations. Additional tests will follow shortly which were made in an attempt to discover the importance of each hypothesis.

(3) Moderate statistical support was found for including a variable measuring the volume of new issues of corporate bonds or of corporate bonds and equities for the month of observation of the yield spread plus the two preceding it. The interpretation placed on this was that when the market becomes congested with new issues competing for investment funds, underwriters foresee greater difficulty in distributing them and, accordingly, reduce their bids and offering prices for new issues. Thus the yields on new issues are increased above those on comparable seasoned issues. However, the levels of the significance and consistency of the results were not great enough to lend any certainty to the hypothesis.

(4) The level of seasoned yields had no explanatory power in the Moody regression of spread corrected for coupon, but it was statistically significant with a positive regression coefficient in the coupon-corrected Homer regression.

(5) No statistical support was found for the hypothesis that underwriters' pricing policies might be affected by the speed of sale of recent issues, as measured by the ratio of slow-selling to total new issues in the recent past.

(6) No statistical support was found for the hypothesis that money

market conditions, as measured by the Treasury bill rate, affect the new-seasoned spread.

ANALYSIS OF SUBPERIODS. During the earlier stages of this study, regressions similar to those covering the full period, January 1952–December 1963, were run separately for periods of rising yields and periods of falling yields using the Moody data. Similarly, separate regressions were run for each of three complete specific cycles in interest rates.[61] These subperiod regressions are presented in Tables 5-9 and 5-10. The yield variables M_{30}, M_{56}, M_{57}, and M_{58} are somewhat different from those used before, but not importantly. Exact definitions are given in the Appendix. On the whole, the same variables that explain the variation in yield spreads in the full period seem to explain most of the variation in each of the subperiods as well. The following are the main points suggested by the subperiod regressions.

(1) The volume measure showed an inconsistent pattern in the subperiod runs, as it had in variously specified equations covering the whole period. In coupon-corrected equations that included the bill rate, volume was significant at the .01 level in the first two interest rate cycles, as it was during periods of rising yields, but it was not in the third interest rate cycle or in periods of falling yields. (In the regression uncorrected for coupon, volume was not significant in runs that included the bill rate in either subperiod or full-period regressions.)

(2) In regressions that do not include bill yields, the coefficients of the change-in-yield variables were of the same general order of magnitude during periods of rising yields and those of falling yields, and during the individual interest rate cycles, as they were during the entire period. In coupon-corrected regressions that included bill yields, however, the coefficients of the change-in-yield variables were considerably smaller for the separate interest rate cycles than for the period as a whole. This was most notably the case for the more remote change-in-yield variables.

(3) In each of the three interest rate cycles, but not in the regressions for periods of rising and falling yields, the Treasury bill rate

---

[61] The periods of rising rates were January 1952 through May 1953, April 1954 through October 1957, July 1958 through September 1959, and January through December 1963. The periods of falling rates were September 1953 through March 1954, November 1957 through June 1958, and October 1959 through January 1963. The first interest rate cycle was January 1952 through March 1954, the second was March 1954 through June 1958, and the third was June 1958 through January 1963.

proved to be statistically significant at the .05 level; and in the case of
the second and third cycles it was statistically significant at the .01
level (Table 5-10). As noted above, when the bill rate was added to the
regressions for the first and second cycles, though not the third one, it
considerably reduced the significance of some of the change-in-yield
variables, since the correlation of the bill rate and the change-in-yield
variables is considerably higher in the individual interest rate cycles
than in the whole period. Since very strong support has already been
found for the change-in-yield variables, it might be that the bill rate is
acting as a proxy for those variables and is statistically significant for
that reason.

TABLE 5-9. Summary of Full Period and Subperiod Regressions for Moody
New-Seasoned Spreads With and Without Corrections for Coupon Differences

	Full Period		Period of Rising Rates		Period of Falling Rates	
Equation	(1) M_1	(2) M_2	(3) M_1	(4) M_2	(5) M_1	(6) M_2
		Part A				
b_1 for M_{10} (coupon differences)	.279	—	.292	—	.378	—
b_2 for M_{30} (change in yields)	.485	.510	.474	.645	.328	.446
b_3 for M_{56}	.250	.239	.235	.313	.083	.145
b_4 for M_{57}	.136	.224	.136	.255	−.040	.250
b_5 for M_{58}	.157	.210	.096	.144	.131	.257
b_6 for V_{60} (volume)	−.016	.043	.004	.056	−.056	.049
Constant	−.010	−.005	−.003	−.037	−.067	−.020
t for b_1	11.934	—	9.696	—	9.034	—
t for b_2	9.428	12.257	6.501	11.950	4.346	6.497
t for b_3	5.035	5.892	3.463	5.991	1.056	1.963
t for b_4	3.113	6.343	2.132	5.497	−.553	3.830
t for b_5	4.362	7.542	2.527	4.590	2.321	5.082
t for b_6	−.707	2.238	.136	2.176	−1.664	1.536
Number of observations	128	128	77	77	57	57
Mean of yield spread	.172	.096	.222	.143	.114	.042
S.D. of yield spread	.230	.150	.238	.149	.229	.160
S.E. of estimate	.100	.085	.082	.075	.103	.103
Multiple correlation coefficient	.906	.831	.943	.874	.906	.787
F statistic of multiple correlation coefficient	92.02	54.25	94.08	45.81	37.96	16.57

(continued)

TABLE 5-9 (concluded)

Equation	Interest Rate Cycle #1		Interest Rate Cycle #2		Interest Rate Cycle #3	
	(1) M_1	(2) M_2	(3) M_1	(4) M_2	(5) M_1	(6) M_2
Part B						
b_1 for M_{10} (coupon differences)	−.151	−	.314	−	.459	−
b_2 for M_{30} (change in yield)	.795	.357	.426	.464	.375	.639
b_3 for M_{56}	.555	.125	.163	.118	.178	.352
b_4 for M_{57}	.374	.186	.069	.164	.086	.329
b_5 for M_{58}	.327	.027	.102	.160	−.018	.191
b_6 for V_{60} (volume)	.001	.064	.023	.159	−.012	−.003
Constant	.175	−.021	−.020	−.182	−.247	.062
t for b_1	−1.094	−	17.065	−	15.287	−
t for b_2	6.048	6.948	12.456	7.948	6.948	9.997
t for b_3	4.909	2.163	5.376	2.205	3.493	5.601
t for b_4	4.677	3.493	2.376	3.376	1.925	5.762
t for b_5	3.427	.515	3.461	3.447	−.595	5.246
t for b_6	.043	2.302	.948	4.087	−.542	−.088
Number of observations	21	21	44	44	54	54
Mean of yield spread	.131	.070	.256	.148	.154	.069
S.D. of yield spread	.161	.096	.250	.159	.227	.164
S.E. of yield estimate	.034	.040	.043	.077	.060	.084
Multiple correlation coefficient	.985	.933	.987	.890	.968	.874
F statistic of multiple correlation coefficient	74.107	20.157	235.602	28.879	118.221	31.094

NOTE: See Appendix for definition of symbols.

AUTOCORRELATED ERRORS. A statistical problem encountered in the regressions used in the study is autocorrelation of the residual error terms. Although Durbin-Watson statistics were not computed for the residuals of the regressions run in the main part of this study, some checks showed that the Durbin-Watson statistics were typically between 1.2 and 1.6. This indicates a highly significant, positive first-order autocorrelation of the residuals.

Autocorrelation of errors does not introduce a bias into the least-squares estimates of the true parameters as long as the model is not autoregressive. However, even in the nonautoregressive case the statistical significance of the regression coefficients, as measured by their t-values, is overstated because of the underestimation of the standard errors of the regression coefficients computed by ordinary least-squares. Moreover, if the regression equation with autocorrelated

TABLE 5-10. Summary of Regressions by Interest Rate Cycle for Moody New-Seasoned Yield Spread Corrected for Coupon, Including Treasury Bill Rate as an Independent Variable

| | Interest Rate Cycle | | | |
	#1	#2	#3	Entire Period
b_1 for M_{30} (change in yields)	.259	.433	.628	.509
b_2 for M_{56}	.035	.066	.314	.235
b_3 for M_{57}	.078	.012	.269	.217
b_4 for M_{58}	−.014	.001	.073	.204
b_5 for V_{60} (volume)	.055	.103	.017	.0409
b_6 for T_{20} (bill yields)	.104	.095	.074	.0051
Constant	−.186	−.266	−.180	−.0134
t of b_1	3.975	8.786	10.415	12.13
t of b_2	.517	1.417	5.166	5.67
t of b_3	1.121	.221	4.635	5.50
t of b_4	−.285	.010	1.316	6.34
t of b_5	2.167	2.934	.592	2.07
t of b_6	2.113	4.175	2.694	.43
Number of observations	21	44	54	128
Mean of yield spread	.070	.148	.069	.096
S.D. of yield spread	.096	.159	.164	.150
S.E. of estimate	.004	.064	.079	.086
Multiple correlation coefficient	.950	.926	.892	.831
F statistic of multiple correlation coefficient	21.419	37.378	30.499	44.94

NOTE: See Appendix for definition of symbols.

errors is autoregressive, the least-squares estimates of the regression coefficients will be biased, even asymptotically.

Because of autocorrelation, the significance levels of the regression coefficients are lower than those indicated by the *t*-values listed. Second, the autocorrelation suggests that some errors may have been made in the specification of the relationship tested. That is, some significant variables may have been omitted or the form of the variables or the equation may be imperfect. Third, the coefficients of the change-in-yield variables may involve a bias, as already noted.

TIME REQUIRED FOR SEASONING. The above analysis of yield spreads is based on the assumption that there are no systematic differences between new and outstanding issues, other than coupon rate differences, that would account for any significant part of the spread. This implies that any spread which exists at the time of issue, after correction for coupon differences, should disappear after the new issue has been outstanding long enough for the market to equilibrate itself. Does the spread in fact vanish after the new bond has become seasoned? And, if so, how long does this take?

In order to make this part of the study meaningful, we had to select periods when new-seasoned spreads were reasonably high and remained high, so that the closing of the yield gap between individual recent issues and seasoned averages would not merely reflect the elimination of yield spreads between new and seasoned issues generally. The periods chosen were March through May 1953, May 1956 through March 1957, and June through September 1959.

The average yield spread on Aa utilities for all new issues during these periods was 9.0 basis points after correction for coupon. The average spread on these issues one month after the issue date was 3.8 basis points. After two months the spread was 3.1 basis points, after three months it was −1.0 basis points, and from then through the eighth month the average fluctuated within a narrow range above and below zero.

On the average, initial yield spreads on utilities thus appear to be eliminated within two to three months of the date of issue. White, using a somewhat different procedure, arrived at a similar conclusion.[62] Homer, in describing the recent issue market, wrote that "for a period up to, say, three months it [the volume of trading in a recent issue] will continue far larger than for seasoned bonds. At about that point trading activity will die out, and the issue will take its place as just one more seasoned utility." [63]

In addition, we carried out a brief study of the seasoning time required on federal obligations. The paucity and heterogeneity of new issues made it difficult to interpret the available data, but the indication seems to be that the new issue yield spread disappears somewhere between two and four months after issue. Our procedure was first to measure the monthend differences between the yields of bonds issued during the month and the corresponding point on the government yield curve. Omitting bills, certificates, and the $1\frac{1}{2}$ per cent note series, there was a positive yield spread in thirty-eight cases and a negative yield

[62] White, p. 133.
[63] Homer, July 20, 1965 Letter.

spread in ten cases between March 1951 and December 1960.[64] The total spread among the bonds showing a positive spread was 352 basis points; the total for those showing a negative spread was 28 basis points. During the second month after issue the spread declined on twenty-seven issues and increased on seven; the decline was 164 basis points and the increase was 27. By the end of the third month twenty-eight issues had shown a decline in spread from that at the end of the first month, and eight showed an increase. In basis points the decline from the end of the first month was now 244. During the fourth month there was no change in the number of recent issues for which the spread had changed since time of issue, but the total spread declined 12 more basis points net. In the fifth month after issue the spread declined on three more issues, and the net spread in basis points did not change. From that time on the behavior of spreads was random.

These tests confirm that yield spreads are not due to systematic differences in the characteristics of new and outstanding issues (other than coupon rate), and tend to support a hypothesis explaining spreads in terms of market imperfections. The fact that the spreads persist for a period of two to three months after issue suggests that market imperfections prevent more rapid arbitrage. The tests are not inconsistent, however, with the hypothesis which attributes yield spreads partly to underwriting risk. The regression results, moreover, are consistent with both hypotheses. We now turn to three additional tests designed to evaluate these two hypotheses, as well as throw light on the connection between the new issue, recent issue, and seasoned issue markets.[65]

UNDERWRITING RISKS VERSUS MARKET IMPERFECTIONS AS AN EXPLANATION OF YIELD SPREADS. The first two of the following three tests deal with the market imperfections hypothesis, and the third deals with the underwriting risk hypothesis.

(1) Suppose new issue yields turn downward from month t to month $t + 1$, but that even in month $t + 1$ these yields are above those on seasoned bonds in month t. If yields in the seasoned issue market lag behind those in the new issue market, seasoned yields would continue

---

[64] The yield curves used in this study were those prepared by the Morgan Guaranty Trust Company.

[65] William H. White states in his study that "even though the amplitude of variation of the yields on seasoned bonds is smaller than that on new issues, the yields on the two types of bonds are closely synchronized in regard to the timing of peaks, troughs, and major discontinuous changes." White, p. 136.

to rise when new issue yields are above them, attempting to close the spread, despite the falling rates on new issues. If, on the other hand, seasoned yields turn downward along with new issue yields even though the new issue yields in month $t + 1$ exceed the seasoned yields in month t, it can be inferred that seasoned yields are directly influenced by yield-determining conditions and are not simply following a distributed lag adjustment toward their equilibrium level.

Using the Moody corporate Aa series on seasoned issues and new issues with the same coupon rate as the bonds in the seasoned average,[66] the seasoned yields continued to rise in twenty-two of the thirty-one cases where the new issue yield turned downward while remaining above the level of seasoned yields; the reverse occurred in nine of the thirty-one cases. Nothing conclusive can be inferred from this test, but it suggests that the seasoned market lags the new issue market and, therefore, supports the market imperfections hypothesis.

(2) Is the correlation between changes in seasoned yields and changes in new issue yields the month before higher than the correlation between changes in new issue yields and changes in seasoned yields the month before? An affirmative answer would support the hypothesis that seasoned yields tend to lag.

In the Moody Aa corporate series for the period from 1952 through 1963 (with the new issue series corrected for coupon as described above), virtually no correlation was found between the first-differences (one-month changes) of new issue yields and those of seasoned yields for the preceding month, but there was a substantial correlation (.50) between the first-differences of seasoned yields and those of new issue yields for the preceding month. The correlation between first-differences of new and seasoned yields for the same month was only slightly higher (.55).[67] Thus, when the first-difference in seasoned yields is regressed on the change in new issue yields in the same month and the preceding one the coefficient of multiple correlation is very high (.83), and can be raised slightly (to .86) by the addition of the new issue rate change for the second month earlier.[68]

[66] This latter series was derived by adding to Moody's seasoned series the new-seasoned spread measured between Moody's new issue series and the series for the yield on seasoned bonds with the same coupon rate as the new issue. The adjustment affected the correlations very little.

[67] There was no correlation between the first differences of new issue yields and those of new issue yields for the previous month, indicating that in predicting changes in seasoned yields the change in new issue yields for the previous month is not simply a proxy variable for the simultaneous new issue yield change.

[68] It is possible that some of this correlation may be explained by the fact that the new issue yield change of the preceding month is a proxy for the change in seasoned yields of

The preceding two experiments support the conclusion that market forces operate more rapidly on new issue yields than on seasoned ones. Seasoned yield movements appear to follow new issue yield movements with a distributed lag. The tests thus support the hypothesis that frictions in the seasoned issue market are a cause of new-seasoned yield spreads. They do not, however, preclude a role for the underwriting risk hypothesis. The third test involves an examination of the behavior of yields on recently issued bonds after their prices are freed from syndicate price maintenance agreements.

(3) If new issue yields are higher than yields on outstandings because of underwriters' pricing policies, issues recently released from syndicate should decline relative to new issues. A direct comparison of yields on recently released issues with new issue yields is not possible because there are not enough new issues, in the weeks following termination of a syndicate, with which to compare the yield on the newly released issue. Instead, the test examines the behavior of yields on recent issues during periods of some length when new issue yields were predominantly rising and new-seasoned spreads were large. If the yields on issues recently released from syndicate fell during such periods, this would provide strong support for the underwriting risk hypothesis.

Using the yield data for A, Aa, and Aaa utilities in the weekly issues of *Moody's Bond Survey,* we found the percentage of bond issues whose yields fell in the first week following the end of syndicate price maintenance agreements, and the change from offering yield during the first week, first two weeks, and first three weeks after release from syndicate. Table 5-11 shows these data for each of six periods between 1956 and 1966. The bottom line shows the average three-week change in new issue yields during these periods and can be compared to the line above it showing three-week changes on recently released issues.

It is evident from the first line of Table 5-11 that the yields on a substantial number of bonds fell immediately after the termination of the syndicate despite the fact that new issue yields were predominantly rising. Because of the erraticism of new issue yields, some of the decline in yields on recent issues could be due to short periods of falling new issue yields during the longer periods of rising yields. However, in four of the six periods more than half of the recent issues fell — well above what one would expect from erratic movements in new issue yields. Furthermore, comparing the lower two lines in every one of the six periods, the average yield change on recently released issues in

the preceding month. There is more autocorrelation in seasoned than in new issue yields.

TABLE 5-11. Changes in Yields on Recent Issues After Termination of Syndicate Price Maintenance Agreements, Compared With Yield Changes on All New Issues (*yield changes in basis points*)

	Feb. 28, 1956–Jan. 30, 1957	Feb. 5, 1957–June 27, 1957	Aug. 27, 1957–Nov. 20, 1957	April 22, 1959–Aug. 26, 1959	Sept. 14, 1960–Dec. 9, 1960	July 14, 1965–June 30, 1966
(1) Per cent of bond issues whose yields fell in the first week after the end of price maintenance agreements	53	57	73	62	40	35
(2) Average change in yield from offering yield on issues recently released from syndicate:						
(a) during first week	0.0	0.3	−1.8	1.3	1.9	2.8
(b) during first two weeks	−0.2	0.7	−5.0	−0.2	4.1	2.6
(c) during first three weeks	−3.4	0.6	−1.5	1.5	3.0	3.1
(3) Average three-week change in new issue yields	7.2	10.7	0.5	6.7	8.5	6.4

the three weeks following syndicate termination was either negative or, if positive, far less than the average three-week change in new issue yields.

The test thus suggests that there is, indeed, some tendency for underwriters to underprice new issues. This test is limited, however, to periods of rising new issue yields. It should be remembered, moreover, that evidence also exists that some of the new-seasoned spread is caused by imperfections in the capital markets. Thus, both hypotheses, the one concerning the pricing policies of underwriters and that concerning market imperfections, appear to have some validity.

THE SPREAD UNDER STABLE MARKET CONDITIONS. What conditions would lead to the elimination of the yield spread? It is tempting to approach this question through the regression equations, but this would place on the equations a burden they clearly are not equipped to handle. The value of the constants, for example, varies considerably among the different equations.

Nevertheless, the evidence gathered here on the determinants of the spread suggests that it would be close to zero under stable market conditions. With one possible exception the three determinants of a positive spread discussed above presuppose rising market rates. Under stable markets, coupon rates on new issues would be similar to those on seasoned issues; [69] frictions in the market for seasoned bonds would have no importance; and underwriters would not have to incorporate a premium in their offering yields based on an extrapolation of past yield increases. Of course, the underwriters' aversion to risk might be such that they will always include some "sweetener" in their offering yield. However, if this differential consistently resulted in extra profits under stable market conditions, competition among underwriters would quickly erode it away. [70]

The time series on yield differences during a few periods of rate stability are consistent with these speculations. During the second half of 1954, yield levels were stable and the yield differential hovered around zero (see Charts 5-1 and 5-2). Again in the relatively stable period from June 1962 to June 1963, yield differentials were only slightly positive on balance in the Homer series and slightly negative on balance in the Moody's series. This implies that the positive yield

---

[69] Yields would have to be stable for a fairly long period, of course, for this to hold true.

[70] It could make a difference in this regard whether the market was stable, or unstable but without trend.

spreads during the period 1952–63 reflect largely, if not entirely, the tendency for yields to rise on balance over that period.

Our explanation of yield spreads suggests further that a prolonged period of falling yields would result in predominantly negative spreads. Coupon rates on new issues would be lower than those on outstandings, and thus would cause a negative spread. Past yield declines, furthermore, would tend to generate a negative spread if market frictions prevented the prompt adjustment of yields on outstandings. The pricing policy of underwriters could also contribute to a negative spread if they tended to extrapolate past rate declines and if competition between them was intense. Evidence from the 1930's appears to confirm this. Comparison of a series of Moody Aa seasoned utility yields with new issue yields on Aa utilities revealed that, on the average, spreads were negative in 1931 and from 1933 to 1937.[71]

Appendix

KEY TO SYMBOLS

TYPE OF SERIES

Note: All yield series are monthly unless designated with a subscript q for quarterly.

B Bankers Trust, series of yields on Grade 2 public utility bonds.

C_q Avery Cohan, series of yields on Aa public utility bonds. Quarterly.

F Federal Reserve, series of yields on long-term U.S. government bonds.

G Salomon Brothers and Hutzler, series of yields on long-term U.S. government bonds.

H Sidney Homer, series of yields on Aa public utility bonds.

K Mortimer Kaplan, series of yields on "recently issued" Aa corporate bonds.

M Moody, series of yields on Aa corporate bonds.

S Ratio of volume of slow selling to total newly issued Aaa, Aa and A public utilities.

T Treasury bills, ninety-day, series of yields.

V Volume of newly issued securities.

---

[71] Braddock Hickman offers an alternative explanation, namely, the inability of agency ratings to keep up with market views. Since new issues came chiefly from firms with better prospects than others with similar ratings, their lower yield could be attributed in part to differences in investment quality among equally rated bonds. Braddock Hickman, *Corporate Bond Quality and Investor Experience,* Princeton for NBER, 1958, p. 298. See also William H. White, p. 127.

X Symbol used in the tables summarizing the regression equations to stand for the letter corresponding to the series studied. For example, X_{10} stands for M_{10} when used in a table for Moody data.

SUBSCRIPTS FOR SERIES

1–4 New-seasoned yields spreads, new issue yield minus seasoned issue yield; or underwriting yield spread.

10 Coupon difference, average new minus average seasoned issue coupon.

20–22 Level of yields, current month.

30–58 Change in new issue yields over various periods.

60–65 Variables relating to volume of new issues.

q Quarterly series.

Full Glossary

B BANKERS TRUST SERIES

B_1 Spread between yield on newly issued Bankers Trust Company Grade 2 public utilities and yield on seasoned Moody Aa public utilities. In percentage points. Both series are monthly averages of yields with issues weighted by volume in the case of the new issue average. (Sources: data obtained from Bankers Trust Company; *Moody's Bond Survey*)

B_{10} Average coupon difference between newly issued Bankers Trust Grade 2 utilities and seasoned Moody Aa utilities, 1957–63; average coupon difference on Moody Aa corporates, new versus seasoned issues, 1951–56. All in percentage points. (Sources: Bankers Trust Company; *Moody's Bond Survey*)

B_{20} Yield on newly issued Bankers Trust Company Grade 2 public utilities. In percentage points. (Source: Bankers Trust Company)

B_{30}–B_{41} B_{30} is the change in yield on new Bankers Trust Grade 2 utilities during the past month, measured as current yield minus yield of preceding month. B_{31} is the change for the month before the last, B_{32} is the change for the month before that, and so forth for B_{33} through B_{41}. In percentage points. (Source: Bankers Trust Company)

C_q COHAN SERIES (QUARTERLY)

C_{q20} Yield on newly issued Cohan Aa public utilities. The Cohan series consists of quarterly averages of yields on newly issued thirty-year Aa public utility mortgage bonds which were sold to underwriters at competitive bidding. In percentage points. (Source: Avery B. Cohan, "Yields on New Underwritten Corporate Bonds, 1935–1958," *The Journal of Finance,* December, 1962, and data supplied directly to us for 1959–60)

F FEDERAL RESERVE SERIES

F_{21} Yield on outstanding long-term U.S. government bonds, Federal Reserve series. Yields are monthly averages of daily quotations. (Source: *Federal Reserve Bulletin*)

F_{30}–F_{53} F_{30} is the change in yield on outstanding long-term government bonds, Federal Reserve series, current yield minus yield of preceding month. F_{31} is the change for the month before last, F_{32} is the change for the month before that, and so forth for F_{33} through F_{53}. (Source: *Federal Reserve Bulletin*)

G SALOMON BROTHERS AND HUTZLER

G_{21} Yield on outstanding long-term U.S. government bonds, Salomon Brothers and Hutzler series. Yields are for the first of the month. (Source: Salomon Brothers and Hutzler, "An Analytical Record of Yields and Yield Spreads")

G_{30-53} G_{30} is the change in yield on outstanding long-term government bonds, Salomon Brothers and Hutzler series, current yield minus yield of preceding month. G_{31} is the change for the month before last, G_{32} is the change for the month before that, and so forth for G_{33} through G_{53}. (Source: Salomon Brothers and Hutzler)

H HOMER SERIES

H_1 Spread between the yield on Homer's newly issued callable Aa public utilities and the yield on Homer's seasoned callable Aa public utility bonds with $2\frac{3}{4}$–$2\frac{7}{8}$ per cent coupon. In percentage points. Both the new issue and seasoned issue series are for yields as of the first of each month. (Source: Salomon Brothers and Hutzler; Mark W. Frankena)

H_2 Spread between the yield on new callable issues of Aa public utility bonds, Homer series, and the yield on seasoned callable Aa public utility bonds of current coupon. The yield on seasoned bonds of current coupon means the estimated yield on seasoned bonds with coupon rate equal to that on new issues for that date. This yield is calculated by interpolation and extrapolation of yields on seasoned bonds in various coupon groups. In percentage points. The series are for the first of the month. (Source: Salomon Brothers and Hutzler; Mark W. Frankena)

H_{10} Difference between average coupon on newly issued Homer Aa utilities and the $2\frac{3}{4}$–$2\frac{7}{8}$ per cent coupon rate. (Source: data obtained from Sidney Homer and Mark W. Frankena)

H_{20} Yield on new issues, callable Aa public utility bonds, Homer series. (Source: Salomon Brothers and Hutzler)

H_{21} Yield on seasoned issues with $2\frac{3}{4}$–$2\frac{7}{8}$ coupon, callable Aa public utility bonds, Homer series. (Source: Salomon Brothers and Hutzler; Mark W. Frankena)

H_{22} Yield on seasoned issues with coupon rate equal to that on new issues, callable Aa public utility bonds, Homer series. (Source: Salomon Brothers and Hutzler; Mark W. Frankena)

H_{30}–H_{41} H_{30} is the change in yield on new Aa public utility bonds, Homer series, current yield minus yield of preceding month. H_{31} is the change for the month before last, H_{32} is the change for the month before that, and so forth for H_{33} through H_{41}. (Source: Salomon Brothers and Hutzler)

H_{56} Change in yield on newly issued Aa public utility bonds, Homer series, yield in preceding month minus average yield for two to three months preceding. In percentage points. (Source: Salomon Brothers and Hutzler)

H_{57} Change in yield on newly issued Aa public utility bonds, Homer series, average yield of two to three months preceding minus average yield for four to six months preceding. In percentage points. (Source: Salomon Brothers and Hutzler)

H_{58} Change in yield on newly issued Aa public utility bonds, Homer series, average yield for four to six months preceding minus average yield for seven to twelve months preceding. In percentage points. (Source: Salomon Brothers and Hutzler)

K   KAPLAN SERIES

K_1 Spread between yield on Kaplan recently issued Aa corporate bonds and yield on Moody's seasoned Aa corporate bonds. In percentage points. The Kaplan series is for monthly averages of Friday yields for recently issued bonds and the Moody series is for monthly averages of yields. (Sources: *Moody's Bond Survey* and data from Mortimer Kaplan, Federal Housing Administration)

K_{10} Average coupon difference between Kaplan recently issued Aa corporates and Moody seasoned Aa corporates. (Sources: Moody's Investors' Service; Mortimer Kaplan)

K_{20} Yield on recently issued Aa corporates, Kaplan series. (Source: Mortimer Kaplan)

K_{30}–K_{33} K_{30} is the change in yield on recently issued Aa corporate bonds, Kaplan series, current yield minus yield of preceding month. K_{31} is the change for the month before last, K_{32} is the change for the month before that, and K_{33} is the change for the month before that. In percentage points. (Source: Mortimer Kaplan)

M   MOODY SERIES

M_1 Spread between yield on newly issued Aa corporates and yield on seasoned Moody Aa corporates. Newly issued yields are Moody's specially computed averages of offering yields on new issues (other than convertibles, issues with warrants, and equipment trusts), weighted by amounts offered. Seasoned yields are Moody's monthly average (averages of daily figures) and includes yields on securities with various coupon rates. Figures are in percentage points. (Source: *Moody's Bond Survey*)

M_2 Spread between the yield on newly issued Aa corporates, Moody series, and the yield on seasoned Aa corporates with coupon rate equal to that on new issues. In percentage points. (Source: Moody's Investors' Service)

M_4 Moody new-seasoned yield spread as described under M_1 *plus* underwriter spread, which is the difference between the yield to maturity calculated from the offering price and the yield to maturity calculated from the price at which the issue was sold to the underwriter. Underwriter spread thus measures the difference between the investor's return to maturity and the actual interest cost to the borrower. The underwriter spread is an average for newly issued Aa corporates weighted by size of issue.

M_{10} Difference between average coupon on newly issued Moody Aa corporates and average coupon on seasoned Moody Aa corporates. (Source: *Moody's Bond Survey*)

M_{20} Yield on newly issued Aa corporates, Moody series. (Source: *Moody's Bond Survey*)

M_{21} Yield on seasoned Aa corporates, Moody series. (Source: *Moody's Bond Survey*)

M_{22} Yield on seasoned Aa corporates with coupon rate equal to that on new issues, Moody series. (Source: derived from data supplied by Moody's Investors Service)

M_{30}–M_{41} M_{30} is the change in yield on newly issued Aa corporates, Moody series, current yield minus yield of preceding month. M_{31} is the change for the month before last, M_{32} is the change for the month before that, and so forth for M_{33} through M_{41}. In percentage points. (Source: *Moody's Bond Survey*)

M_{56} Change in yield on newly issued Aa corporates, Moody series, yield in preceding month minus average yield for two to three months preceding. In percentage points. (Source: *Moody's Bond Survey*)

M_{57} Change in yield on newly issued Aa corporates, Moody series, average yield of two to three months preceding minus average yield for four to six months preceding. In percentage points. (Source: *Moody's Bond Survey*)

M_{58} Change in yield on newly issued Aa corporates, Moody series, average yield for four to six months preceding minus average yield for seven to twelve months preceding. In percentage points. (Source: *Moody's Bond Survey*)

S SLOW-SELLING ISSUES

S_{60} Ratio of volume of slow-selling to total new Aaa, Aa and A public utility issues. Ratio applies to month preceding the observation of yield spread being explained. (Source: data from Sidney Homer)

S_{61} Ratio of volume of slow-selling to total new Aaa, Aa and A public utility issues. Ratio applies to next to last month before the observation of yield spread being explained. (Source: Sidney Homer)

T TREASURY BILLS

T_{20} Monthly average of yields on newly issued three-month Treasury bills. In percentage points. (Source: *Federal Reserve Bulletin*)

T_{21} Yield on newly issued three-month Treasury bills on the Monday nearest the first of each month. In percentage points. (Source: *Federal Reserve Bulletin*)

V VOLUME OF NEW ISSUED SECURITIES

V_{60} Volume of newly issued corporate securities, including bonds and equities, issued in the current and preceding month. In billions of dollars. (Source: *Federal Reserve Bulletin*)

V_{61} Volume of newly issued corporate securities, including bonds and equities, issued in the current and the two preceding months. In billions of dollars. (Source: *Federal Reserve Bulletin*)

V_{62} Volume of newly issued corporate securities, including bonds and equities, issued in the current and three preceding months. In billions of dollars. (Source: *Federal Reserve Bulletin*)

V_{63} Volume of newly issued corporate securities, including bonds and equities, issued in the two preceding months. In billions of dollars. (Source: *Federal Reserve Bulletin*)

V_{64} Volume of newly issued corporate bonds, including public offerings and private placements, issued in the current and two preceding months. In billions of dollars. (Source: *Federal Reserve Bulletin*)

V_{65} Volume of newly issued corporate bonds, including public offerings and private placements, issued in the three preceding months. In billions of dollars. (Source: *Federal Reserve Bulletin*)

TABLE B_1. Spread Between Yield on Newly Issued Bankers Trust Company Grade 2 Public Utilities and Yield on Seasoned Moody Aa Public Utilities

	January	February	March	April	May	June	July	August	September	October	November	December
1952	.21	.27	.25	.15	.16	.19	.17	.19	.22	.18	.16	.13
1953	.12	.18	.20	.27	.33	.35	.27	.26	.28	.15	.10	.12
1954	.10	.02	.05	.06	.09	.04	.03	.07	.10	.05	.06	.08
1955	.12	.12	.16	.13	.17	.11	.17	.33	.11	.07	.11	.14
1956	.08	.07	.22	.30	.30	.21	.38	.65	.51	.47	.54	.51
1957	.64	.44	.51	.60	.80	1.02	.75	.66	.53	.60	.55	.38
1958	.02	.15	.41	.17	.28	.24	.24	.45	.51	.25	.25	.35
1959	.37	.21	.15	.27	.40	.29	.29	.35	.60	.42	.53	.58
1960	.23	.44	.31	.38	.39	.19	.15	.19	.23	.23	.37	.45
1961	.10	.04	.02	.28	.22	.30	.18	.18	-.02	-.14	.03	.08
1962	.03	-.04	-.10	-.14	-.17	-.10	-.07	-.06	-.16	-.11	-.10	-.12
1963	-.12	-.11	-.05	.03	.01	-.01	-.02	-.02	.01	-.04	-.02	.04

TABLE B_{20}. Yield on Newly Issued Bankers Trust Company Grade 2 Public Utilities

	January	February	March	April	May	June	July	August	September	October	November	December
1951	2.75	2.81	2.96	3.16	3.21	3.45	3.35	3.12	3.10	3.21	3.27	3.28
1952	3.27	3.28	3.30	3.17	3.18	3.23	3.22	3.25	3.28	3.26	3.21	3.18
1953	3.23	3.36	3.42	3.62	3.83	3.92	3.68	3.64	3.70	3.42	3.30	3.33
1954	3.24	3.05	2.98	3.00	3.06	3.04	3.02	3.05	3.10	3.04	3.05	3.07
1955	3.13	3.18	3.25	3.21	3.28	3.23	3.30	3.50	3.32	3.25	3.28	3.37
1956	3.25	3.20	3.38	3.60	3.64	3.55	3.75	4.13	4.12	4.16	4.30	4.35
1957	4.51	4.25	4.31	4.40	4.65	4.96	4.85	4.91	4.84	4.92	4.85	4.43
1958	3.75	3.83	4.14	3.89	3.97	3.94	4.03	4.42	4.75	4.54	4.50	4.57
1959	4.64	4.52	4.45	4.67	4.96	4.96	4.93	4.95	5.32	5.22	5.21	5.28
1960	5.00	5.12	4.90	4.92	4.96	4.77	4.69	4.55	4.59	4.65	4.82	4.94
1961	4.58	4.44	4.36	4.65	4.63	4.75	4.71	4.75	4.57	4.42	4.57	4.64
1962	4.58	4.52	4.43	4.35	4.26	4.34	4.42	4.43	4.30	4.30	4.30	4.26
1963	4.25	4.25	4.29	4.38	4.37	4.35	4.37	4.38	4.42	4.39	4.42	4.50

TABLE C_{Q20}. Yield on Newly Issued Cohan Aa Public Utilities, by Quarters

	First	Second	Third	Fourth
1952	3.22	3.17	3.18	3.13
1953	3.35	3.69	3.68	3.33
1954	3.06	3.02	3.02	3.03
1955	3.15	3.23	3.32	3.30
1956	3.24	3.58	3.96	4.25

	First	Second	Third	Fourth
1957	4.37	4.58	4.79	4.72
1958	3.96	3.87	4.18	4.47
1959	4.49	4.85	4.86	5.15
1960	4.90	4.85	4.60	4.80

TABLE H_1. Spread Between the Yield on Homer's Newly Issued Callable Aa Public Utilities and the Yield on Homer's Seasoned Callable Aa Public Utility Bonds With $2\frac{3}{4}$–$2\frac{7}{8}$ Per Cent Coupon

	January	February	March	April	May	June	July	August	September	October	November	December
1952	.14	.11	.08	.14	.08	.12	.13	.12	.14	.10	.08	.10
1953	.07	.06	.15	.17	.26	.26	.27	.25	.19	.22	.08	.08
1954	.13	.01	−.01	.03	.04	.09	.01	.03	.06	.06	.04	.06
1955	.04	.08	.08	.13	.10	.12	.06	.07	.17	.12	.08	.13
1956	.09	.08	.03	.23	.37	.28	.39	.47	.45	.37	.50	.47
1957	.62	.64	.53	.61	.57	.75	.73	.71	.49	.54	.76	.43
1958	.34	.15	.39	.34	.37	.29	.33	.43	.46	.40	.31	.46
1959	.42	.40	.20	.20	.13	.45	.37	.30	.41	.52	.56	.63
1960	.59	.32	.58	.44	.42	.38	.35	.39	.30	.40	.49	.63
1961	.29	.06	.20	.32	.42	.42	.43	.20	.26	.12	.15	.20
1962	.21	.13	.15	.09	.09	.06	.11	.10	.05	.11	.13	.15
1963	.13	.05	.13	.12	.14	.10	.07	.10	.10	.08	.10	.12
1964	.11	.09	.06	.09	.05	.07	.04	.04	.07	.07	.07	.09
1965	.06	.02	.09	.09	.08	.17	.13	.15	.18	.17	.11	.15
1966	.15	.21	.35	.14	.43	.62	.60	.57	.84	.54	.66	.85
1967	.62	.29	.61	.42	.67	.56						

TABLE H_2. Spread Between the Yield on New Callable Issues of Aa Public Utility Bonds, Homer Series, and the Yield on Seasoned Callable Aa Public Utility Bonds of Current Coupon

	January	February	March	April	May	June	July	August	September	October	November	December
1952	.14	.09	.08	.08	.02	.07	.09	.09	.09	.05	.06	.06
1953	.07	.08	.06	.10	.15	.18	.13	.10	.12	.05	.03	.06
1954	.05	-.06	-.06	-.02	-.02	.04	-.03	-.03	.03	.01	-.01	.01
1955	-.02	.05	.05	.09	.08	.10	.06	.06	.12	.09	.04	.11
1956	.06	.07	.02	.15	.21	.12	.15	.20	.17	.11	.20	.25
1957	.20	.17	.10	.14	.13	.19	.21	.30	.15	.08	.24	.05
1958	.11	.04	.11	.14	.11	.00	.10	.16	.28	.13	.12	.20
1959	.18	.17	.09	.07	.04	.25	.23	.13	.13	.21	.12	.13
1960	.22	.03	.15	.04	.01	.04	.07	.11	.03	.04	.11	.21
1961	-.01	-.05	.05	.11	.16	.12	.08	.00	.14	.06	.06	.13
1962	.14	.05	.10	.05	.04	.02	.08	.11	.05	.06	.02	.07
1963	.06	.03	.04	.03	.08	.07	.05	.04	.04	.05	.05	.06
1964	.04	.01	.04	.05	.03	.05	.00	-.01	.04	.03	.03	.05
1965	.02	-.01	.03	.03	.02	.07	.04	.05	.05	.07	.03	.05
1966	.05	.05										

TABLE H_{10}. Average Coupon Rate on Homer Newly Issued, Callable Aa Public Utilities [a]

	January	February	March	April	May	June	July	August	September	October	November	December
1952	$3\frac{3}{8}$	$3\frac{1}{4}$	$3\frac{1}{4}$	$3\frac{1}{4}$	$3\frac{1}{4}$	$3\frac{1}{4}$	$3\frac{1}{4}$	$3\frac{1}{4}$	$3\frac{1}{4}$	$3\frac{1}{4}$	$3\frac{1}{4}$	$3\frac{1}{4}$
1953	$3\frac{1}{4}$	$3\frac{3}{8}$	$3\frac{1}{2}$	$3\frac{5}{8}$	$3\frac{7}{8}$	$3\frac{7}{8}$	$3\frac{3}{4}$	$3\frac{3}{4}$	$3\frac{5}{8}$	$3\frac{5}{8}$	$3\frac{3}{8}$	$3\frac{3}{8}$
1954	$3\frac{3}{8}$	$3\frac{1}{8}$	3	3	$3\frac{1}{8}$	$3\frac{1}{4}$	$3\frac{1}{8}$	$3\frac{1}{8}$	$3\frac{1}{8}$	$3\frac{1}{8}$	$3\frac{1}{8}$	$3\frac{1}{8}$
1955	$3\frac{1}{8}$	$3\frac{1}{4}$	$3\frac{1}{4}$	$3\frac{1}{4}$	$3\frac{1}{4}$	$3\frac{3}{8}$	$3\frac{1}{4}$	$3\frac{3}{8}$	$3\frac{1}{2}$	$3\frac{3}{8}$	$3\frac{3}{8}$	$3\frac{3}{8}$
1956	$3\frac{3}{8}$	$3\frac{1}{4}$	$3\frac{1}{4}$	$3\frac{1}{2}$	$3\frac{3}{4}$	$3\frac{5}{8}$	$3\frac{3}{4}$	4	$4\frac{1}{8}$	$4\frac{1}{8}$	$4\frac{1}{4}$	$4\frac{3}{8}$
1957	$4\frac{1}{4}$	$4\frac{1}{2}$	$4\frac{3}{8}$	$4\frac{1}{8}$	$4\frac{3}{8}$	$4\frac{5}{8}$	$4\frac{7}{8}$	5	$4\frac{7}{8}$	$4\frac{7}{8}$	5	$4\frac{1}{2}$
1958	$3\frac{7}{8}-4$	$3\frac{3}{4}$	$4\frac{1}{8}$	4	$3\frac{7}{8}$	4	4	$4\frac{3}{8}$	$4\frac{5}{8}$	$4\frac{5}{8}$	$4\frac{3}{4}$	$4\frac{5}{8}$
1959	$4\frac{5}{8}$	$4\frac{3}{4}$	$4\frac{3}{8}$	$4\frac{5}{8}$	$4\frac{5}{8}$	$4\frac{1}{8}$	5	5	5	$5\frac{1}{4}$	$5\frac{1}{4}$	$5\frac{1}{4}$
1960	$5\frac{1}{4}$	5	$5\frac{1}{8}$	$4\frac{7}{8}$	5	5	$4\frac{7}{8}$	$4\frac{5}{8}$	$4\frac{1}{8}$	$4\frac{3}{4}$	$4\frac{3}{4}$	5
1961	$4\frac{5}{8}$	$4\frac{3}{8}$	$4\frac{3}{8}$	$4\frac{5}{8}$	$4\frac{3}{4}$	$4\frac{3}{4}$	5	$4\frac{3}{4}$	$4\frac{3}{4}$	$4\frac{1}{2}-\frac{5}{8}$	$4\frac{5}{8}$	$4\frac{5}{8}$
1962	$4\frac{5}{8}$	$4\frac{5}{8}$	$4\frac{1}{8}$	$4\frac{3}{8}$	$4\frac{3}{8}$	$4\frac{3}{8}$	$4\frac{3}{8}$	$4\frac{1}{2}$	$4\frac{3}{4}$	$4\frac{3}{8}$	$4\frac{3}{8}$	$4\frac{3}{8}$
1963	$4\frac{3}{8}$	$4\frac{1}{4}$	$4\frac{3}{8}$	$4\frac{3}{8}$	$4\frac{3}{8}$	$4\frac{3}{8}$	$4\frac{3}{8}$	$4\frac{3}{4}$	$4\frac{3}{4}$	$4\frac{3}{8}$	$4\frac{1}{2}$	$4\frac{1}{2}$
1964	$4\frac{5}{8}$	$4\frac{1}{2}$	$4\frac{3}{8}$	$4\frac{5}{8}$	$4\frac{5}{8}$	$4\frac{1}{2}$	$4\frac{1}{2}$	$4\frac{1}{2}$	$4\frac{1}{2}$	$4\frac{5}{8}$	$4\frac{1}{2}$	$4\frac{5}{8}$
1965	$4\frac{5}{8}$	$4\frac{1}{2}$	$4\frac{5}{8}$	$4\frac{5}{8}$	$4\frac{5}{8}$	$4\frac{5}{8}$	$4\frac{5}{8}$	$4\frac{5}{8}$	$4\frac{3}{4}$	$4\frac{3}{4}$	$4\frac{3}{4}$	$4\frac{7}{8}$
1966	5	5										

[a] The difference between the average coupon rate on newly issued Homer Aa utilities and the $2\frac{1}{4}-\frac{7}{8}$ per cent coupon rate is derived by subtracting $2\frac{1}{4}$ per cent from the following coupon rates.

TABLE H_{20}. Yield on New Issues, Callable Aa Public Utility Bonds, Homer Series

	January	February	March	April	May	June	July	August	September	October	November	December
1951	2.80	2.80	2.90	3.05	3.10	3.20	3.35	3.20	3.01	3.14	3.23	3.30
1952	3.28	3.13	3.18	3.19	3.15	3.19	3.21	3.21	3.20	3.19	3.17	3.13
1953	3.19	3.26	3.40	3.45	3.75	3.78	3.73	3.60	3.65	3.50	3.22	3.30
1954	3.23	3.05	2.90	2.93	3.00	3.10	3.00	3.00	3.05	3.03	3.00	3.02
1955	3.00	3.14	3.20	3.20	3.20	3.25	3.20	3.25	3.40	3.30	3.22	3.32
1956	3.25	3.20	3.15	3.45	3.70	3.57	3.73	3.90	4.07	4.01	4.20	4.30
1957	4.50	4.40	4.22	4.29	4.35	4.62	4.85	5.00	4.81	4.78	4.97	4.47
1958	3.94	3.70	4.00	4.00	3.90	3.85	3.95	4.25	4.60	4.57	4.42	4.55
1959	4.60	4.65	4.37	4.47	4.59	5.05	4.95	4.85	5.00	5.25	5.15	5.15
1960	5.25	4.95	5.10	4.85	4.88	4.90	4.80	4.60	4.47	4.65	4.75	5.00
1961	4.60	4.32	4.32	4.52	4.75	4.75	4.85	4.65	4.75	4.55	4.52	4.60
1962	4.65	4.55	4.55	4.40	4.29	4.29	4.39	4.47	4.30	4.30	4.26	4.28
1963	4.28	4.19	4.27	4.27	4.39	4.35	4.32	4.35	4.35	4.38	4.40	4.43
1964	4.50	4.42	4.39	4.50	4.48	4.48	4.44	4.42	4.45	4.47	4.47	4.50
1965	4.45	4.39	4.47	4.48	4.48	4.59	4.56	4.60	4.67	4.70	4.66	4.80
1966	4.90	4.98	5.30	5.15	5.50	5.67	5.67	5.77	6.35	6.05	6.00	6.20
1967	5.85	5.20	5.70	5.55	5.80	5.95						

TABLE H_{21}. Yield on Seasoned Issues With $2\frac{3}{4}$–$2\frac{7}{8}$ Coupon, Callable Aa Public Utility Bonds, Homer Series

	January	February	March	April	May	June	July	August	September	October	November	December
1952	3.14	3.02	3.10	3.05	3.07	3.07	3.08	3.09	3.06	3.09	3.09	3.03
1953	3.12	3.20	3.25	3.28	3.49	3.52	3.46	3.35	3.46	3.28	3.14	3.22
1954	3.10	3.04	2.91	2.90	2.96	3.01	2.99	2.97	2.99	2.97	2.96	2.96
1955	2.96	3.06	3.12	3.07	3.10	3.13	3.14	3.18	3.23	3.18	3.14	3.19
1956	3.16	3.12	3.12	3.22	3.33	3.29	3.34	3.43	3.62	3.64	3.70	3.83
1957	3.88	3.76	3.69	3.68	3.78	3.87	4.12	4.29	4.32	4.24	4.21	4.04
1958	3.60	3.55	3.61	3.66	3.53	3.56	3.62	3.82	4.14	4.17	4.11	4.09
1959	4.18	4.25	4.17	4.27	4.46	4.60	4.58	4.55	4.59	4.73	4.59	4.52
1960	4.66	4.63	4.52	4.41	4.46	4.52	4.45	4.21	4.17	4.25	4.26	4.37
1961	4.31	4.26	4.12	4.20	4.33	4.33	4.42	4.45	4.49	4.43	4.37	4.40
1962	4.44	4.42	4.40	4.31	4.20	4.23	4.28	4.37	4.25	4.19	4.13	4.13
1963	4.15	4.14	4.14	4.15	4.25	4.25	4.25	4.25	4.25	4.30	4.30	4.31
1964	4.39	4.33	4.33	4.41	4.43	4.41	4.40	4.38	4.38	4.40	4.40	4.41
1965	4.39	4.37	4.38	4.39	4.40	4.42	4.43	4.45	4.49	4.53	4.55	4.65
1966	4.75	4.77	4.95	5.01	5.03	5.05	5.07	5.20	5.51	5.51	5.34	5.35
1967	5.23	4.91	5.09	5.07	5.13	5.39	5.66	5.68	5.75	5.75		

TABLE H_{22}. Yield on Seasoned Issues of Current Coupon, Callable Aa Public Utility Bonds, Homer Series

	January	February	March	April	May	June	July	August	September	October	November	December
1952	3.14	3.04	3.10	3.11	3.13	3.12	3.12	3.12	3.11	3.14	3.11	3.07
1953	3.12	3.18	3.34	3.35	3.60	3.60	3.60	3.50	3.53	3.45	3.19	3.24
1954	3.18	3.11	2.96	2.95	3.02	3.06	3.03	3.03	3.02	3.02	3.01	3.01
1955	3.02	3.09	3.15	3.11	3.12	3.15	3.14	3.19	3.28	3.21	3.18	3.21
1956	3.19	3.13	3.13	3.30	3.49	3.45	3.58	3.70	3.90	3.90	4.00	4.05
1957	4.30	4.23	4.12	4.15	4.22	4.43	4.64	4.70	4.66	4.70	4.73	4.42
1958	3.83	3.66	3.89	3.86	3.79	3.85	3.85	4.09	4.32	4.44	4.30	4.35
1959	4.42	4.48	4.28	4.40	4.55	4.80	4.72	4.72	4.87	5.04	5.03	5.02
1960	5.03	4.92	4.95	4.81	4.87	4.86	4.73	4.49	4.44	4.61	4.64	4.79
1961	4.61	4.37	4.27	4.41	4.59	4.63	4.77	4.65	4.61	4.49	4.46	4.47
1962	4.51	4.50	4.45	4.35	4.25	4.27	4.31	4.36	4.25	4.24	4.24	4.21
1963	4.22	4.16	4.23	4.24	4.31	4.28	4.27	4.31	4.31	4.33	4.35	4.37
1964	4.46	4.41	4.35	4.45	4.45	4.43	4.44	4.43	4.41	4.44	4.44	4.45
1965	4.43	4.40	4.44	4.45	4.46	4.52	4.52	4.55	4.62	4.63	4.64	4.76
1966	4.85	4.93										

TABLE K_1: Spread Between Yield on Kaplan Recently Issued Aa Corporate Bonds and Yield on Moody Seasoned Aa Corporate Bonds

	January	February	March	April	May	June	July	August	September	October	November	December
1952	.13	.10	.13	.16	.17	.15	.16	.14	.11	.10	.06	.07
1953	.18	.18	.16	.16	.26	.34	.29	.27	.26	.15	.11	.02
1954	-.02	.01	-.04	.01	-.03	-.03	-.03	-.03	-.01	-.03	-.04	-.04
1955	-.01	.03	.03	.02	.03	.06	.07	.06	.07	.07	.02	.02
1956	.02	-.01	.04	.15	.16	.19	.22	.31	.25	.19	.15	.21
1957	.30	.45	.51	.52	.51	.66	.65	.54	.48	.51	.47	.32
1958	.47	.07	.23	.14	.10	.07	.11	.17	.22	.18	.10	.22
1959	.26	.24	.18	.16	.18	.21	.15	.18	.35	.31	.38	.42
1960	.32	.25	.31	.27	.29	.25	.17	.16	.20	.20	.20	.28
1961	.21	.10	.04	.13	.14	.22	.15	.10	.03	-.01	-.03	-.02
1962	-.06	-.08	-.10	-.15	-.16	-.18	-.15	-.16	-.15	-.14	-.13	-.11
1963	-.13	-.11	-.09	-.03	-.02	-.04	-.07	-.09	-.05	-.07	-.06	-.04

TABLE K_{10}. Average Coupon Rate on Kaplan Recently Issued Aa Corporates [a]

	January	February	March	April	May	June	July	August	September	October	November	December
1952	3.38	3.33	3.33	3.32	3.30	3.27	3.30	3.31	3.30	3.25	3.25	3.25
1953	3.25	3.31	3.40	3.41	3.64	3.86	3.89	3.88	3.82	3.71	3.63	3.43
1954	3.41	3.33	3.16	3.09	2.99	3.05	3.07	3.11	3.10	3.12	3.10	3.12
1955	3.13	3.13	3.17	3.18	3.20	3.27	3.30	3.31	3.38	3.38	3.29	3.31
1956	3.33	3.30	3.29	3.39	3.55	3.62	3.65	3.75	3.89	3.98	3.86	4.08
1957	4.33	4.52	4.44	4.36	4.40	4.69	4.86	4.87	4.92	4.97	4.93	4.82
1958	4.67	3.88	4.09	4.09	4.04	3.94	3.94	3.99	4.22	4.47	4.48	4.55
1959	4.59	4.68	4.56	4.52	4.58	4.82	4.89	4.88	5.01	5.22	5.34	5.33
1960	5.28	5.21	5.10	4.93	4.93	4.99	4.90	4.88	4.73	4.60	4.66	4.88
1961	4.94	4.76	4.58	4.50	4.62	4.65	4.74	4.78	4.80	4.75	4.68	4.58
1962	4.58	4.57	4.57	4.48	4.33	4.28	4.28	4.40	4.45	4.39	4.38	4.36
1963	4.36	4.33	4.29	4.31	4.41	4.43	4.38	4.34	4.34	4.36	4.37	4.43

[a] The difference between the average coupon rate on Kaplan recent issues and the average coupon rate on Moody seasoned Aa corporates, is derived by subtracting the average coupon rate on seasoned Moody Aa corporates from the following coupon rates.

TABLE K_{20}. Yield on Recently Issued Aa Corporates, Kaplan Series

	January	February	March	April	May	June	July	August	September	October	November	December
1951	2.70	2.73	2.91	3.01	2.99	3.07	3.09	3.01	2.99	2.97	3.19	3.23
1952	3.18	3.11	3.16	3.17	3.17	3.18	3.20	3.20	3.18	3.18	3.12	3.12
1953	3.27	3.32	3.34	3.45	3.67	3.84	3.71	3.66	3.69	3.48	3.38	3.30
1954	3.20	3.13	2.99	3.01	3.00	3.03	3.01	3.00	3.03	3.01	3.00	3.00
1955	3.05	3.13	3.16	3.15	3.18	3.20	3.21	3.26	3.29	3.26	3.20	3.24
1956	3.21	3.15	3.22	3.45	3.50	3.54	3.61	3.81	3.88	3.88	3.91	4.06
1957	4.19	4.28	4.31	4.31	4.34	4.64	4.75	4.75	4.74	4.79	4.76	4.40
1958	4.28	3.84	4.01	3.92	3.88	3.85	3.94	4.15	4.42	4.39	4.31	4.40
1959	4.48	4.48	4.41	4.48	4.64	4.77	4.73	4.76	5.04	5.07	5.08	5.16
1960	5.09	4.96	4.93	4.85	4.90	4.85	4.73	4.60	4.61	4.64	4.67	4.78
1961	4.69	4.50	4.38	4.50	4.55	4.67	4.68	4.67	4.62	4.55	4.51	4.54
1962	4.49	4.48	4.43	4.34	4.27	4.26	4.34	4.33	4.31	4.27	4.27	4.27
1963	4.24	4.25	4.25	4.32	4.34	4.32	4.32	4.31	4.36	4.36	4.38	4.42

TABLE M_1. Spread Between Yield on Newly Issued Moody Aa Corporates and Yield on Seasoned Moody Aa Corporates

	January	February	March	April	May	June	July	August	September	October	November	December
1952	.09	.04	.23	.13	.14	.19	.15	—	—	.09	.03	.09
1953	.15	.25	.22	.30	.47	—	.26	.23	.42	-.13	.01	.02
1954	-.03	-.09	-.12	-.01	.03	-.06	—	-.06	.07	-.06	.06	-.02
1955	.08	.04	.15	—	.09	.06	.29	.30	.10	.06	.05	.10
1956	—	-.01	.09	.42	.28	.20	.59	.62	.35	.35	.54	.45
1957	.47	.43	.50	.50	.59	.90	.59	.68	.53	.63	.40	.35
1958	-.09	.15	.31	.07	.10	.03	.15	.54	.48	.31	.26	.32
1959	.37	.11	.17	.27	.42	.42	.35	.35	.79	.36	.51	.42
1960	.15	.33	.12	.36	.27	.16	.09	-.02	.21	.18	.27	.47
1961	.04	—	.03	.19	.15	.27	.12	.15	-.09	-.11	-.06	.00
1962	.00	-.05	-.13	-.14	-.15	-.18	-.07	-.10	-.19	-.15	-.16	-.06
1963	-.17	-.09	-.08	.02	-.02	-.05	-.04	-.07	-.06	-.04	-.03	.03
1964	-.04	-.08	.03	—	-.04	-.03	-.08	-.07	.02	—	—	.00
1965	—	-.03	.03	-.01	.02	.07	.03	.11	.08	-.01	.04	.12
1966	.07	.22	.30	.10	.15	.49	.52	.50	.32	.29	.32	.45
1967	.09	.08	.22	.17	.30	.26	.24	.42	.22	.39	—	.45

TABLE M_2. Spread Between the Yield on Newly Issued Aa Corporates, Moody Series, and the Estimated Yield on Seasoned Aa Corporates, Coupon Rate Equal to That on New Issues

	January	February	March	April	May	June	July	August	September	October	November	December
1952	.05	.00	.14	.11	.10	.12	.13	—	—	.03	-.03	.10
1953	.08	.20	.12	.18	.20	—	.06	.13	.09	-.16	.03	.05
1954	-.02	-.09	-.08	-.01	.01	-.02	—	-.06	.06	-.06	.05	-.02
1955	.06	.03	.15	—	.09	.06	—	.22	.06	.04	.05	.08
1956	—	.00	.06	.40	.19	.12	.21	.46	.12	.04	.38	.27
1957	.29	.28	.32	.29	.20	.58	.34	.35	.17	.44	.19	.15
1958	-.05	.10	.16	-.02	.00	.01	.05	.26	.30	.12	.10	.12
1959	.19	.03	.07	.15	.26	.30	.25	.25	.72	.22	.35	.28
1960	.06	.24	-.08	.12	.08	-.04	-.11	.00	-.01	-.18	-.08	.18
1961	-.175	—	-.07	.06	.06	.20	.02	.12	-.145	-.16	-.11	-.02
1962	.02	-.03	-.105	-.06	-.10	-.03	.025	.02	.00	-.02	-.03	.07
1963	-.09	.04	.01	.09	.05	.03	.05	.01	.015	.03	.035	.08

TABLE M_4. Moody New-Seasoned Yield Spread as Described Under M_1 Plus Underwriter Spread [a]

	Jan-uary	Feb-ruary	March	April	May	June	July	Au-gust	Sep-tember	Octo-ber	Novem-ber	Decem-ber
1952	.080	.020	.040	.049	.043	.032	.070	—	—	.030	.037	.043
1953	.030	.048	.032	.059	.046	—	.040	.040	.009	.030	.030	.030
1954	.030	.029	.119	.015	.025	.052	.070	.030	.029	.034	.035	.020
1955	.032	.030	.030	—	.033	.026	—	.030	.030	.030	.024	.039
1956	—	.030	.027	.050	.045	.040	.033	.060	.053	.050	.042	.040
1957	.057	.048	.040	.050	.050	.073	.059	.050	.051	.040	.057	.057
1958	.050	.040	.047	.050	.050	.042	.050	.055	.058	.053	.050	.042
1959	.047	.040	.047	.063	.055	.042	.040	.044	.074	.070	.009	.051
1960	.050	.046	.042	.059	.050	.045	.050	.057	.052	.055	.051	.045
1961	.040	.050	.050	.059	.053	.053	.040	.050	.040	.040	.045	.056
1962	.040	.050	.048	.040	.050	.048	.045	.043	.040	.040	.040	.040
1963	.030	.040	.036	.038	.036	.046	.040	.046	.057	.040	.050	.033

[a] Underwriter spread is the difference between the yield to maturity calculated from the offering price and the yield to maturity calculated from the price at which the issue was sold to the underwriter.

TABLE M_{10}. Difference Between Average Coupon on Newly Issued Moody Aa Corporates and Average Coupon on Seasoned Moody Aa Corporates

	January	February	March	April	May	June	July	August	September	October	November	December
1952	.33	.25	.42	.31	.33	.26	.17	—	—	.35	.31	.24
1953	.43	.47	.46	.66	.92	—	.69	.52	.70	.14	.27	.27
1954	.22	-.05	-.14	-.04	.03	-.11	—	.02	.02	-.01	.08	.03
1955	.10	.14	.20	—	.20	.14	—	.50	.25	.23	.10	.29
1956	—	.10	.19	.60	.54	.48	.57	.92	.96	.96	1.21	1.21
1957	1.245	1.12	1.18	1.18	1.31	1.71	1.54	1.78	1.57	1.59	1.46	1.11
1958	.45	.67	.85	.57	.59	.57	.85	1.29	1.09	.995	1.045	.96
1959	1.14	.795	.89	.94	1.33	1.37	1.29	1.25	1.855	1.54	1.58	1.58
1960	1.265	1.30	1.09	1.255	1.255	1.13	.86	.61	.92	.84	.98	1.19
1961	.815	—	.69	.94	.865	1.065	.94	.975	.60	.64	.64	.85
1962	.725	.66	.56	.475	.40	.305	.475	.44	.35	.285	.285	.305
1963	.12	.305	.24	.35	.35	.28	.26	.215	.245	.325	.345	.455

TABLE M_{10a}. Average Coupon Rate on Newly Issued Moody Aa Corporates

	January	February	March	April	May	June	July	August	September	October	November	December
1952	3.2083	3.125	3.300	3.189	3.214	3.281	3.1875	—	—	3.250	3.208	3.1875
1953	3.375	3.416	3.458	3.656	3.916	—	3.750	3.625	3.8125	3.250	3.375	3.375
1954	3.333	3.062	2.968	3.083	3.145	3.000	—	3.125	3.125	3.100	3.1875	3.125
1955	3.2083	3.250	3.3125	—	3.312	3.250	—	3.625	3.375	3.375	3.250	3.4375
1956	—	3.250	3.343	3.750	3.687	3.625	3.718	4.083	4.125	4.125	4.375	4.375
1957	4.4375	4.312	4.375	4.375	4.500	4.906	4.729	4.968	4.900	4.916	4.791	4.437
1958	3.775	4.000	4.187	3.900	3.925	3.906	4.187	4.625	4.625	4.575	4.625	4.541
1959	4.718	4.375	4.531	4.587	5.000	5.041	5.000	4.958	5.562	5.250	5.291	5.3125
1960	5.000	5.041	4.833	5.000	5.000	4.875	4.625	4.375	4.687	4.6875	4.825	5.000
1961	4.625	—	4.500	4.750	4.675	4.875	4.750	4.875	4.500	4.5416	4.5416	4.750
1962	4.625	4.5625	4.4583	4.375	4.300	4.333	4.500	4.470	4.375	4.3125	4.3125	4.375
1963	4.1875	4.375	4.3125	4.4166	4.4166	4.350	4.375	4.333	4.3625	4.4375	4.4583	4.5833

TABLE M_{10b}. Average Coupon on Seasoned Moody Aa Corporates

	January	February	March	April	May	June	July	August	September	October	November	December
1952	2.88	2.88	2.88	2.88	2.88	3.02	3.02	3.02	3.02	2.90	2.90	2.95
1953	2.95	2.95	3.00	3.00	3.00	3.06	3.06	3.11	3.11	3.11	3.11	3.11
1954	3.11	3.11	3.11	3.12	3.12	3.11	3.11	3.11	3.11	3.11	3.11	3.10
1955	3.11	3.11	3.11	3.11	3.11	3.11	3.11	3.13	3.13	3.15	3.15	3.15
1956	3.15	3.15	3.15	3.15	3.15	3.15	3.15	3.16	3.16	3.16	3.16	3.16
1957	3.19	3.19	3.19	3.19	3.19	3.19	3.19	3.19	3.33	3.33	3.33	3.33
1958	3.34	3.34	3.33	3.33	3.33	3.33	3.33	3.33	3.53	3.58	3.58	3.58
1959	3.58	3.58	3.64	3.64	3.67	3.67	3.71	3.71	3.71	3.71	3.71	3.735
1960	3.735	3.745	3.745	3.745	3.745	3.745	3.77	3.77	3.77	3.84	3.84	3.81
1961	3.81	3.81	3.81	3.81	3.81	3.81	3.81	3.90	3.90	3.90	3.90	3.90
1962	3.90	3.90	3.90	3.90	3.90	4.025	4.025	4.025	4.025	4.025	4.025	4.07
1963	4.07	4.07	4.07	4.07	4.07	4.07	4.12	4.12	4.12	4.12	4.12	4.13

TABLE M_{20}. Yield on Newly Issued Aa Corporates, Moody Series

	January	February	March	April	May	June	July	August	September	October	November	December
1951	2.82	2.85	2.95	3.16	3.10	3.46	—	3.01	—	3.16	3.29	3.25
1952	3.14	3.05	3.26	3.14	3.14	3.22	3.19	—	—	3.17	3.09	3.14
1953	3.24	3.39	3.40	3.59	3.88	—	3.68	3.625	3.85	3.20	3.28	3.30
1954	3.19	3.03	2.91	2.99	3.06	3.00	—	2.97	3.11	2.98	3.10	3.02
1955	3.14	3.14	3.28	—	3.24	3.20	—	3.50	3.32	3.25	3.23	3.32
1956	—	3.15	3.27	3.72	3.62	3.55	3.68	4.12	3.98	4.04	4.30	4.30
1957	4.36	4.26	4.30	4.29	4.42	4.88	4.69	4.89	4.79	4.91	4.69	4.43
1958	3.72	3.92	4.09	3.85	3.88	3.81	3.98	4.52	4.68	4.52	4.47	4.50
1959	4.59	4.35	4.40	4.59	4.88	4.98	4.93	4.93	5.48	5.12	5.21	5.16
1960	4.92	5.04	4.74	4.94	4.88	4.76	4.65	4.42	4.62	4.62	4.74	4.97
1961	4.52	—	4.37	4.56	4.56	4.72	4.65	4.72	4.50	4.45	4.48	4.56
1962	4.55	4.51	4.40	4.35	4.28	4.26	4.42	4.39	4.27	4.26	4.24	4.32
1963	4.20	4.27	4.26	4.37	4.34	4.31	4.35	4.33	4.35	4.39	4.41	4.49
1964	4.45	4.38	4.50	—	4.46	4.48	4.42	4.42	4.50	—	—	4.50
1965	—	4.43	4.51	4.47	4.51	4.59	4.59	4.70	4.71	4.65	4.73	4.92
1966	4.90	5.12	5.35	5.20	5.25	5.65	5.77	5.88	5.90	5.84	5.78	5.93
1967	5.39	5.26	5.45	5.43	5.72	5.89	5.96	6.18	6.09	6.40		

TABLE M_{21}. Yield on Seasoned Aa Corporates, Moody Series

	January	February	March	April	May	June	July	August	September	October	November	December
1952	3.05	3.01	3.03	3.01	3.00	3.03	3.04	3.06	3.07	3.08	3.06	3.05
1953	3.09	3.14	3.18	3.29	3.41	3.50	3.42	3.39	3.43	3.33	3.27	3.28
1954	3.22	3.12	3.03	3.00	3.03	3.06	3.04	3.03	3.04	3.04	3.04	3.04
1955	3.06	3.10	3.13	3.13	3.15	3.14	3.14	3.20	3.22	3.19	3.18	3.22
1956	3.19	3.16	3.18	3.30	3.34	3.35	3.39	3.50	3.63	3.69	3.76	3.85
1957	3.89	3.83	3.80	3.79	3.83	3.98	4.10	4.21	4.26	4.28	4.29	4.08
1958	3.81	3.77	3.78	3.78	3.78	3.78	3.83	3.98	4.20	4.21	4.21	4.18
1959	4.22	4.24	4.23	4.32	4.46	4.56	4.58	4.58	4.69	4.76	4.70	4.74
1960	4.77	4.71	4.62	4.58	4.61	4.60	4.56	4.44	4.41	4.44	4.47	4.50
1961	4.48	4.40	4.34	4.37	4.41	4.45	4.53	4.57	4.59	4.56	4.54	4.56
1962	4.55	4.56	4.53	4.49	4.43	4.44	4.49	4.49	4.46	4.41	4.40	4.38
1963	4.37	4.36	4.34	4.35	4.36	4.36	4.39	4.40	4.41	4.43	4.44	4.46
1964	4.49	4.46	4.47	4.49	4.50	4.51	4.50	4.49	4.48	4.50	4.49	4.50
1965	4.48	4.46	4.48	4.48	4.49	4.52	4.56	4.59	4.63	4.66	4.69	4.80
1966	4.83	4.90	5.05	5.10	5.10	5.16	5.25	5.38	5.58	5.55	5.46	5.48
1967	5.30	5.18	5.23	5.26	5.42	5.63	5.72	5.76	5.87	6.01		

TABLE M_{22}. Yield on Seasoned Aa Corporates of Current Coupon, Coupon Rate Equal to That on New Issues, Moody Series

	January	February	March	April	May	June	July	August	September	October	November	December
1952	3.09	3.05	3.12	3.03	3.04	3.10	3.06	—	—	3.14	3.12	3.04
1953	3.16	3.19	3.28	3.41	3.68	—	3.62	3.49	3.76	3.36	3.25	3.25
1954	3.21	3.12	2.99	3.00	3.05	3.02	—	3.03	3.05	3.04	3.05	3.04
1955	3.08	3.11	3.13	—	3.15	3.14	—	3.28	3.26	3.21	3.18	3.24
1956	—	3.15	3.21	3.32	3.43	3.43	3.47	3.66	3.86	4.00	3.92	4.03
1957	4.07	3.98	3.98	4.00	4.22	4.30	4.35	4.54	4.62	4.47	4.50	4.28
1958	3.77	3.82	3.93	3.87	3.88	3.80	3.93	4.26	4.38	4.40	4.37	4.38
1959	4.40	4.32	4.33	4.44	4.62	4.68	4.68	4.68	4.76	4.90	4.86	4.88
1960	4.86	4.80	4.82	4.82	4.80	4.80	4.76	4.42	4.63	4.80	4.82	4.79
1961	4.70	—	4.44	4.50	4.50	4.52	4.63	4.60	4.65	4.61	4.59	4.58
1962	4.53	4.54	4.51	4.41	4.38	4.29	4.40	4.37	4.27	4.28	4.27	4.25
1963	4.29	4.23	4.25	4.28	4.29	4.28	4.30	4.32	4.34	4.36	4.38	4.41

TABLE S$_{60}$. Ratio of Volume of Slow-Selling to Total New Aaa, Aa and A Public Utility Issues [a]

	January	February	March	April	May	June	July	August	September	October	November	December
1952	1.000	.000	1.000	.757	.809	.481	.524	1.000	1.000	.629	.298	1.000
1953	.429	.647	.519	.743	.772	.515	.482	.615	.717	.739	.909	.846
1954	.588	.395	.868	.868	.591	.859	.917	.954	.949	.169	1.000	.194
1955	.969	.828	.862	1.000	.933	1.000	.766	1.000	.082	1.000	.372	1.000
1956	.560	.000	.787	.793	.709	.931	.901	.275	.078	.571	.671	.833
1957	.467	.216	.764	.102	.737	.601	.279	.440	.288	.848	.962	.113
1958	.000	.772	.802	.794	.958	1.000	.941	.292	.677	.000	.685	.636
1959	1.000	.547	1.000	1.000	1.000	.386	.190	1.000	1.000	.000	.483	.110
1960	.746	.500	1.000	.791	.812	1.000	.813	1.000	1.000	.000	.950	.684
1961	.595	.655	.830	.769	.818	.598	.828	.411	1.000	.947	.799	.772
1962	.000	.778	.951	.731	1.000	.776	.758	.476	.586	1.000	.295	1.000
1963	.568	1.000	.477	.747	.781	.985	1.000	1.000	1.000	1.000	1.000	.636

[a] Ratio applies to month preceding the observation of yield spread being explained.

6

Interest Rates and Bank Reserves —
A Reinterpretation of the Statistical
Association   *Phillip Cagan*

I. Introduction

Many studies of banking have found that reserve ratios are correlated
with interest rates; the relationship has become the centerpiece of
theoretical and econometric models of the financial sector linking the
supply of money to market developments. A currently popular interpretation of the association is that banks equate the marginal advantages of additional free reserves and earning assets; the two substitute for each other in bank portfolios depending upon the cost of
borrowing reserves and the rate of return on assets. Given the quantity
of unborrowed reserves provided by the monetary authorities, a relation between free reserves and interest rates helps determine the
supply of bank deposits.

That an association exists between reserves and interest rates has
long been noted in U.S. data. While the interest-rate data need no
special comment, the data on reserves do. Before 1914, the association
pertained to excess reserves (vault cash and balances with reserve

NOTE: Circulation of an earlier version of this study in 1966 elicited many comments
which were most useful in preparing this revision. I wish to thank in particular Karl
Brunner, Richard Davis, Peter Frost, Jack Guttentag, George Morrison, Anna Jacobson
Schwartz, Robert Shay and William L. Silber. The conclusions are entirely mine, of
course.

I am also indebted for supervision of the computations to Josephine Trubek and Jae
Won Lee, research assistants, and to Martha T. Jones in the data processing department,
at the National Bureau.

agents minus required reserves); at that time there was no central bank to create and lend reserves. Since 1914, when Federal Reserve Banks began providing a discount window for member banks, it has pertained to excess reserves and member-bank borrowing from Reserve Banks, or to free reserves (excess reserves minus borrowing). The association for both periods—before and after 1914—is similar, as will be shown later. The explanation given for the phenomenon, however, has turned completely around. Until the late 1930's, most studies (such as the well-known work of Riefler [39] and Tinbergen [45] [1]) assumed that the association reflected an effect of the reserve ratio on interest rates. Then, following Turner's 1938 criticism [46] of Riefler's study, the direction of influence was reversed—interest rates were thought to affect reserve ratios. The new explanation was expressed in terms of the marginal advantages to banks of free reserves and other assets. This later view has come to monopolize opinion. The Appendix to this chapter briefly surveys empirical studies on this subject, documenting the shift in interpretation.

Evidence on the association is examined in Section II. Section III tests the earlier explanation and Section IV the later explanation. Both are found to be inadequate. Finally, Section V discusses and tests another interpretation of the association. The conclusion is that the pursuit of short-run profits motivated bank borrowing much more strongly in the 1920's than it did in the 1950's, but such behavior accounts for little, if any, of the association in either period. The explanation offered here is that bank borrowing from the Federal Reserve increases as monetary conditions tighten, because the banks are striving to accommodate their regular loan customers. Interest rates appear to play a small role in the variations of deposit growth due to changes in free reserves.

II. Interest Rates and Reserve Ratios: The Statistical Association

The association referred to above pertains mainly to short-run cyclical movements. There have been long-run movements in the excess reserve (or free reserve) ratio of banks, but they reflect institutional developments or special circumstances.[2] We may focus on short-run

[1] Bracketed numbers refer to works cited in the references following the Appendix to this chapter.

[2] Long-run movements are discussed in my *Determinants and Effects of Changes in the Money Stock* [7].

movements by grouping the data according to the stages of business cycles. Chart 6-1 presents National Bureau reference cycle patterns of the free reserve ratio of member banks [3] and the commercial paper rate, which behaves similarly to the Treasury bill rate typically used in this comparison. The patterns for the two series tend to move inversely. Although far from perfect, the association is fairly strong for most periods. The amplitude of cyclical movements in the reserve ratio has varied, however. They were large in the 1920's and even larger in the 1930's, but were quite small in the 1950's. Short-term interest rates fluctuated with roughly the same amplitude in the 1950's as they did in the 1920's, but with a much smaller amplitude in the intervening period. A sharp decline in the early 1930's brought short-term rates to very low levels, where they remained with only minor changes during that decade and most of the next.

The strongest evidence of an inverse association is provided by the data for the 1920's, the period studied by Riefler. The period since World War II, to which most recent studies are confined, has produced a smaller variety of cyclical patterns and, so far, less revealing evidence. The difference in the relation over time can be seen in Chart 6-2, which presents a scatter diagram of changes from stage to stage of the reference cycle patterns 1919–61. The chart distinguishes the three periods discussed. The points for the middle period 1933–38 show no correlation. Those for 1919–33 show the strongest correlation, though four observations in particular for that period (dated on the chart) stand out as extremes. The points for the latest period also show a negative correlation, but with a much flatter slope than that for the 1920's. The flatter slope reflects the smaller amplitude of fluctuation in the free reserve ratio after World War II compared with the 1920's, given the roughly unchanged amplitude of fluctuation in short-term interest rates.

Although Charts 6-1 and 6-2 show little association for the 1930's and early 1940's, that period is often cited as dramatic proof of such an association. After 1933, banks stopped borrowing from Federal Reserve Banks and accumulated excess reserves at a rapid pace, while short-term interest rates fell sharply, creating a nice inverse association between the two series for the period as a whole. The changes

---

[3] Although many studies of the association do not divide reserves by deposits, it is desirable to do so, particularly when examining data for long time periods.

Data on member-bank free reserves have been published by the Board of Governors of the Federal Reserve System since 1929; earlier figures used here are estimates of the National Bureau.

CHART 6-1. Reference Cycle Patterns of Member-Bank Free Reserve Ratio and Commercial Paper Rate, 1919–61

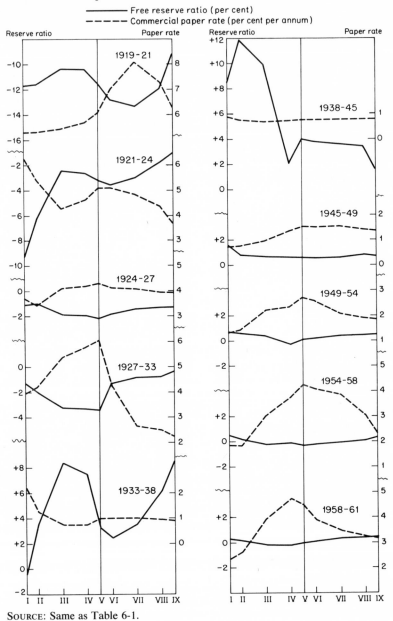

———— Free reserve ratio (per cent)
— — — — Commercial paper rate (per cent per annum)

SOURCE: Same as Table 6-1.

CHART 6-2. Member-Bank Free Reserve Ratio and Commercial Paper Rate, Changes Between Reference Stages in Percentage Points

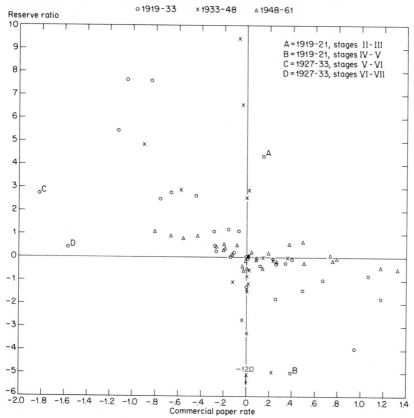

SOURCE: Same as Table 6-1.

from stage to stage in Chart 6-2 hide this longer-run association during those years.

The continuing increase in excess reserves after 1933 can be attributed to a combination of two quite different influences, both of a special nature and both difficult to quantify. The first influence reflects the cost of investing in short-term securities, supplemented during that decade by the lack of demand for loans and the risk of investing in long-term securities. Banks normally profit by investing funds which, for the time being, exceed needed working balances. To take care of fluctuations in reserves, banks buy short-term securities for short holding periods, as excess funds permit. At very low yields on those securities, however, the transaction costs (broadly interpreted) of buying and selling may equal or exceed the return; excess funds will then be held idle. If the break-even point for most banks were as high as 1 per cent on Treasury bills and commercial paper, it would help explain the sharp rise in the excess reserve ratio after 1933 when those short-term rates fell below that level,[4] even though the changes from stage to stage in Chart 6-2 reveal no relation.

Transaction costs undoubtedly did not exceed the return on loans and bonds, however. Beyond some moderate amount, depending upon the circumstances of each individual bank, excess reserves are not needed to meet expected drains. If the preceding argument were to explain an accumulation beyond that amount in the 1930's, it would have to be that the demand for bank loans was limited, and that bonds appeared unattractive to banks at the low yields then available because of the danger of capital losses if yields later increased. (The situation changed in 1942 when the Federal Reserve began to support U.S. bond prices, preventing any increase in yields while the policy continued.) This danger does not seem to have been sufficient to explain why banks did not purchase bonds during the 1930's. After all, yields continued to fall throughout the decade and there was little prospect of a major rise. It cannot, however, be ruled out as a minor reason for the accumulation of excess reserves.

A second influence on excess reserves during that period was the shattering experience of the financial crisis which culminated in the complete suspension of bank operations for one week in March 1933. For many years thereafter, banks remained extremely reluctant to acquire any but the highest-grade assets, which were limited in supply. There is considerable evidence to support this interpretation.[5] Banks shifted their portfolios after 1933 toward cash and short-term earning assets which were highly liquid and low in risk, and continued to do so until the wartime support policy of the Reserve Banks made long-term bonds substantially more liquid. This shift produced an unusually large accumulation of excess reserves.

---

[4] This argument is presented and tested by Peter A. Frost [17]. This period has also been interpreted as providing unique evidence for the existence of a "liquidity trap" for banks (that is, a flattening of their demand curve for reserves at very low rates), on the argument that the large increases in the ratio after the mid-1930's were accompanied by very low, virtually constant short-term interest rates (see Horwich [24], and the references cited therein).

[5] It is discussed by Friedman and Schwartz [16], Chapter 9, and was stressed by me [7]. Also see the supporting evidence presented by George R. Morrison [31], Chapters 3–5.

The 1930's and 1940's wove together some very special circumstances, making interpretation difficult. They do not provide clear evidence on the behavior of banks in ordinary times. Moreover, in the 1920's and 1950's the amount of excess reserves and the amplitude of their fluctuation were usually too small to warrant our attention; most of the fluctuation in free reserves ratios reflected borrowing from Reserve Banks. The subsequent analysis concentrates on the borrowing during those two decades, though for comparison 1929–38 is included in some regressions for the full period (with the two world wars excluded).

Many of the patterns in Chart 6-1 portray a standard response to cycles in business activity—interest rates conforming positively and the reserve ratio inversely—which raises a question of spurious association. These two variables may appear to be related solely because they both conform to business cycles. Corresponding cyclical movements in two variables tempt us to infer that they are directly related, but such evidence by itself is weak: Since many variables conform to business cycles, cyclical movements in each of them can be attributed to a wide variety of possible relationships. This is true of reserve ratios and interest rates, which may display associated cyclical fluctuations for many reasons. Changes between successive stages, as shown in Chart 6-2, suppress the serial correlation existing in the monthly series and make trends less prominent, but common cyclical influences of a possibly spurious nature may still remain. One way to remove such influences is to hold the average cyclical pattern constant by means of dummy variables. Since reference cycles have nine stages, we need seven dummy variables, one for each of seven of the eight stage-to-stage changes (one less than the total number to avoid overdetermining the regression). The dummy variables represent separate constant terms for each stage change and absorb any covariation in the other variables which would result from a common cyclical pattern. This is equivalent to fitting eight separate regressions with the requirement that all of them have the same regression coefficient for the nondummy variables.

Table 6-1 reports the correlations of stage-to-stage changes, with and without dummy variables, for various periods. The interest series are the main short-term rates available which appear relevant to the management of bank reserves. The atypical 1938–48 period of bond pegging is excluded, and the very different decades following the two world wars are shown separately. The table reveals a high negative association, confirming earlier studies. For the much cited 1948–61

TABLE 6-1. Correlation Between Free Reserve Ratio and Interest Rates, Changes Between Reference Cycle Stages

Period, Banks, and Interest Rate	Simple Correlation Coefficient (and t value)	Partial Correlation Coefficient (and t value), Holding Common Cyclical Movements Constant [a]
1874–1914 [b]		
New York City Clearing House Banks		
Commercial paper rate	−.49(4.9)	−.36(3.3)
Call money rate	−.47(4.7)	−.32(2.8)
Log of call money rate [c]	−.53(5.3)	
Reserve City National Banks		
Commercial paper rate	−.16(1.4)	−.06(0.5)
Call money rate	−.09(0.8)	−.03(0.3)
Country National Banks		
Commercial paper rate	−.30(2.8)	−.21(1.8)
Call money rate	−.16(1.5)	−.06(0.5)
1919–61, Member Banks [d]		
1919–61 excluding 1938–48		
Commercial paper rate	−.58(5.8)	−.64(6.3)
Treasury bill rate	−.52(4.7)	−.60(5.6)
Bank loan rate	−.58(5.7)	−.57(5.3)
1919–29		
Commercial paper rate	−.86(8.7)	−.90(8.8)
Treasury bill rate	−.82(6.6)	−.87(6.9)
Bank loan rate	−.82(7.4)	−.80(5.9)
1948–61		
Commercial paper rate	−.60(3.8)	−.13(0.6)
Treasury bill rate	−.70(5.0)	−.34(1.6)
Bank loan rate	−.53(3.2)	−.09(0.4)

SOURCE: Excess reserve ratio. New York City Clearing House Banks (excess lawful money reserves to net deposits): 1874–1908, A. P. Andrew, *Statistics for the United States, 1867–1909,* National Monetary Commission, 1910, Table 28; 1909–14, *Commercial and Financial Chronicle* seasonally adjusted monthly data kindly supplied by George R. Morrison from data cards for his *Liquidity Preference of Commercial Banks* [31]. Noncentral Reserve city and country national banks (lawful money plus deposits with reserve agents to net deposits, minus required reserve ratio): *Annual Report of the Comptroller of the Currency,* various years, seasonally adjusted call-date data.

Free reserve ratio of member banks (excess reserves minus Federal Reserve discounts and advances as ratio to demand deposits adjusted plus time deposits): NBER estimates from data in *Banking and Monetary Statistics* and *Federal Reserve Bulletin*

period, however, the dummy variables reduce the correlation to insignificance, indicating that the association then cannot be distinguished from a common response of the variables to business cycles. Yet, for the 1920's the correlation remains highly significant despite the inclusion of dummy variables, suggesting that the 1948–61 correlation probably is, after all, genuine though weak. As can be seen from Chart 6-2, the observations for the 1920's dominate the correlation for the post-World War I period as a whole.

Before World War I, the association is strong only for banks in New York City. One reason for its weak appearance elsewhere is that the two interest-rate series, both compiled from New York City quota-

NOTES TO TABLE (CONTINUED)

(member bank deposits 1948–61 supplied by Board of Governors of Federal Reserve System), seasonally adjusted monthly data.

Call money rate: January 1948–December 1961, *Survey of Current Business;* February 1936–December 1947, FRB; January 1878–January 1936, Frederick R. Macaulay, *Some Theoretical Problems Suggested by the Movements of Interest Rates, Bond Yields and Stock Prices in the United States Since 1856,* NBER, New York, 1938.

Commercial paper rate: February 1936–December 1961, computed from weekly data in *Commercial and Financial Chronicle;* January 1878–January 1936, Macaulay.

Treasury bill rate: FRB. (Treasury notes and certificates to 1929, three-month bills thereafter.)

Bank loan rate: IQ 1939–IVQ 1961, FRB; January 1928–December 1938, unpublished data supplied by Board of Governors of the Federal Reserve System; January 1919–December 1927, *B&MS.*

Regression observations are changes between nine successive NBER reference stage averages of monthly seasonally adjusted data.

[a] Multiple regression equation (col. 2) is

$$\Delta r_0 = \alpha \Delta \left(\frac{R_f}{D} \right) + \sum_{1}^{7} \delta_s U_s + \text{constant}$$

where r_0 is the interest rate, R_f/D the reserve ratio, and U_s the seven dummy variables, one for each successive pair of reference stages except the last. The operator Δ denotes changes between reference-stage averages. U_s is unity if the observation pertains to that pair of stages, otherwise zero; α and δ_s are regression coefficients. Signs of the t values, which pertain to the associated regression coefficients, have been dropped.

[b] Period begins with stage change VI–VII of 1870–79 reference cycle for New York banks and with VIII–IX of that cycle for the other banks, and ends with VIII–IX of 1912–14 cycle.

[c] Excludes seven extreme observations: 1879–85 VII–VIII; 1885–88 II–III; 1891–94 VI–VII and VI–VIII; 1894–97 II–III; and 1904–08 VI–VII and VII–VIII.

[d] Period begins with initial trough of 1919–21 cycle or peak of 1945–49 cycle and ends with peak of 1927–33 cycle or terminal trough of 1958–61 cycle, except that the Treasury series begins with 1920 peak. Exclusion refers to period from 1938 trough to 1948 peak.

tions, were less relevant to other Reserve city and country banks. Excess reserves of interior banks depended primarily on the local demand for loans. When the demand was high, excess reserves were low; and conversely. Only if the interior demand for loans and the commercial paper or call loan rates had the same movements are the correlations in Table 6-1 likely to be as high for the interior banks as for those in New York City.

Although the various interest rates give similar results, the regression using call money rates in logarithmic form produces a better fit for the earlier period (despite the exclusion of seven extreme observations which, if included, would make the correlation even higher). The logarithmic form is justified for the earlier period by nonlinearity at both ends of the relation: The excess reserve ratio had a lower limit imposed by national bank reserve requirements (the banking system could not acquire more reserves through domestic borrowing, since there was no central bank to provide them). And, when short-term rates were below 1 per cent, very large increases in the ratio may have been associated with small declines in rates because, as suggested earlier, costs of temporarily investing excess reserves may have exceeded the low return available. There is less reason for nonlinearity in the later period. The free reserve ratio of member banks has no practical limits (the ratio can be and usually is negative, and an upper theoretical limit of unity or so is never approached). Also, the only period with very low interest rates—1933–48—has been excluded. Since excess reserves have been quite small except for the 1930's, any important nonlinearity would have to pertain to borrowing. A tendency of the Federal Reserve to constrain borrowing, just when banks want to increase it, might produce a nonlinear relationship. Chart 6-2 gives but a slight suggestion of nonlinearity for the 1920's, however, and none for the 1950's. To keep the analysis of the two periods comparable, linear regressions have been used throughout.

In general, the evidence demonstrates an association between reserve ratios and interest rates which has a long history and cannot be dismissed as a product of common cyclical patterns. It appears to reflect a direct relationship between the two variables.

III. Critique of the Earlier Interpretation

Many writers have pointed to the association summarized by Table 6-1, and most of those before Turner attributed it to monetary effects on interest rates. Although never spelled out, the basic hypothesis was that a tight reserve position forces banks to restrict credit, and a position of ease allows them to expand. Hence, low reserves in relation to deposits lead to high interest rates, and conversely. How the effect on rates occurs, however, was never clarified, and suggestions of various mechanisms can be found in the literature.

In some early writings on the association it was implied that low reserve ratios lead the public to expect tight credit, and conversely for high ratios. The public then takes steps which somehow produce the expected behavior of interest rates. We may be skeptical, however, that such expectations would be held with much regularity unless banks did affect interest rates directly.

Tinbergen's view was that banks simply post a loan rate reflecting their reserve position. As reserves tighten, banks post higher rates, and conversely as reserves loosen. But this view oversimplifies banking practice in the United States and elsewhere. Such insularity from the demand side is true in part for only a few U.S. rates (such as consumer loan rates and the prime loan rate) and to only a limited extent for the average bank loan rate, used here. "Administrative pricing" of bank rates cannot explain the association for commercial paper and Treasury bill rates, which are determined on the open market.

If reserve ratios affect market interest rates, the connection presumably occurs through the supply of loanable funds. A high growth rate of the money stock increases the supply of loanable funds in relation to the demand, thus lowering interest rates, and conversely. The association will carry over to the free reserve ratio, however, only insofar as the ratio is a determinant of monetary growth, as was implied by Riefler's formulation. He contended that undesired changes in reserves resulting from open-market operations and currency or gold flows are largely offset in the first instance by member-bank borrowing — an increase if banks initially lose reserves or a decrease if they gain. By tradition as well as by Federal Reserve insistence, borrowing should be infrequent and, when justified, temporary; member banks in debt therefore take immediate steps to build up reserves by restricting credit. When total borrowing rises, the banking system restricts credit and the money market tightens. Thus, when the volume of borrowing is high (free reserve ratio low), interest rates are high, and conversely — reflecting an inverse effect of the growth rate of the money stock on interest rates.

On a theoretical level such an explanation seems plausible. On an empirical level, it also has merit — up to a point. An earlier study of mine found a significant inverse effect by the rate of growth of the money stock on interest rates [8]. And the free reserve ratio is positively correlated with the rate of deposit growth. But are these relationships strong enough to account for the high association between the reserve ratio and interest rates in Table 6-1? In the Riefler interpretation, that association is an indirect reflection of separate relations between each of the two variables and the growth rate of deposits. Therefore, it should disappear when deposit growth is held constant. A test of this hypothesis is reported in Table 6-2. The partial correlations with deposit growth held constant (col. 4) are only slightly smaller than the simple correlations of Table 6-1 (reproduced here in col. 1), indicating that the direct association between the free reserve ratio and interest rates far outweighs any indirect association via deposit growth. The hypothesis fails. The statistical reason for the small difference between columns 1 and 4 is that the postulated correlations with deposit growth (cols. 2 and 3) are much weaker than the correlations in column 1 which they are supposed to explain.

There is an alternative formulation of the Riefler theory. The association between the free reserve ratio and interest rates might reflect a relation between interest rates and the public's demand to hold money. Earlier writers sometimes seem to have had such an explanation in mind. The demand to hold money depends upon interest rates, and a change in the money stock affects market rates as the public buys or sells financial assets to remain on its demand curve. If the reserve ratio were a good proxy for the total money stock, the association between the ratio and interest rates would reflect those portfolio adjustments. But this formulation has serious drawbacks. First of all, the correlations of Table 6-1 do not hold wealth or income constant, as is required to measure the demand for money balances properly. Secondly, the reserve ratio is not consistently a good proxy for the level of deposits, which depends mainly upon the level of reserves made available to the banking system. Moreover, when we use the level of deposits in Table 6-2 in place of their growth rate, the correlations (not shown) are very similar to those presented there and also fail to support the Riefler theory.

Of course, some effect of the kind Riefler and other earlier writers proposed may be at work, since changes in reserve ratios affect deposit growth to some extent and thus affect interest rates through the supply of loanable funds. We may conclude, however, that such effects are not the main explanation of the high correlations in Table 6-1. We

TABLE 6-2. Correlations Between Free Reserve Ratio, Interest Rate, and Growth Rate of Deposits, Changes Between Reference Cycle Stages

Period and Interest Rate	Simple Correlation Coefficient			Partial Correlation Coefficient
	Free Reserve Ratio and Interest Rate (1)	Deposit Growth and		Free Reserve Ratio and Interest Rate, Holding Deposit Growth Constant (4)
		Interest Rate (2)	Free Reserve Ratio (3)	
1919–29				
Commercial paper rate	−.86	−.31	.49	−.85
Treasury bill rate	−.82	−.65	.64	−.69
1946–61				
Commercial paper rate	−.60	−.60	.39	−.50
Treasury bill rate	−.70	−.65	.39	−.64

SOURCE: Same as Table 6-1. Deposit growth is monthly percentage change in member-bank demand and time deposits.

NOTE: Coverage and data are the same as corresponding correlations of Table 6-1. Observations are changes between successive reference stage averages of monthly data.

The two correlations in column 3 for the earlier period are different only because the expansion phase of the 1919–21 cycle is omitted for Treasury bills.

are led to examine the main current interpretation, discussed in the next section.

IV. Examination of the Recent Interpretation

Since the 1930's most writers have completely reversed the Riefler interpretation. Instead of the free reserve ratio somehow influencing interest rates, the effect is now viewed as running from rates to the ratio. This new view, as argued above, seems justified by the evidence. The rationale for the effect has, however, taken a particular form. Banks are thought to adjust their reserve positions by borrowing from Reserve Banks, primarily to maximize short-run profits. When market rates rise, so does the income foregone by holding excess reserves idle, intensifying the inducement to keep reserves low and to borrow (assuming the borrowing rate does not rise commensurately). Since borrowing accounted for most of the fluctuation in free reserves in the 1920's and 1950's, the new view as applied to those periods is mainly a theory of borrowing. It denies Riefler's thesis that banks eschew indebtedness and borrow only to meet temporary reserve deficiencies. As Turner contended, banks may honor the tradition against unnecessary borrowing, but always with half an eye on the foregone profits. Consequently, when market rates rise, banks make do with smaller reserves, taking greater chances of being caught short, and so find it necessary to borrow more often.

A DIRECT TEST OF THE PROFIT THEORY. This theory implies that after 1914 the free reserve ratio was more closely correlated with the difference between the market and the discount rate than with the market rate by itself, since the profit depends upon the return from lending minus the cost of borrowing. Table 6-3 presents the partial correlation coefficients of the free reserve or borrowing ratio with both the interest rate and its differential over the discount rate, each as a separate variable. For all periods, the market rates themselves account for virtually all the association observed in the previous tables. This is true when sectors of member banks are treated separately (also shown), and when the period of the excess profits tax (June 30, 1950, to December 30, 1953) is given a separate constant term by means of a dummy variable (not shown). The results are also the same when the 1919–21 cycle, which had unusually high levels of borrowing and two extreme observations (see Chart 6-2), is excluded (not shown). The short-run profit motive as represented by the differential rate either is not significant or, when significant, has the wrong sign (in theory the differential should affect free reserves inversely and borrowing positively).

The regressions using the ratio of borrowing to deposits take account of the objection that the banks which hold most of the excess reserves seldom borrow and may behave differently. Treating borrowing by itself, however, gives the same results (with opposite sign), because its cyclical variations dominate those in excess reserves (except during the 1930's and 1940's, omitted here). The combination of time and demand deposits in the denominator of the ratio may also raise objections, because time deposits are less subject to unexpected withdrawals and seldom give banks cause for borrowing. Using demand deposits instead of total deposits in the denominator of the ratio, however, gives similar results (not shown). Finally, substitution of the federal funds rate for the discount rate in the regressions also gives similar results (not shown).[6]

Many studies have reported weak, though significant, negative coefficients for the differential rate, which simply reflects the correlation of the differential with the market rate (the discount rate has less amplitude of fluctuation). The correlation coefficient between the commercial paper or Treasury bill rate and the corresponding differential rate was about +.5 for stage changes in the 1920's and 1950's. The bank-loan-rate differential, on the other hand, has a positive correlation with the free reserve ratio, because the loan rate moves sluggishly and its differential is dominated by the discount rate. Since it gives the wrong sign, the loan differential has understandably not been reported in published studies.

The differential rate is clearly the relevant one for bank profits, rather than the level of the market rate; yet the correlation is all with the rate level. It may be argued that the differential rate is not entirely appropriate for the profit theory on the grounds that informal pressures by Federal Reserve officials to discourage banks from borrowing have not been taken into account here. Undoubtedly such pressures on banks vary over the cycle, and, conceivably, they reduce the correlation shown by the differential rate. Yet, such pressures probably intensify just when the profit incentive to borrow is

---

[6] The federal funds rate is relevant here only if the reserve position of banks lending federal funds, unlike that of borrowers, is not influenced by the funds rate. This is not likely, but it is a possibility. Otherwise, the behavior of lenders and borrowers of federal funds cancels out in the aggregate reserves of member banks.

TABLE 6-3. Regression of Free Reserve or Borrowing Ratio on Interest Rates and Their Differential Over the Discount Rate, Changes Between Reference Cycle Stages (*partial correlation coefficient and* t *value*)

	Free Reserve Ratio and		Borrowing Ratio and	
	Rate	Differential	Rate	Differential
All Member Banks				
1919–61 excl. 1938–48				
Commercial paper rate	−.56(5.5)	+.07(0.6)		
Treasury bill rate	−.55(5.1)	+.24(2.0)		
Bank loan rate	−.47(4.3)	+.13(1.0)		
1919–29				
Commercial paper rate	−.85(8.0)	+.19(1.0)	+.85(8.0)	−.17(0.9)
Treasury bill rate	−.86(7.6)	+.48(2.5)	+.85(7.5)	−.49(2.6)
Bank loan rate	−.74(5.6)	+.38(2.0)	+.74(5.5)	−.37(2.0)
1948–61				
Commercial paper rate	−.48(2.7)	−.02(0.1)	+.48(2.7)	+.08(0.4)
Treasury bill rate	−.53(3.2)	−.10(0.5)	+.55(3.3)	+.18(0.9)
Bank loan rate	−.42(2.3)	+.16(0.8)	+.50(2.9)	−.07(0.3)
Member Banks by Sector, 1948–61				
New York City				
Commercial paper rate	−.36(2.0)	+.08(0.4)		
Treasury bill rate	−.37(2.0)	−.02(0.1)		
Bank loan rate	−.22(1.1)	+.20(1.0)		
Chicago				
Commercial paper rate	−.47(2.7)	+.13(0.7)		
Treasury bill rate	−.49(2.8)	+.07(0.3)		
Bank loan rate	−.40(2.2)	+.15(0.8)		
Reserve cities				
Commercial paper rate	−.43(2.4)	−.05(0.2)		
Treasury bill rate	−.49(2.8)	−.17(0.9)		
Bank loan rate	−.39(2.1)	+.14(0.7)		
Country				
Commercial paper rate	−.51(2.9)	−.12(0.6)		
Treasury bill rate	−.57(3.5)	−.11(0.5)		
Bank loan rate	−.50(2.9)	+.11(0.6)		

SOURCE: Discount rate is that of Federal Reserve Bank of New York: January 1922–December 1961, Board of Governors of the Federal Reserve System, *Annual Report,* various years, and *Federal Reserve Bulletin;* November 1914–December 1921, simple averages of weighted rates on commercial, agricultural and livestock paper from FRB, *Discount Rates of the Federal Reserve Banks, 1914–21.* Reserve ratios by sectors, *Federal Reserve Bulletin,* monthly data seasonally adjusted by NBER. Other data are the same as for Table 6-1.

highest. When the discount rate is high enough to discourage borrowing, persuasion is superfluous. If the pressures partially offset borrowing for profit without eliminating it, the differential rate would still be the appropriate variable. The absence of correlation in Table 6-3 suggests that official persuasion effectively stifles the desire to borrow for short-run profit. That indeed was Riefler's contention, though his explanation relied on the traditional belief that borrowing was incompatible with sound banking, rather than on the Federal Reserve's restraint of banks' desire to borrow when it was profitable.

There is no simple way to quantify variations in official pressures against borrowing. We may conjecture that the pressure steps up, both when the differential rate rises (which increases the incentive to borrow) and when market rates rise and the credit market tightens (for reasons to be discussed in Section V). If so, the absence in Table 6-3 of a variable representing such pressure weakens the partial correlation of both independent variables; which of them is more greatly affected is hard to judge. Nevertheless, it seems unlikely that this omission can explain away the insignificance of the differential rate. Certainly none of the many studies attributing an important effect to the differential rate on borrowing contend that its importance is evident only after taking the degree of pressure into account.[7]

Another objection to Table 6-3 might be that the short-run profit incentive is represented in the regressions by the difference between the market and discount rates, thus assuming that their regression

NOTES TO TABLE (CONTINUED)

NOTE: Regression equations have the form:

$$\frac{B}{D_m} \text{ or } \frac{R_f}{D_m} = \alpha r_0 + \beta(r_0 - r_b) + \text{constant}$$

where r_0 and r_b are the open market and borrowing (discount) rates, B and R_f are member-bank borrowed and free reserves, and D_m member-bank deposits. α and β are regression coefficients. The regressions were run as first differences between reference stages, that is, each observation is the change between successive stage averages of monthly data.

Periods are the same as for previous tables (for Treasury bills, excluding 1919–20 expansion stages).

Signs of the t values, which pertain to the associated regression coefficients, have been dropped.

[7] A partial exception is a series of articles by Murray Polakoff, who has argued that borrowing is constrained beyond a certain point during periods of monetary tightness. He suggests that the relation between the free reserve ratio and the differential rate at such times is curvilinear. See [35], [36], and especially [37].

coefficients have opposite signs equal in magnitude. Because of official pressures against borrowing or a variety of other reasons, the two rates may conceivably affect the free reserve ratio by different amounts. If the profit theory is to be supported, however, the market rate should have a negative effect and the discount rate a positive effect on the ratio, since in theory they affect short-run profits in opposite directions. Table 6-4 shows that the data also fail to support this more general formulation of the profit theory. The market rate has a negative coefficient as required, but the discount rate tends to have a negative

TABLE 6-4. Regression of Free Reserve Ratio on Market and Discount Rates, Changes Between Reference Cycle Stages

Market Rate and Period	Partial Correlation Coefficient (and *t* value)	
	Market Rate	Discount Rate
1919–29		
Commercial paper rate	−.51(3.0)	−.19(1.0)
Treasury bill rate	−.48(2 5)	−.48(2.5)
Bank loan rate	−.40(2.2)	−.38(2.0)
1948–61		
Commercial paper rate	−.34(1.8)	.02(0.1)
Treasury bill rate	−.54(3.2)	.10(0.5)
Bank loan rate	−.18(0.9)	−.16(0.8)

SOURCE: Same as for Table 6-3, all member banks.

coefficient as well (reflecting its covariation with market rates). Two of the coefficients are positive, but the very low level of significance indicates that they do not differ statistically from zero. An increase in the discount rate simply does not have a perceptible depressing influence on bank borrowing from Reserve Banks as is implied by the profit theory.

The high (negative) correlation between the free reserve ratio and market interest rates in Tables 6-3 and 6-4, and the apparent absence of any influence by the discount rate, can be more simply explained by *long-* rather than short-run profit incentives. Banks rightly concern themselves with their position in the market over the long run and at all times wish to accommodate the loan demand of their regular customers; to do so when credit tightens requires selling securities, running down excess reserves, and borrowing. (A variable to take account of loan demand will be used in Section V.) That effect amply accounts for the observed association in Table 6-1, and borrowing motivated by changes in the differential rate (Table 6-3) does not contribute to the explanation. The often cited correlation of the free reserve ratio with the differential rate alone reflects the correlation between the ratio and the market rate, and cannot be offered as evidence for a short-run profit theory of bank borrowing.

If the differential rate has a measurable effect on bank behavior, it must be found in some other way. The subsequent analysis examines the data for such an effect.

TESTS BASED ON A DISCREPANCY BETWEEN ACTUAL AND DESIRED RESERVES. *The Effect on Deposit Growth.* The preceding analysis assumes that desired and actual free reserves are always equal, whereas in fact they may not be. A sophisticated version of the borrowing-for-profit theory, first presented by Meigs [30], distinguishes between actual and desired levels of the free reserve ratio (denoted by $\dfrac{R_f^a}{D_m}$ and $\dfrac{R_f^d}{D_m}$, where D_m is member-bank deposits). The desired ratio depends inversely on the difference between the open-market rate (r_0) and the borrowing (discount) rate (r_b):

$$\frac{R_f^d}{D_m} = -\phi(r_0 - r_b), \tag{1}$$

where ϕ is positive. The rate of change of member-bank deposits is made proportional to the existing discrepancy between the actual and the desired ratio:

$$\frac{d\log_e D_m}{dT} = \gamma \left(\frac{R_f^a}{D_m} - \frac{R_f^d}{D_m} \right). \tag{2}$$

Substituting (1) into (2), we have

$$\frac{d\log_e D_m}{dT} = \gamma \left(\frac{R_f^a}{D_m} + \phi \left[r_0 - r_b \right] \right), \tag{3}$$

where γ and ϕ are positive. Hence deposit expansion is related positively to the rate differential and the free reserve ratio. Put into this terminology, Riefler's theory would be equivalent to assuming that the desired free reserve ratio is a constant.

Regressions based on this equation and two others, discussed subsequently, are presented in Table 6-5. For purposes of measurement,

TABLE 6-5. Regression of Deposit Growth on the Rate Differential and Other Variables, Changes Between Reference Cycle Stages

Period and Interest Rate	Equation Number	Partial Regression Coefficient (and t value)			
		$\dfrac{R_f}{D_m}$ (1)	$r_{CP} - r_b$ or $r_{TB} - r_b$ (2)	$\dfrac{d\log_e R_u}{dT}$ (3)	$\dfrac{D_m}{R_u}\left(-d\,\dfrac{R_q}{D_m}\right)/\dfrac{}{dT}$ (4)
1919–29					
Commercial paper rate	3	4.8(3.0)	6.5(0.8)		
	4	4.6(2.8)	4.8(0.6)	−.02(1.0)	
	5	4.7(3.3)	−5.8(0.7)	−.01(0.7)	.12(2.9)
Treasury bill rate	3	3.1(3.5)	−4.0(1.4)	−.03(2.9)	
	4	2.2(2.7)	−7.0(2.6)	−.03(2.9)	
	5	2.5(2.7)	−6.8(2.5)	−.03(2.3)	.02(0.6)
1922–29					
Commercial paper rate	3	4.2(2.1)	−6.4(1.2)		
	4	4.8(3.0)	−0.3(0.1)	.09(3.3)	
	5	5.2(2.9)	0.4(0.1)	.10(3.0)	.08(0.5)
Treasury bill rate	3	2.8(1.6)	−7.2(2.8)		
	4	3.8(2.3)	−3.5(1.3)	.07(2.5)	
	5	3.9(2.0)	−3.4(1.2)	.07(2.0)	.01(0.1)
1948–61					
Commercial paper rate	3	4.7(1.7)	−3.4(1.2)		
	4	4.4(1.5)	−4.0(1.3)	−.06(0.9)	
	5	2.7(1.1)	−2.7(1.1)	.27(2.6)	.35(3.6)
Treasury bill rate	3	1.7(0.6)	−5.6(2.4)		
	4	1.5(0.5)	−5.7(2.4)	−.05(0.9)	
	5	2.5(0.9)	−1.9(0.7)	.25(2.0)	.32(2.7)

SOURCE: Reserve ratio and interest rates, same as for Tables 6-1 to 6-4; deposit growth, same as Table 6-3; required reserves, based on same sources as free reserves; unborrowed reserves, for 1919–29, high-powered money from Friedman and Schwartz [16, Table B3], revised and extended, *minus* member-bank borrowing and currency outside banks (equals unborrowed reserves at Federal Reserve Bank *plus* vault cash of all banks), and for 1948–61, member-bank reserves at Federal Reserve Banks *minus* borrowing.

NOTE: Regressions are based on text equations 3, 4, and 5, plus a constant term, not shown. Dependent variable is monthly percentage change in member-bank demand and time deposits, annual percentage rate. Independent variables are defined by column:

(1) free reserve ratio (ratio of member-bank free reserves to demand and time deposits), per cent;

(2) differential rate (commercial paper or Treasury bill rate *minus* discount rate), per cent per annum;

banks are assumed to begin to respond immediately to any discrepancy between the actual and desired ratio, so that the average rate of deposit growth during a given month reflects the average discrepancy in that month. The assumption seems appropriate for monthly data, since banks are more likely to act on the basis of their current reserve position than on that of the previous month or quarter. Yet, while the response begins immediately, it may not be completed within one month, but only with time approximates a full adjustment. The regressions therefore measure a continuing process of adjustment. Because the variables are averaged for reference stages, however, and then put into first-difference form as in previous tables to avoid spurious correlation, the data reflect the average effect on deposit growth of the discrepancy during reference stages (usually several months or more in duration).

In regressions based on equation (3), the regression coefficients estimate the effect of a 1-percentage point change in the ratio or the rate differential on the annual percentage rate of deposit growth. The free reserve ratio has the correct sign (and for commercial paper is highly significant with t well above 2.0 in the earlier period), but the rate differential is not significant and mostly has the wrong sign (it should be positive). The regressions appear to pick up the negative effect of monetary growth on interest rates, which hides whatever positive effect the differential rate would have on the desired free reserve ratio and, thence, on deposit growth.

One suggested way of isolating the latter effect is to take account of some of the other factors determining deposit growth, since the reserve ratio is not the only factor or even the most important one. Accordingly, we may, following Meigs, add the growth rate of unborrowed reserves,

NOTES TO TABLE (CONTINUED)

(3) growth rate of unborrowed reserves (monthly percentage change in bank reserves *minus* borrowed reserves), annual percentage rate;

(4) contribution of required reserves to growth rate of deposits — see footnote 8 (monthly change in ratio of member-bank required reserves to total deposits, with sign reversed, *times* the ratio of deposits to unborrowed reserves), annual percentage rate.

The regressions were run as first differences between reference stages, that is, each observation is the change between successive stage averages of monthly values of the variables shown in table heading.

The first and last periods are the same as for previous tables (for Treasury bills 1919–29, excluding 1919–20 expansion stages). The 1922–29 period begins March 1922 with the change between stages III and IV of the 1921–24 cycle.

Signs of t value have been dropped.

R_u, to the equation:

$$\frac{d\log_e D_m}{dT} = \gamma \left(\frac{R_f^a}{D_m} + \phi[r_0 - r_b] \right) + \Theta \frac{d\log_e R_u}{dT}, \qquad (4)$$

and, following Davis [11],[8] also the contribution to deposit growth of changes in the required reserve ratio:

$$\frac{d\log_e D_m}{dT} = \gamma \left(\frac{R_f^a}{D_m} + \phi[r_0 - r_b] \right) + \Theta \frac{d\log_e R_u}{dT} + \eta \frac{D_m}{R_u} \left(\frac{-d\dfrac{R_q}{D_m}}{dT} \right), \qquad (5)$$

where Θ and η are positive. These two variables are added to the regressions in Table 6-5. For the later period, unborrowed reserves are

---

[8] The contribution of changes in requirements may be derived as follows. By definition, total reserves of member banks comprise required R_q and excess reserves R_e:

$$R_u + B \equiv R_q + R_e,$$

or

$$R_u \equiv R_q + R_f,$$

where $R_f \equiv R_e - B$.

Dividing by member-bank deposits and rearranging the terms gives

$$D_m \equiv \frac{R_u}{\dfrac{R_q}{D_m} + \dfrac{R_f}{D_m}}.$$

To derive rates of change, we may take natural logarithms and differentiate with respect to time:

$$\frac{d\log_e D_m}{dT} \equiv \frac{d\log_e R_u}{dT} + \frac{D_m}{R_u} \left(\frac{-d\dfrac{R_q}{D_m}}{dT} \right) + \frac{D_m}{R_u} \left(\frac{-d\dfrac{R_f}{D_m}}{dT} \right).$$

In this form the growth rate of deposits is the sum of three parts, the contribution of the growth rate of unborrowed reserves and that of changes in the required and free reserve ratios. The factor D_m/R_u converts changes in the reserve ratios into units that represent their contribution to the growth rate of deposits. (The factor can be omitted if we deal with changes in the dollar amount of reserves rather than in ratios.)

This formulation disregards currency flows on the assumption that the Reserve Banks supply whatever quantity of currency the public desires, offsetting entirely the effect of currency flows on bank reserves. Otherwise, changes in the ratio of currency held by the public to deposits affect reserves and deposit growth. The Reserve Banks have often, though by no means always, offset changes in the currency ratio; they certainly did not at certain crucial times like 1929–33. And a currency offset could not be expected at all in the period before 1914. (In that earlier period, too, B was zero.)

While the analysis here follows current practice in ignoring currency flows, the appropriateness of doing so requires further study, particularly for the earlier period.

defined as member-bank deposits at Federal Reserve Banks less borrowing. For the early 1920's, however, that definition makes no sense. Such reserves were then negative: borrowing exceeded bank deposits at Federal Reserve Banks, which was possible because vault cash was an important component of bank reserves. The series used for the 1920's therefore includes the vault cash of all banks (nonmember-bank vault cash cannot be readily excluded). This series has always been positive but, in 1920 and 1921, it was quite small. By 1922 reserves held at Federal Reserve Banks had increased appreciably, and vault cash was relatively less important. Table 6-5 therefore also reports regressions for 1922–29, to exclude the first two years of the decade when borrowing was nearly as large as total reserves; the unborrowed residual was small then, and its monthly percentage changes were volatile.

The two added variables show significant effects on deposit growth, though for the earlier period changes in the required reserve ratio [9] are only important in 1919 (this year covered only by the commercial paper regressions). The volatile changes in unborrowed reserves during the early 1920's produce an apparent negative effect in the regressions which turns positive when those years are omitted. In terms of long-run effects, the coefficients of these last two variables should, by the above formulation, be positive and approximately unity. They estimate pure numbers, since the dependent variable is measured in the same units. A continual increase in unborrowed reserves or decrease in required reserves will add to the growth rate of deposits unless continually offset by increases in the free reserve ratio.

The estimated effects of these variables in the table are all well below unity, presumably because of lags. In the short run, changes in unborrowed reserves are partly or largely unforeseen. They would affect deposit growth gradually and only after a period of adjustment, whereas banks can be expected to expand deposits right along with anticipated, regular increases in unborrowed reserves. A regression coefficient below unity for this variable therefore indicates that the changes were not fully anticipated. (Meigs [30] suggests that the rate of change of unborrowed reserves may also affect the desired level of free reserves. Banks may be comfortable with a lower ratio during periods of rapid growth in unborrowed reserves. Consequently, besides the direct effect on deposit growth, a higher growth rate of re-

---

[9] In the earlier period changes in the required ratio reflected shifts in deposits between reserve classes and between time and demand deposits. In the later period, changes in legal requirements also occurred.

serves would gradually lead to a once-and-for-all reduction in the free reserve ratio and to a higher rate of deposit growth while the reduction was taking place. This effect would tend to make the regression coefficient of changes in unborrowed reserves higher, however, not lower.) The coefficient may also be less than unity insofar as the Federal Reserve partly offsets member-bank borrowing through deliberate changes in unborrowed reserves; this will be discussed later.

However we interpret these regressions, the interest-rate differential gives no evidence of a positive effect on deposit growth. Regressions of the form (4) and (5) or close variants are often used in studies of banking behavior.[10] The differential rate sometimes turns out to be significant with the correct sign, though usually the association is weak. The only major differences between this and other studies are the omission of data after the 1961 trough and the allowance for common cyclical patterns in the variables. Significant correlations using data in monthly or quarterly form need not reflect a genuine relationship but simply a tendency of the variables to move similarly over business cycles in response to a variety of cyclical influences. In Table 6-5 the common cyclical pattern in the variables has practically been eliminated by taking changes between reference-stage averages (dummy variables to remove any remaining common cyclical pattern were not used), and the differential rate is either insignificant or has the wrong sign.

These results indicate that responses of the desired free reserve ratio to the differential rate are not strong enough to register clearly on deposit growth. The next two subsections show why such responses may not affect deposit growth and explore an alternative way of measuring them.

The Problem of Interdependence Between Open-Market Operations and Borrowing. Many econometric models of the monetary system do not allow for a dependence of Federal Reserve open-market operations on member-bank borrowing. To be sure, unborrowed reserves are usually included in equations like (4) and (5), but only to take account of a dependence running in the other direction: Open-market operations make reserves temporarily flush or tight, which leads some banks to reduce or step up borrowing, as the case may be, until they can accommodate their portfolios to the new conditions. Later, when banks have had time to adjust to the change in reserves, the free

[10] See for example Meigs [30]; Brunner and Meltzer [4], especially Table 5; Davis [10] and [11]; and Teigen [44]. See also Rangarajan and Severn [38], who use the market (not the differential) rate, and conclude that it has no discernible effect on deposit growth.

reserve ratio returns to the desired level determined by other considerations. Those adjustments are consistent with the explanation of borrowing given by Riefler. It is appropriate to allow for them in measuring the effect of the differential rate. But there is no reason to ignore a mutual dependence. The privilege of borrowing helps individual banks avoid temporary stringencies, but it is not supposed to compromise the over-all objectives of monetary policy. The Federal Reserve may also engage in open-market sales — as well as persuasion — to offset borrowing which interferes with the desired monetary policy. To the extent that borrowing is thereby offset, it, as well as the corresponding reduction in unborrowed reserves, will have no observable effect on deposit growth. If we measure the effect of the differential rate on desired free reserves by means of their induced contribution to deposit growth, we in effect assume that the Federal Reserve does not offset the contribution. This assumption underlies much recent econometric research on the determinants of the money supply and deserves attention.[11]

The fact of the matter is that changes in unborrowed reserves and the free reserve ratio are highly correlated inversely (as shown by Table 6-6) especially when changes in the required reserve ratio are held constant. Since the variables are all measured in the same units, the negative coefficients of about unity indicate that the contributions to deposit growth of unborrowed and free reserves offset each other and also that unborrowed reserves offset changes in requirements. (Since the data pertain to concurrent monthly changes, there is no implication that the offsets are permanent.) It is true that the two independent variables, as measured, contain unborrowed reserves in the denominator. That might tend to increase the negative correlation with the dependent variable, but probably not a great deal. The dependent variable is monthly changes in unborrowed reserves which, except perhaps for the early 1920's, behave quite differently than the ratio D_m/R_u contained in the two independent variables. Nor do the high correlations reflect similar cyclical patterns in the variables. When dummy variables are used to absorb the common cyclical fluctuations, the results (not shown) are virtually the same.

---

[11] Whether valid or not, the assumption does not affect the argument made by Meigs [30] that free reserves are a misleading indicator of bank behavior; their level does not predict how rapidly banks are going to expand loans or deposits. When the growth of unborrowed reserves is high, banks might keep the actual free reserve ratio low, and by that indicator monetary policy might appear to be tight; while in fact the desired ratio may be even lower, leading to rapid monetary growth. Nothing said here denies this point.

TABLE 6-6. Regression of the Growth Rate of Unborrowed Reserves on the Contribution to Deposit Growth of the Free and Required Reserve Ratios, Changes Between Reference Cycle Stages

	Simple or Partial Regression Coefficient (and t value)		
Period	$\dfrac{D_m}{R_u}\left(\dfrac{-d\,\dfrac{R_f}{D_m}}{dT}\right)$	$\dfrac{D_m}{R_u}\left(\dfrac{-d\,\dfrac{R_q}{D_m}}{dT}\right)$	Adj. R^2
1919–29	−.80(6.7)		.62
	−.88(8.9)	−.86(3.8)	.75
1922–29	−1.17(8.4)		.80
	−1.10(12.8)	−1.70(5.3)	.93
1948–61	.35(0.7)		.00
	−1.00(6.1)	−.89(14.5)	.89

SOURCE: Same as for Table 6-5.

NOTE: Dependent variable of regressions is growth rate of unborrowed reserves (monthly percentage change in bank reserves at Reserve Banks *minus* borrowed reserves), annual percentage rate. Constant term is not shown. Independent variables, by column, are:

(1) Contribution of free reserves to growth rate of deposits — see footnote 8 (monthly change in ratio of member-bank free reserves to total deposits, with sign reversed, *times* the ratio of deposits to unborrowed reserves), annual percentage rate.

(2) Contribution of required reserves to growth rate of deposits — see footnote 8 (same as col. 1 except with required instead of free reserves), annual percentage rate.

The regressions were run as first differences between reference stages, that is, each observation is the change between successive stage averages of monthly values of the variables shown in the table heading.

Periods are the same as for Table 6-1.

Signs of t values have been dropped.

These results are indeed to be expected. Open-market operations are used to offset sudden and undesired changes in bank reserves. For example, they help counteract the immediate effects of changes in legal requirements, allowing banks time to make adjustments. Banks borrow when open-market sales disturb reserves, but that response alone seems insufficient to explain the high correlation. In addition, the Federal Reserve counteracts the effect on deposits of any borrowing which does not agree with monetary objectives. It is true that the Reserve Banks have never announced an explicit policy of offsetting bank borrowing, but they nevertheless pursue such a policy indirectly in the normal course of countering undesired expansions or lapses in deposit growth. The correlation between free and unborrowed reserves therefore reflects an influence running in both directions.

For the short-run profit theory of borrowing, however, it is irrelevant that induced changes in desired free reserves, as found in Table 6-5, do not affect deposit growth. Because of open-market operations and other factors affecting deposit growth, it is better to test the theory directly, as is done below.

The Effect on Free Reserves. Another difficulty with equations (3)–(5), mentioned earlier, is that they ignore the inverse effect of monetary growth on interest rates. That effect would tend to counteract the positive relation assumed in those equations and helps to explain why the coefficients of the differential rate in Table 6-5 are sometimes negative. Because of that difficulty and the interdependence just discussed, we may examine the effects of the differential rate on the contribution of the free reserve ratio to deposit growth, rather than on the total growth itself. We may retain the general hypothesis that banks respond to the discrepancy between the desired and the actual free reserve ratio. The equation then is

$$\frac{D_m}{R_u}\left(\frac{-d\,\dfrac{R_f^a}{D_m}}{dT}\right) = \gamma\left(\frac{R_f^a}{D_m} + \phi[r_0 - r_b]\right). \tag{6}$$

Table 6-7 reports regressions of this form,[12] as well as with the addition of changes in unborrowed and required reserves. The contribution of the free reserve ratio to deposit growth is practically the same as the change in the ratio with the sign reversed. The difference is the factor D_m/R_u, which as pointed out in footnote 8 converts changes in the ratio into their effect on deposit growth. The assumption behind this formulation is that a given discrepancy between the actual and desired ratios leads banks to produce — other things remaining the same — a commensurate change in the growth rate of deposits rather than in the reserve ratio *per se*. The two effects will usually be roughly equivalent, however, thus rendering the distinction of little importance. Large

[12] See footnote 8 for derivation of dependent variable. Variants of (6) were also used by Meigs [30]; as well as by de Leeuw [12]; Goldfeld [18]; and Goldfeld and Kane [19].

TABLE 6-7. Regression of the Contribution to Deposit Growth of Free Reserves on the Differential Rate and Other Variables, Changes Between Reference Cycle Stages

Period and Interest Rate	Partial Regression Coefficient (and t value)				
	$\dfrac{R_f}{D_m}$ (1)	$r_{CP} - r_b$ or $r_{TB} - r_b$ (2)	$\dfrac{d\log_e R_u}{dT}$ (3)	$\dfrac{D_m}{R_u}\left(\dfrac{-d\,\dfrac{R_q}{D_m}}{dT}\right)$ (4)	Adj. R^2 (5)
1922–29					
Commercial paper rate	8.3(0.7)	55.3(1.9)	—		.08
	11.2(0.9)	55.9(1.9)	—	0.7(0.8)	.06
	4.2(0.8)	9.8(0.6)	−.68(7.1)	—	.79
	−3.0(0.7)	−3.4(0.3)	−.85(10.7)	−1.5(4.0)	.90
Treasury bill rate	15.6(1.5)	46.8(3.2)	—	—	.34
	18.1(1.7)	46.7(3.2)	—	0.6(0.8)	.32
	7.3(1.3)	14.6(1.6)	−.61(6.3)	—	.81
	−0.6(0.1)	5.0(0.7)	−.80(9.1)	−1.3(3.6)	.90
1948–61					
Commercial paper rate	−0.3(0.1)	−1.7(0.4)	—	—	.00
	0.7(0.2)	−1.2(0.3)	—	−.10(1.4)	.00
	−0.7(0.2)	−2.2(0.6)	−.07(0.8)	—	.00
	2.4(1.2)	−4.6(2.2)	−.69(7.6)	−.65(7.9)	.69
Treasury bill rate	4.6(1.1)	5.5(1.8)	—	—	.04
	4.6(1.2)	4.7(1.5)	—	−.08(1.1)	.05
	4.4(1.1)	5.4(1.7)	−.05(0.6)	—	.02
	2.2(0.9)	−3.1(1.4)	−.72(6.6)	−.71(6.7)	.66

SOURCE: Same as for Table 6-5.

NOTE: Regressions are based on text equation (6) and variants, plus a constant term, not shown. For derivation of monetary variables, see footnote 8. Dependent variable is contribution of free reserves to growth rate of deposits (same as Table 6-6), annual percentage rate. Independent variables (see Table 6-5) are, by column:

(1) free reserve ratio, per cent;
(2) differential rates, per cent per annum;
(3) growth rate of unborrowed reserves, annual percentage rate;
(4) contribution of required reserves to growth rate of deposits, annual percentage rate.

The regressions were run as first-differences between reference stages, that is, each observation is the change between successive stage averages of monthly values of the variables shown in table heading.

Periods are the same as for previous tables.

Signs of t values have been dropped.

differences did occur in 1920 and 1921 when unborrowed reserves were very small and, as before, those years have been excluded for that reason.

The regressions with the highest multiple correlations are those including changes in unborrowed reserves and legal requirements. As explained in the preceding subsection, however, the former can be expected to overstate the response of banks to open-market operations and hide the true effects of the other variables. It should perhaps be omitted.[13] There is no parallel reason for omitting changes in the required reserve ratio, since those changes induce temporary borrowing and presumably reflect distributional shifts in deposits or policy actions with long-run objectives in mind, rather than provide a short-run offset to borrowing. With changes in unborrowed reserves excluded, the differential rate is positive and significant ($t \geq 2.0$) for Treasury bills 1922–29, and on the borderline of significance for bills 1948–61 and commercial paper 1922–29. If we test the profit theory by adding the market rate to these regressions (not shown), the coefficient of the differential rate remains about the same in size and significance, unlike the version of the theory in Table 6-3 which failed that test. The addition of dummy variables also makes little difference here, unlike the correlations in Table 6-1 for the 1948–61 period. These results therefore provide some evidence of a short-run profit theory of borrowing.

Based on the Table 6-7 estimates, however, the lure of such profits has been sharply constrained since the 1920's. If we compare the earlier and later periods for the first two Treasury bill regressions (which exclude changes in unborrowed reserves), we see that the coefficient of the differential rate was nine times larger in the 1920's (47 compared with 5). The coefficient measures the effect on deposit growth: the change produced in the annual percentage rate of deposit growth for a 1-percentage point change in the differential. Column 2 divided by column 1 gives an estimate of ϕ in equation (6): the effect on the desired free reserve ratio (in percentage points). By the same comparison, that effect was two and a half times larger in the 1920's. The decline in magnitude is not surprising, considering how much larger were the fluctuations in borrowing during the 1920's for similar variations in the differential rate. Ironically, economists began to

---

[13] One could, of course, set up a more complicated equation that allowed for mutual interaction between bank borrowing and open-market operations, but that seems unnecessary for present purposes.

attach importance to borrowing by banks for short-run profit well after the heyday of such activity had passed.

The estimate of ϕ for Treasury bills 1948–61 is slightly above unity (5.5/4.6), indicating that a 1-percentage point rise in the bill-discount differential—the typical change from cyclical trough to peak in the 1950's (see Chart 6-3, below)—increased the desired free reserve ratio about 1 percentage point, not a large amount. To be sure, because of the delayed adjustment, this induced an increase in the contribution to deposit growth of 5.5 per cent per year (the estimate of $\gamma\phi$ in col. 2), but open-market operations apparently offset most or all of it, as indicated by the negative estimate when changes in both unborrowed and required reserves are included.

The partial correlations of the differential rate in Table 6-7 (not shown) range from +.66, for the first two Treasury bill regressions in the earlier period, to below zero (for the negative coefficients). On the whole they are much smaller than the corresponding correlations relating the free reserve ratio to the level of interest rates in Table 6-1, which are also much more significant and therefore more reliable. While that association originally attracted the attention of economists and eventually led to the short-run profit theory, it cannot be adequately explained as a reflection of equation (6) or its variants. Indeed, the statistical relations measured by Tables 6-1 and 6-7 appear to be practically independent of each other.

V. Reinterpretation

The preceding results seem paradoxical at first. The strong association observed between the free reserve ratio and interest rates appears to reflect neither the contribution of the ratio to deposit growth nor the effect of differential rates on the desired ratio. Those two interpretations, however, do not exhaust the possibilities. In particular, they disregard an important characteristic of bank behavior: the effort to retain the loyalty of regular customers by accommodating requests for loans so far as possible even when funds are scarce. Such behavior has been noted.[14]

Experience generally shows that tightness in the availability of credit to bank customers is related to a large volume of member bank discounts outstanding,

[14] The first quotation is from [2], p. 46, the second by George W. McKinney, Jr. [29], p. 27. For similar statements see Robinson [40], Hodgman [23], Kane and Malkiel [25], and Goldfeld [18], pp. 15–16.

and easy credit conditions to a small volume of borrowing from Reserve Banks.

> . . . the typical banker is acutely aware of his responsibilities to his customers and to his community, and is far more interested in establishing and maintaining long-term customer relations and providing his community with funds to meet its legitimate credit needs than he is in short-run profit considerations.

In striving to satisfy the demand of regular customers for loans, banks will, when necessary, lend whatever funds they can obtain by reducing excess reserves, selling securities, and borrowing. When loan demand expands, therefore, it is met by reducing the free reserve ratio, regardless of the discount rate and the effect on short-run profits. When, at some later time, loan demand weakens and funds become plentiful, banks settle into a more relaxed and easy reserve position. The costs of accommodating customers at "acceptable" loan rates frequently requires giving up maximum current profits, which banks willingly subordinate to the more important purpose of retaining the loyalty of their regular clientele over the long run.

To be sure, when banks need funds, they undoubtedly seek to acquire them in the cheapest way. That they try to maximize profits or minimize losses at all times is not at issue here. The question is how to explain the high correlation between borrowing and interest rates. Probably no one would deny the importance to banks of accommodating customers, yet most time-series studies have overlooked this simple explanation of the correlation. Short-term interest rates serve as a proxy for the intensity of pressure put on bank officials by regular borrowers, since market rates reflect changes in the demand for short-term funds, part of which represents a demand for bank loans.[15]

The pressure to make loans varies over time, not only because the demand for loans fluctuates, but also because banks do not charge a rate that clears the market. Loan officers could let high rates drive away the excess demand when reserves become tight, but by all accounts they prefer instead to ration credit. Bank loan rates do move with the market to a considerable extent, but usually not enough to clear it. Credit rationing leaves an unsatisfied demand in excess of supply and creates a group of disgruntled customers pressing to borrow more. The intensity of over-all pressure will depend upon a variety of factors, an important one being the level of market rates. In view of the widely acknowledged concern of banks to retain customer

---

[15] The first writer to attribute the association to loan demand, so far as I know, is Irving Fisher [15]. See the quotation of his in the Appendix.

loyalty, the high correlation of short-term interest rates with the reserve ratio (Table 6-1) in itself supports this interpretation.

Market rates may be an imperfect indicator of the intensity of customer pressure on banks. Consequently, the test of Table 6-3 may be biased against the short-run profit theory of borrowing, since the market rate is also correlated with the market-discount rate differential (a result of infrequent changes in the discount rate). The market rate might, as an imperfect proxy for the degree of credit rationing, spuriously reduce the partial correlation between the differential rate and the reserve ratio. Perhaps, if we took account in another way of the pressure on banks to accommodate customers, an effect of the market-discount rate differential might come to light.

Unfortunately, there are no ready measures of shifts in the demand curve for bank loans. We must improvise. Besides the level of market rates, two makeshift indicators of the pressure on banks to expand credit suggest themselves. The prevalence of credit rationing suggests one: the difference between the market rate and the average bank loan rate. The first rate reflects what banks could charge (for a given supply), and the second what they do charge, at least directly. To be sure, loan rates usually exceed the rate on commercial paper or Treasury bills, because these instruments entail less risk than the average bank loan does. Nevertheless, since market rates fluctuate with shifts in the demand curve for loans, the differential between the market and the loan rate measures variations both in excess demand and in the pressure on banks to expand loans. Thus the market-discount rate differential may be reinterpreted: In the partition of $r_0 - r_b$,

$$(r_0 - r_l) + (r_l - r_b),$$

the first term (the market-loan rate differential) measures the excess demand for bank loans, and the second term (the loan-discount rate differential) measures the gross profit to banks in borrowing from Reserve Banks.

Another indicator is the volume of loans as a proportion of earning assets. Banks devote an increasing portion of their total resources to loans as the pressure mounts, even though they satisfy only part of the total demand. The assumption underlying this indicator is that rejected applications for loans increase approximately as fast as do approvals.

Admittedly, these two indicators are rough. We cannot expect them to remain nicely proportional to the pressure on banks to expand loans. They nevertheless provide an alternative to market rates as measures of that pressure, and so allow a partly independent test of the relative importance of the two interpretations of bank borrowing.

Table 6-8 presents the results of such a test. One set of regressions makes use of the foregoing partition, in which the loan-discount rate differential represents the incentive to borrow for short-run profits. That variable does poorly (its coefficient is not even negative for the

TABLE 6-8. Regression of Free Reserve Ratio on Rate Differential and Two Proxies for Intensity of Loan Demand, Changes Between Reference Cycle Stages

	Partial Regression Coefficient (and t value)				Total Corre-
	Loan Demand		Differential Rate		lation
Period and Market Rate (r_0)	$r_0 - r_l$ (1)	$\dfrac{L}{L+I}$ (2)	$r_l - r_b$ (3)	$r_0 - r_b$ (4)	Coeffi- cient
1919–29					
Commercial paper rate	−2.2(3.5)	—	+0.6(0.8)	—	.76
	—	−.42(3.3)	—	−0.9(1.1)	.62
Treasury bill rate	−1.3(2.5)	—	+1.5(2.1)	—	.71
	—	−.71(5.9)	—	−0.8(1.8)	.80
1948–61					
Commercial paper rate	−0.4(2.3)	—	−0.0(0.0)	—	.55
	—	−.04(2.3)	—	−0.2(1.0)	.56
Treasury bill rate	−0.4(3.1)	—	−0.0(0.2)	—	.63
	—	−.04(2.9)	—	−0.4(2.9)	.69

SOURCE: Ratio of loans to total earning assets: for later period all commercial banks, for earlier period reporting member banks, *Federal Reserve Bulletin,* monthly data seasonally adjusted by NBER. Other data are the same as for Tables 6-1 and 6-3.

NOTE: Dependent variable is ratio of member-bank free reserves to demand and time deposits, per cent. Constant term is not shown. Independent variables are, by column:

(1) Commercial paper or Treasury bill rate *minus* average bank loan rate, per cent per annum.

(2) Ratio of loans to total loans and investments, per cent.

(3) Average bank loan rate *minus* discount rate, per cent per annum.

(4) Commercial paper or Treasury bill rate *minus* discount rate, per cent per annum.

The regressions were run as first-differences between reference stages, that is, each observation is the change between successive stage averages of monthly values of the variables shown in table heading.

Periods are the same as for previous tables (for Treasury bills 1919–29, excluding 1919–20 expansion stages).

Signs of t values have been dropped.

earlier period, although it should be), and it appears to have no relation to borrowing. Consequently, the market-discount rate differential
was used to represent the profit incentive in the other set of regressions, in which the loan ratio represents the intensity of loan demand.
The two independent variables in that set are related (their simple correlation coefficient is +.30 for the earlier period and +.51 for the later
period), but not so closely as to preclude measuring their separate
effects.

The loan-demand variables are highly significant. Their regression
coefficients imply that customer pressure affected the reserve ratio
much less in the 1950's than in the 1920's, consistent with the much
freer borrowing allowed in the earlier period. The total correlation coefficients are nearly as high as the simple correlations between the
ratio and the corresponding market rates in Table 6-1. The Table 6-8
regressions appear to capture most of that association, which the short-
run profit theory attributes to the effect of differential rates alone.
Judged by the levels of significance, however, the loan-demand
variables are more important, with one exception: the later regression
for bills in which the two variables have equal significance. The differential rates mostly have the correct negative coefficient, but only for
the exception is it significant ($t \geq 2.0$), though it is on the borderline in
in the second Treasury bill regression for the earlier period. The results are similar to Table 6-7 in that the coefficient for the differential
rate is larger for the earlier period.

The evidence of Table 6-8 on the short-run profit incentive is only
tentative. A better proxy for loan demand might well reduce the coefficient of the differential rate. The results of using the market rate
as the proxy (Tables 6-3 and 6-4) suggest such a possibility. Yet those
results may underestimate the profit effect, as was suggested, because
the market rate might, if Reserve Banks put restrictions on borrowing,
sometimes indicate the true return in borrowing for short-run profit
better than the differential rate does. Since the market rate may thus
represent both reasons for borrowing and the other proxies for loan
demand may be inadequate, the importance of the profit effect is hard
to assess. Presumably it lies part way between the effects shown by
Tables 6-3 and 6-8.

The relative importance of loan demand and the differential rate can
be assessed from their regression coefficients and amplitudes of fluctuation. In the later period, for example, the ratio of loans to total assets
usually rose about 10 percentage points from trough to peak of reference expansions, and the bill-discount rate differential about 1 per-

centage point. The regression coefficient of the differential rate is ten times that of the loan ratio (bottom line, Table 6-8). Therefore, their effects on the free reserve ratio over reference expansions were about equal, each producing a total change in the reserve ratio of roughly 0.4 percentage points. For the earlier period, the effects were larger and the loan ratio was absolutely and relatively much more important. For commercial paper rates in both periods, the loan ratio was relatively more important than the differential rate.

Since we find that borrowing depends in part upon the bill-discount rate differential, at least for the later period, does that mean that the funds are used to acquire Treasury bills? Clearly not. Chart 6-3 shows that bank holdings of Treasury bills did not follow movements in the bill-discount rate differential during the 1950's. Bill holdings tended to rise in the last half of reference contractions, when the profit incentive to borrow—and borrowing itself (see Chart 6-1)—actually reached a cyclical low point. The bill-discount rate differential was seldom positive in the post-World War II period; when it was, bank holdings of bills were not at their cyclical peaks (the 1950–53 expansionary years, when the excess profits tax was in effect, are a partial exception). A comparison of cyclical movements therefore denies that the differential rate influenced the purchase of Treasury bills. By all indications, bills serve as a dispensable reservoir of lending power to meet cyclical variations in loan demand.[16] What is true of bills is generally true of other security holdings. Banks both run off securities and borrow from Reserve Banks to finance an expansion of loans.

The bill-discount rate differential nevertheless does better than the other series in reflecting the short-run profit from loans. The *loan*-discount rate differential itself shows no relation to borrowing from Reserve Banks, largely because banks prefer to ration credit rather than to charge what the market will bear at the moment. But the average loan rate may not, when funds are tight, fully register changes in the *short-run* return produced by higher compensating balances and the selection of loans with lower risk. As a result, the bill rate may more accurately represent changes in the total return from loans. The ques-

---

[16] Since pressure for loans leads banks to reduce bill holdings as well as the free reserve ratio, it is also tempting to argue that loan demand is the source, via changes in the nonbank supply of bills, of the corresponding movements in the bill rate. Hence the bill rate and the free reserve ratio would be inversely correlated, though not directly as cause and effect. One difficulty with this interpretation, however, is that the bill holdings of banks do not have a regular (inverse) cyclical pattern (Chart 6-3), while the bill rate has a regular positive pattern (see [8]). The argument therefore appears weak.

tion here is not what banks do with borrowed funds — mainly they expand loans, but whether they borrow only when the desired accommodation of long-standing customers strains resources or also, as the evidence in part suggests, when the rate differential makes it particularly attractive.

CHART 6-3. Reference Cycle Patterns of Treasury Bill Holdings of All Commercial Banks and Bill-Discount Rate Differential, 1948–61

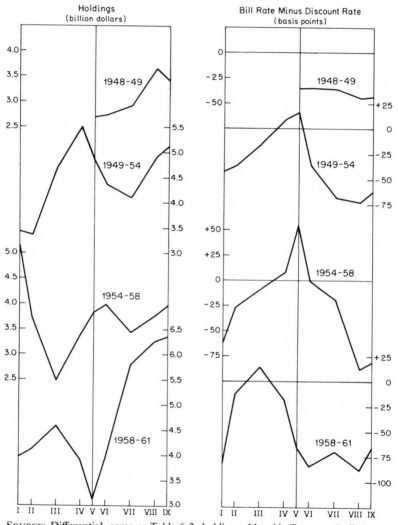

SOURCE: Differential, same as Table 6-3; holdings, *Monthly Treasury Bulletin*.

Whether we interpret the effect of the differential rate in these regressions to be large or small, it seems clear that the major part of bank borrowing reflects simply a desire to accommodate customers, without regard to short-run profits. That is shown by the high correlation (Table 6-8) between the free reserve ratio and the loan-demand variable, holding the differential rate constant. Such borrowing appears to be the main explanation for the long-noted association between interest rates and bank reserves. While loan demand may well explain most of the association before World War I, the evidence developed here does not directly apply to that period. The discount window did not exist and we cannot readily distinguish between the two roles of interest rates at that time: as proxy for loan demand and as the foregone return on excess reserves.[17] For the 1920's and since World War II, when borrowing from Reserve Banks has provided most of the fluctuation in free reserves, the distinction can be made because the second role is played by the market-discount rate differential, not by the market rate itself. For these later periods at least, loan demand should be accorded primary emphasis in a theory of bank borrowing and the free reserve ratio. The effect of interest rates on free reserves has, on the whole, been less important. Their effect appears to be very important only because the rates happen to be good proxies for customer pressures on banks to expand loans.

VI. Summary

Statistical studies of the behavior of bank reserves have had an unusually long history relative to other empirical work in economics. During the past half-century economists have become increasingly aware of a high correlation between reserve ratios and short-term interest rates. An earlier interpretation, expounded most fully by Riefler, attributed the association to the influence of bank reserves on financial markets. Though never adequately spelled out, this view may be formulated as saying that easy or tight reserves produce a high or low contribution, respectively, by banks to the growth rate of deposits, which shifts the supply curve of loanable funds and affects market interest rates accordingly. The rates are thus inversely related to the reserve

---

[17] The pre-1914 period is further complicated by the fact that many reserve agents paid interest on deposit reserves held with them by other banks. The rate paid, however, was a standard 2 per cent and, as far as I can determine, changed little. A rise in market rates, therefore, still increased the incentive to reduce excess reserves.

ratio of the banking system. Beginning with Turner's 1938 criticism of Riefler's study, opinion reversed the direction of influence and, since then, has attributed the association to the effect of market rates on the free reserve ratio. This interpretation regards bankers as equating the marginal contribution to profits of holding excess reserves and earning assets or of borrowing from Reserve Banks. When market rates rise, banks are thought to convert excess reserves into earning assets, and also, if the discount rate does not rise as high, to borrow more. Hence, the free reserve ratio falls as the market-discount rate differential increases.

There is some merit in both explanations of the association, but neither one comes near accounting for it fully: (1) Monetary growth does affect interest rates inversely, but that has nothing to do with the observed association between rates and the reserve ratio. The association is not affected by holding the growth of deposits constant, contrary to the earlier interpretation in which the reserve ratio affects interest rates through the induced changes in bank credit and deposits (Section III). (2) The later interpretation implies that, with the advent of discounting under the Federal Reserve System, the free reserve ratio should be inversely related to the difference between the rate which banks can earn on assets and the discount rate. Yet the free reserve ratio is not correlated with the market-discount rate differential when the market rate itself is held constant (Section IV, first part). The ratio continues to be highly correlated with the level of short-term interest rates.

The alternative interpretation offered here (Section V) puts emphasis on the long-run goals of successful bank management. Personal and business loans provide the most profitable use of bank funds. Studies of banking also stress the overriding concern of management with meeting the credit needs of regular customers. Banks make every effort to accommodate them by selling securities, reducing excess reserves to the minimum, and borrowing from Reserve Banks with only a side glance at the discount rate. Hence, when the demand for loans expands, we observe a rise in interest rates and a decline in the free reserve ratio; and the converse when loan demand slackens. To be sure, banks are constrained to borrow for only short periods at a time. Yet, when the money market tightens and the accommodation of customers strains available funds, banks are forced to borrow more often, and the total borrowing of the system will be greater. That accounts for the major part of the association between the free reserve ratio and interest rates.

Of course, modern bank management seeks to maximize current profits by equating the marginal returns of borrowing and allocating resources among various alternatives, insofar as other considerations permit. But portfolio adjustments are not made in a vacuum. Important long-run and institutional considerations come in—such as preserving the goodwill of long-time customers and official constraints on the purposes and duration of borrowing from the Federal Reserve. Since banks nowadays hold negligible excess reserves, borrowing is one recourse when the demand for loans reaches a cyclical high point.

The data do show an effect on the free reserve ratio of the differential between the Treasury bill rate and the discount rate, holding constant certain other variables (Sections IV, second part, and V). The effect appears to have been much stronger in the 1920's than in the 1950's, as could be inferred from the much larger fluctuations in borrowing in the earlier period (Chart 6-1). Statistical studies of the effect, however, have overstated its strength and importance by making no allowance for common cyclical patterns in the variables and ignoring the varying pressures by bank customers for loans. The differential rate is a rough proxy for those pressures and, when used in regressions as the only interest-rate variable, exhibits a spuriously high correlation with the free reserve ratio.

Banks do not ordinarily borrow to acquire Treasury bills or other securities, as the frequent emphasis in statistical studies on the bill-discount rate differential may suggest. Holdings of such securities, if anything, fall as borrowing increases because both are used to provide funds for meeting an expansion of loans. Moreover, the bill rate usually stood below the discount rate in the 1950's, so the negative differential discouraged using borrowed funds to acquire bills. The bill rate here is apparently a proxy for the total return on loans, and the funds borrowed help banks to fulfill loan commitments. The average loan-discount rate differential shows no such effect, presumably because of credit rationing and the unrecorded returns to banks from compensating balances and other devices for altering charges indirectly.

The statistical association between the reserve ratio and interest rates provides little justification for assuming that changes in the money supply are sensitive to interest rates, as is standard in many current models of the financial system. Although the market-discount rate differential affects the free reserve ratio, changes in the ratio since World War II have accounted for a small part of the variations in deposit growth. To a large extent changes in the ratio are offset by Federal Reserve open-market operations (Section IV, second part). The Federal Reserve itself, of course, might occasionally take steps to limit interest-rate movements by its monetary measures, thus imparting an interest sensitivity to the supply, but it has never systematically pursued such a policy. The cornerstone of the evidence to support allegations of such sensitivity has been the statistical association between interest rates and the reserve ratio, and that association does not carry over to deposit growth (Section IV, second part). Properly interpreted, the data give no indication of an important interest sensitivity in the money supply.

Appendix

HISTORICAL REVIEW OF EARLIER EMPIRICAL STUDIES OF INTEREST RATES AND BANK RESERVES [18]

STUDIES OF THE PRE-1914 MONEY MARKET. A close association between bank reserves and short-term interest rates in New York City has apparently been known to financial observers for some time. "In the pre-war [World War I] days, fluctuations in the surplus reserves of clearing banks were observed with interest by all those who were interested in the state of the money market, for the approach of an exhaustion of the surplus was an announcement of impending restriction" [21, p. 264]. To my knowledge the first published study of the phenomenon was by John P. Norton in 1902 [32]. He examined call money rates and the lawful reserve ratio of New York City Clearing House Banks weekly from 1885 to 1900. The simple correlation between the two was −.52.

Norton assumed that the banks' reserve position largely determines call rates, not the other way around, which agreed with the generally accepted view at the time. Kinley, in the course of his famous study of the independent Treasury [27], attributed to banks' reserve position various short-run effects on the money market, but did not delve into the evidence to support his statements. The only exception I have found is Irving Fisher [15], who expressed a view similar to the findings of this study:

When business is optimistic, . . . the immediate effect is to increase bank loans. These results tend to lessen the ratio of bank reserves to liabilities. Thus the banker is led to raise his rate. It *seems* that the rise merely reflects his reserve situation. But back of this situation is the demand for loans. [Italics his.]

[18] Also see Meigs [30], who reviews the theoretical analysis of this literature.

Writers who subscribed to the other, prevailing view did not elaborate.

In his statistical findings, Norton also showed a three-week lag of call rates behind the reserve ratio, which indicates that changes in the ratio affect interest rates rather than the converse. But this test of timing covered only a two-year period (unspecified), which is too short to provide reliable evidence.

For his study of seasonal variations, Kemmerer [26, table facing p. 40], derived evidence of a negative correlation between the fifty-two weekly seasonal factors in the call money rate and the reserve ratio of New York City Clearing House Banks. The correlation coefficient computed from his data is −.61.

Apparently unaware of Norton's work, Persons [33] published a study in 1924 of the same material but covering a longer period. Persons used the ratio of loans and investments to deposits (which approximates the complement of the reserve ratio) of New York City Clearing House Banks, monthly, 1867–1924. He adjusted the data to remove seasonal variations and a linear trend, which Norton did not do. This series graphically shows a close association (no correlations were computed) with seasonally adjusted commercial paper rates, except for a few periods, attributed by Persons to wars and panics. Comparable call-date data for national banks outside New York City during the same period also correspond to commercial paper rates fairly well over cycles, though not nearly as well month to month. Related comparisons for the pre-1914 period in Table 6-1 of the present study suggest that the correlation is not statistically significant.

The ratio of loans and investments to individual deposits (adjusted for float) of national banks in six geographic regions on call dates, 1901–04, were compared with commercial paper rates. The comparison shows the closest correspondence for New York City banks and the least for the Western and Southern banks. Indeed, there is a clear-cut association only for the New York City banks. (Our results in Table 6-1 confirm this.) This result is consistent with the influence running in either direction. On the one hand, one might argue that New York City banks have the most influence on this interest rate because they dominate the market for commercial paper. On the other hand, one might argue that this rate applies chiefly to the New York money market and so mainly affects the desired reserve levels of banks in that city.

Ayres [1] showed, after smoothing the data by moving averages, that there is a close association between commercial paper rates and the fraction of Treasury currency held outside of banks. The data are monthly figures for the period 1896–1914. Smoothing suppresses changes of a very short-run nature and reveals an association between the cyclical movements. The fraction of currency outside banks, which for the pre-1914 period is the complement of the ratio of reserves to high-powered money, has a close association with commercial paper rates—presumably because it is a fair approximation to the reserve ratio of national banks, at least for cyclical movements. This seems the most plausible way to interpret Ayres' results, as he offers no clear explanation.

In terms of theoretical interpretation, the best of the earlier works is a little-known 1922 article by Seltzer and Horner [42]. They extended the weekly series that Norton used for the period 1885–1900 to the succeeding nine years, 1900–09. For these nine years, they obtained the same correlation coefficient (−.52) that Norton did for the preceding fifteen years.

This is the only earlier work of all I have seen that explicitly interprets the correlation as reflecting a two-way dependence of the reserve ratio on rates *and* of rates on the reserve ratio.[19] For Seltzer and Horner, the reserve ratio measures changes in the "supply factors" affecting the loan market, as it does for Norton, but they also insist that the interest rate acts back upon the reserve ratio to produce a mutual dependence. Since "demand factors" are not represented in their correlation, Seltzer and Horner attribute to these factors the variations in the interest rate not explained by the reserve ratio. When they correlated the weekly data for individual years, the correlation coefficients varied from −.30 to −.68, which the authors explain by the varying strength of "demand factors" in different years.

The interpretation cannot be so simple, however, even in terms of their theoretical framework, as they themselves recognized.[20] In effect, they postulate a supply curve of loanable funds, for which the amount supplied depends upon interest rates (the foregoing studies implicitly assume that this curve is inelastic to changes in interest rates); the whole curve shifts with changes in the reserve ratio (when the ratio is low, loans are curtailed and conversely). Demand is also dependent on interest rates, and shifts in the supply curve

---

[19] Roos and Szeliski [41] did take account of both influences by adding various and sundry variables to their regression equation, but their analysis is so loosely formulated, and their regression variables so shot through with multicollinearity, that an interpretation of their results appears impossible. I seriously doubt that the high correlation coefficients they obtained, covering quite a short period, carry any economic significance.

Their work was inspired by Skinner's results [43], which allegedly show a strong relation between monetary factors and interest rates. He presented his data in graphs without sources or full explanation, so that the results can be neither verified nor interpreted.

[20] Seltzer and Horner argue (pp. 111–112) that "there is an effective limit . . . below which bankers cannot safely reduce their reserves. But as the reserve ratio rises above this limit, bankers have an increasing incentive to lend. . . . The higher the reserve ratios, the lower the rates at which bankers will be willing to lend; the lower the reserve ratios, the higher the rates which must be offered to tempt bankers further to diminish their reserve ratios.

"But, in fact, the situation is really more complex. Demand factors not only operate upon the call rate directly; but the call rate which results from partial or predominant demand influence affects in turn the reserve ratios. The great speculative boom will tend to force call rates upward without a prior decline in the reserve ratio; but the high rates in turn will tempt bankers to diminish their reserves to the minimum ratio compatible with safety or legal requirements. The high rates, in other words, will be partly *cause*, not altogether the effect, of a diminishing reserve ratio." [Italics theirs.]

We should probably interpret them as referring to the *stock* of funds supplied by banks rather than to a *flow* per period of time.

generate observations along the demand curve. But the demand curve may also shift, producing a movement along the supply curve in which loans expand by reducing the reserve ratio and vice versa. The trouble here is that the reserve ratio is serving as proxy for two separate sets of factors: Shifts in the supply curve affect the ratio in the same direction; movements along the curve (due to shifts in the demand curve) affect the ratio inversely. This raises the well-known problem of statistical identification, which they left unresolved.

Seltzer and Horner thought that their study had only historical interest because they believed the association between bank reserves and interest rates disappeared with the advent of Federal Reserve control over bank reserves and ability to stabilize the money market. Yet in the late 1920's, studies of the post-World War I period again found an association, though in a slightly different form.

A later study by Morrison [31] extends the evidence for the pre-1914 period.

STUDIES OF THE POST-1914 MONEY MARKET. Persons' study [33], already cited, covered the early 1920's, for which he also found a good association between the (complement of the) reserve ratio of New York banks and commercial paper rates. This would not be true of the late 1920's nor, especially, since World War II when banks have kept reserves much closer to the minimum required. Burgess [5] was the first to point to the post-1914 association, although in a new form. He showed that there was a close, positive, monthly association during 1923–26 between commercial paper rates and the borrowings (discounts and advances) of member banks from Federal Reserve Banks. In his book [6] published later, he extended the series to the 1922–33 period, for which the conformity is good though far from perfect. Burgess attributed the association to the influence of banks' indebtedness on interest rates. Because of the tradition against borrowing, banks allegedly borrow only temporarily when a reserve drain forces them to, and their ensuing efforts to terminate the debt by contracting loans tighten the money market. Burgess noted that, although borrowing is normally heavy in the closing months of each year, interest rates are not unusually high at that time, which he explained as banks' willingness to loan freely when they know the heavy demand for loans is temporary. A simple theory stating that banks borrow solely for profit does not account for this lapse in the association.

The evidence was discussed at some length in the celebrated book by Riefler [39] in 1930. Riefler's strong insistence that most banks do not borrow for profit appeared to represent the view of most top Federal Reserve officials.[21] His analysis started from a simple graph showing a close association between the borrowings of member banks and three short-term interest rates (for time and call loans, and commercial paper), monthly during 1917–28, with no apparent lag either way. The absence of lags led him to the view that, when

---

[21] See Harris [21, p. 262] and the references cited by him. For more recent views held by the Federal Reserve, however, see [13], [14], and [3].

banks are forced to borrow because of a loss of reserves, they immediately tighten up loans, and short-term rates rise. He noted that banks accounted for two-thirds of short-term loans in 1922 and one-half in 1928. If borrowing depended on profitability, it might lag behind changes in rates.

Borrowing for profit also implies that, without any restrictions on banks, the profit spread would disappear and open-market rates would then approach the discount rate. Although the two rates do exhibit similar movements, this similarity reflects a tendency of the Federal Reserve to adjust the discount rate to the market. Their movements are usually not so close as to prevent banks from making profits. The only rate that stays close to the discount rate is that on acceptances, for which Federal Reserve policy does control the market. The acceptance rate reveals the effect of such control, which other rates do not show.

This argument against the profit theory holds only in the extreme case. If we combine a profit theory with some limited aversion of banks to indebtedness, there is no implication that market rates have to equal the discount rate.

Riefler's argument, which received considerable attention, elicited a mixed reaction. The main issue was whether banks borrow for profit and hence whether the association between borrowings and interest rates reflects the effect of rates (or, better, the differential rate over the discount rate) on borrowing or the effect of borrowing on rates. It is not clear from his evidence which way the direction of influence runs.

Among those writing on the subject before World War II, Currie, Hardy, and Tinbergen supported Riefler's conclusions, while Harris and Turner disputed them.

To determine the response of banks to the level of their indebtedness, Currie [9] examined the association between the borrowings and deposits of different classes of member banks monthly during 1922–31. He found that New York City banks contracted deposits most strongly (by reducing loans and investments) when borrowing was heavy, and the connection between borrowing and deposit contraction was weakest for country banks. In other words, when banks were forced to borrow because of a drain of reserves, they contracted earning assets. The strength of the response varied between country and city banks, as might be expected. His results are marred by the ambiguity of his evidence. It is based on a visual examination of the series, and he made no allowance for common business cycle patterns.

Hardy [20] compared borrowings with the discount rate 1922–31 and found a positive association, whereas the profit theory of borrowing implies a negative one. He explains the positive association by Federal Reserve actions, in which open-market operations and changes in the discount rate occur together. The Reserve Banks sell bonds and raise the discount rate to tighten credit, thus forcing member banks to offset reserve losses by temporarily borrowing at the same time that the discount rate is increased. On the profit theory of borrowing, banks reduce their indebtedness when the discount rate is raised, which would produce an inverse association. This evidence is far from conclusive, however, because Hardy should have used not the level of the discount rate but the differential market rate over the discount rate. Short-term rates are positively correlated with the discount rate.

Tinbergen [45] introduced the concept of "free reserves" (excess reserves minus borrowings). In a scatter diagram he showed that free reserves and a short-term rate of interest—not specified but probably commercial paper rates—have a close linear relation monthly during 1917–37. The relation is negative, since borrowings are subtracted from excess reserves. Actually, the relation for the late 1930's is not linear, but Polak and White [34] demonstrated later that all the points lie along a linear regression function if the interest rate is measured logarithmically. (Logarithms are really only necessary to handle the very low rates of the late 1930's and early 1940's.) As a rationale for the relationship, Tinbergen cited Riefler's study.

Harris [21, Chap. XV] discussed particular episodes (mainly in the late 1920's) when member banks appear to have borrowed for purposes of profit. He drew attention to the lack of a close association between borrowings and short-term rates at various times. Harris contended that the data for certain years can only be explained on the presumption that banks often do borrow or remain in debt for profit.

While Harris questioned the application of Riefler's position to certain periods and in an extreme form to all periods, he did not reject it completely. A major study by Turner [46], however, concluded that the association can be entirely explained by banks' response to changes in the spread between short-term rates and the discount rate. Turner attacked Riefler's argument that borrowing for profit would always keep market rates at the level of the discount rate. This was contrary to fact and was used by Riefler to argue that the profit theory was invalid. Turner rightly countered that this would only happen if banks could and did borrow without limit and if demand factors played no role in determining market rates. Neither of these conditions is likely to hold, nor does the profit theory of borrowing require it to. Riefler's argument therefore rests basically on the assertion, derived from his familiarity with banking practice, that banks do not usually borrow for profit, which Turner disputed. Turner rightly pointed out that interpreting the motivation for borrowing is hazardous. When banks lose reserves, they may rely more on borrowing and less on selling investments, given a favorable profit spread, without breaking the injunction to borrow only for "need." [22]

To determine the direction of influence, Turner examined the relation between borrowings and the profit spread for each of the twelve Federal Reserve districts, monthly during 1922–36. For each district he computed a profit

---

[22] Turner also argued that banks have often held large amounts of bonds at times of sizable indebtedness as proof against Riefler's position that they eschew borrowing except when necessary. This argument is no more convincing than Riefler's. After all, banks might prefer to borrow temporarily for "need" rather than sell bonds if bond prices are at the moment sinking, and not because or only when the profit spread on borrowing is favorable.

spread on borrowing by subtracting the discount rate in the district from the same weighted average of short-term rates used by Riefler. There is no separate short-term rate published for each district. Consequently, since discount rates seldom differ among districts, the profit spread varies very little among districts and disaggregating the twelve districts provides less additional information than one might hope for. Undaunted, Turner compared this spread with the borrowings of banks in each district. The association was closest in the New York, Chicago, Boston and Philadelphia districts; for these he found no lag either way. In the other districts, where the association was lower, he found (based on correlation coefficients) that borrowings lag behind the profit spread by one to five months, suggesting that borrowing depends on profit.

This statistical evidence is really quite weak. The lag occurs only for the weakest correlations, not the highest, and therefore may be spurious. In addition, the correlation for all districts together, which has no lag, is higher than any of the correlations for the districts individually, suggesting that the breakdown by districts provides less information on the relationship than do the aggregate figures. This is inconsistent with the profit theory of borrowing but not with Riefler's position.

Turner's study therefore did not establish that the data favor the profit theory of borrowing over Riefler's interpretation (though Turner thought so), but it did cast a shadow over Riefler's interpretation.

In recent years the empirical study of liquidity preference inspired by Keynes has led to a search for such preferences in all sectors of the economy, including banking. Current studies now assume that the influence runs primarily from interest rates to free reserves and not the other way.[23] The supposition of the earlier work is thus implicitly rejected, though mainly by neglect rather than explicit evidence.

Polak and White's work [34] in 1955 improved on the technical quality of earlier studies and extended the coverage to later years. They presented a scatter diagram, with annual data for 1922–53, of the Treasury bill rate and the ratio of free reserves to total deposits of member banks. The bill rate is measured logarithmically, which appears to make the relationship linear even when the low rates of the late 1930's are included. The observations fit a straight line fairly well — no correlation is computed — indicating that the as-

---

[23] For a recent throwback to the Riefler interpretation, which has been practically extinct since World War II, see [22].

In 1955 Klein and Goldberger [28] presented a scatter diagram using annual data, 1929–52, of percentage changes in the commercial paper rate and the excess reserve ratio of member banks. The relationship is negative but not significant. They view banks as heavily influencing short-term rates through their lending, which creates an inverse dependence of interest rates on banks' ability to lend, as in the older view. However, they regard excess reserves (above average levels) as indicative of a disequilibrium, and depart from the older view by assuming that rates will change in inverse proportion to the degree of disequilibrium. Thus large excess reserves cause banks to lend freely and produce falling rather than low rates.

sociation first noticed by Norton has continued to prevail. Polak and White assumed, however, that they were measuring a simple liquidity preference relation: When market rates are high, banks are encouraged to keep low cash reserves and to borrow, while the incentive progressively weakens as market rates decline. They claimed that they were merely extending Tinbergen's earlier empirical work, but this statement failed to indicate that their rationale for the association is the opposite of Tinbergen's. Hence they should have used the rate differential instead of the level of the rate.

Except for Polakoff [35], who introduced the possibility of a reluctance of member banks to increase borrowing beyond certain limits, the next important development in the profit theory was due to Meigs [30]. He formulated the profit theory in terms of desired and actual reserves, with the desired level depending upon the differential between market rates and discount rate. Since Meigs, this formulation has been applied widely in econometric studies, some of which are cited in the main text.

SUMMARY. These various studies document a close association between free reserves and short-term interest rates. The association is too close and covers too long a period to be accidental. Most of these studies use the same basic data and so do not offer independent evidence, despite the variety of periods covered and the different ways the basic relationship is presented. The underlying association is strong enough to come through no matter how the data are handled and has therefore lent support to a variety of hypotheses. Before the 1930's, the association was generally attributed to the effect of reserves on rates, and since then to the opposite influence.

References

1. Leonard P. Ayres, *Turning Points in Business Cycles,* New York, 1939, p. 142.
2. Board of Governors of the Federal Reserve System, *The Federal Reserve System,* 1961.
3. Karl Brunner and Allan H. Meltzer, *The Federal Reserve's Attachment to the Free Reserve Concept,* Subcommittee on Domestic Finance of the House Committee on Banking and Currency, 88th Cong., 2d Sess., May 7, 1964.
4. ———, "Some Further Investigations of Demand and Supply Functions for Money," *Journal of Finance,* May 1963, 240–283.
5. W. Randolph Burgess, "Factors Affecting Changes in Short Term Interest Rates," *Journal of the American Statistical Association,* June 1927, 195–201.
6. ———, *The Reserve Banks and the Money Market,* New York, 1946.
7. Phillip Cagan, *Determinants and Effects of Changes in the Money Stock 1875–1960,* New York, NBER, 1965, Chap. 4.

8. ——, "Changes in the Cyclical Behavior of Interest Rates," *Review of Economics and Statistics,* August 1966, reprinted as Occasional Paper 100, New York, NBER.

9. Lauchlin Currie, *The Supply and Control of Money in the United States,* Cambridge, Mass., 1935, Chap. VIII.

10. Richard G. Davis, "Open Market Operations, Interest Rates and Deposit Growth," *Quarterly Journal of Economics,* August 1965, 431–454.

11. ——, "Testing Some Variants of the Free Reserves Hypothesis," January 1966, mimeographed.

12. Frank de Leeuw, "A Model of Financial Behavior," in Duesenberry, *et al.* (eds.), *The Brookings Quarterly Econometric Model of the United States,* Chicago, 1965, Chap. 13.

13. Federal Reserve Bank of New York, *Monthly Review,* article on "The Significance and Limitations of Free Reserves," November 1958, 162–167.

14. Federal Reserve Bank of St. Louis, *Review,* article on "Excess Reserves," April 1963, 12.

15. Irving Fisher, *The Theory of Interest,* New York, 1930, 444–450.

16. Milton Friedman and Anna J. Schwartz, *A Monetary History of the United States, 1867–1960,* Princeton for NBER, 1963, Chap. 9.

17. Peter A. Frost, "Banks' Demand for Excess Reserves," unpublished doctoral dissertation, University of California at Los Angeles, 1966.

18. Stephen M. Goldfeld, *Commercial Bank Behavior and Economic Activity: A Structural Study of Monetary Policy in the United States,* New York, 1966.

19. —— and Edward J. Kane, "The Determinants of Member-Bank Borrowing: An Econometric Study," *Journal of Finance,* September 1966, 499–514.

20. Charles O. Hardy, *Credit Policies of the Federal Reserve System,* The Brookings Institution, 1932, Chap. XI.

21. Seymour E. Harris, *Twenty Years of Federal Reserve Policy,* Cambridge, Mass., 1933, Vol. I.

22. John J. Harrington, Jr., "Explaining Changes in the Treasury Bill Rate: The Key Variables," *The Journal of Business,* Seton Hall University, May 1965, 19–28.

23. Donald R. Hodgman, "The Deposit Relationship and Commercial Bank Investment Behavior," *Review of Economics and Statistics,* August 1961, 257–268.

24. George Horwich, "Liquidity Trap in the Thirties: Comment," *Journal of Political Economy,* June 1966, 286–290.

25. Edward J. Kane and Burton G. Malkiel, "Bank Portfolio Allocation, Deposit Variability, and the Availability Doctrine," *Quarterly Journal of Economics,* February 1965, 111–134.

26. Edwin W. Kemmerer, "Seasonal Variations in the New York Money Market," *American Economic Review,* March 1911, 33–49.

27. David Kinley, *The Independent Treasury of the United States and the Relations to the Banks of the Country,* National Monetary Commission, 1910.

28. Lawrence R. Klein and Arthur S. Goldberger, *An Econometric Model of the United States, 1929–1952,* Amsterdam, the Netherlands, 1955, pp. 29–30 and 53.

29. George W. McKinney, Jr., *The Federal Reserve Discount Window,* New Brunswick, N.J., 1960.

30. A. James Meigs, *Free Reserves and the Money Supply,* Chicago, 1962.

31. George R. Morrison, *Liquidity Preferences of Commercial Banks,* Chicago, 1966.

32. John P. Norton, *Statistical Studies in the New York Money-Market,* New York, 1902.

33. Warren M. Persons, "Cyclical Fluctuations of the Ratio of Bank Loans to Deposits, 1867–1924," *Review of Economic Statistics,* October 1924, 260–283.

34. J. J. Polak and William H. White, "The Effect of Income Expansion on the Quantity of Money," International Monetary Fund, *Staff Papers,* August 1955, 422–428.

35. Murray E. Polakoff, "Reluctance, Elasticity, Least Cost, and Member-Bank Borrowing: A Suggested Interpretation," *Journal of Finance,* March 1960, 1–18.

36. ———, "Federal Reserve Discount Policy and Its Critics," in D. Carson (ed.), *Banking and Monetary Studies,* Homewood, Ill., 1963, pp. 210–212.

37. ——— and William L. Silber, "Reluctance and Member-Bank Borrowing: Additional Evidence," *Journal of Finance,* March 1967, 88–92.

38. C. Rangarajan and Alan K. Severn, "The Response of Banks to Changes in Aggregate Reserves," *Journal of Finance,* December 1965, 651–661.

39. Winfield W. Riefler, *Money Rates and Money Markets in the United States,* New York, 1930, Chap. II.

40. Roland S. Robinson, *The Management of Bank Funds,* New York, 1951.

41. Charles F. Roos and Victor S. Von Szeliski, "The Determination of Interest Rates," *Journal of Political Economy,* August 1942, 501–535.

42. Lawrence H. Seltzer and Seward L. Horner, "The Relation of the Percentage of Bank Reserves of National Banks in New York City to the Call Money Loan Rate on the New York Stock Exchange," *Journal of Political Economy,* February 1922, 108–118.

43. Richard D. Skinner, *Seven Kinds of Inflation,* New York, 1937, Chap. VI.

44. R. L. Teigen, "An Aggregated Quarterly Model of the U.S. Monetary Sector," in Karl Brunner (ed.), *Targets and Indicators of Monetary Policy,* forthcoming.

45. Jan Tinbergen, *Business Cycles in the United States of America 1919–32,* League of Nations, 1939, 82–87.

46. Robert C. Turner, *Member-Bank Borrowing,* Columbus, Ohio, 1938.

Index